Fun with the Family™ Las Vegas

Praise for the *Fun with the Family*™ series

"Enables parents to turn family travel into an exploration."

—Alexandra Kennedy, Editor, *Family Fun*

"Bound to lead you and your kids to fun-filled days,
those times that help compose the
memories of childhood."

—Dorothy Jordon, *Family Travel Times*

Help Us Keep This Guide Up to Date

Every effort has been made by the author and editors to make this guide as accurate and useful as possible. However, many changes can occur after a guide is published—establishments close, phone numbers change, hiking trails are rerouted, facilities come under new management, etc.

We would love to hear from you concerning your experiences with this guide and how you feel it could be improved and be kept up to date. While we may not be able to respond to all comments and suggestions, we'll take them to heart, and we'll make certain to share them with the author. Please send your comments and suggestions to the following address:

The Globe Pequot Press
Reader Response/Editorial Department
P.O. Box 480
Guilford, CT 06437

Or you may e-mail us at: editorial@GlobePequot.com

Thanks for your input, and happy travels!

FUN WITH THE FAMILY™ SERIES

fun WITH the Family™

LAS VEGAS

HUNDREDS OF IDEAS FOR DAY TRIPS WITH THE KIDS

LYNN GOYA

THIRD EDITION

INSIDERS' GUIDE ®

GUILFORD, CONNECTICUT

AN IMPRINT OF THE GLOBE PEQUOT PRESS

917.93

Goya

> The prices, hours of operation, and other details listed in this guidebook were confirmed at press time. We recommend, however, that you call establishments before traveling to obtain current information.

INSIDERS' GUIDE®

Copyright © 2002, 2004, 2005 by The Globe Pequot Press

Insiders' Guide is a registered trademark of The Globe Pequot Press.
Fun with the Family is a trademark of The Globe Pequot Press.

Text design by Nancy Freeborn and Linda Loiewski
Maps by Rusty Nelson © The Globe Pequot Press
Spot photography throughout © Photodisc

ISSN 1536-9013
ISBN 0-7627-3491-4

Manufactured in the United States of America
Third Edition/First Printing

To my family of adventurers,
whose middle names must be "What's next?"

Contents

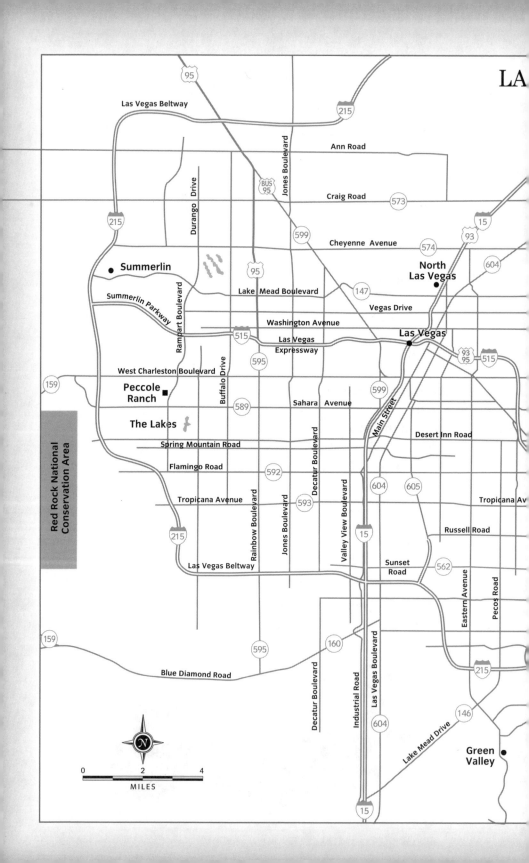

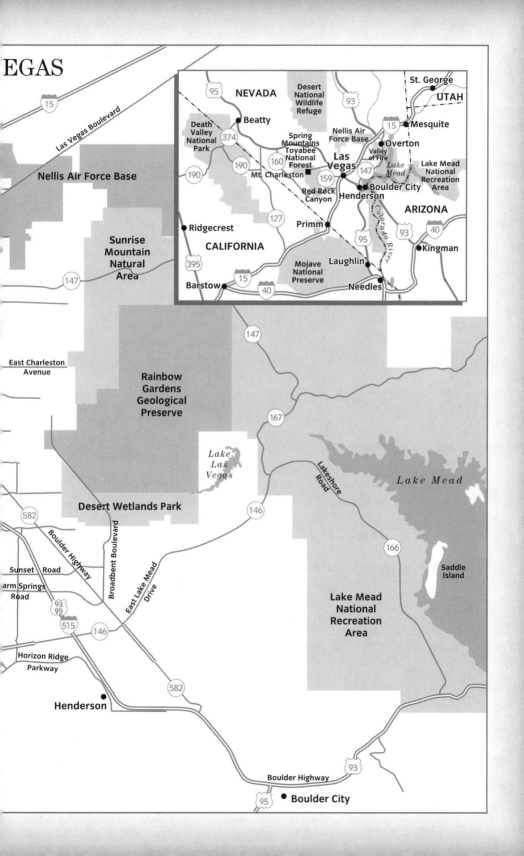

Acknowledgments

I want to thank my family and all of the friends who contributed to this book by sharing their secret haunts, suggesting favorite getaways, and bugging their friends to expand our inside scoop about this area. Particular thanks to those who were willing to trek, splash, look at, listen to, taste, and otherwise explore the Las Vegas Valley with me. Not everything was memorable in a positive way, as they will attest. Thanks also to those businesses and adventurers who are making this area a great place for families and were willing to let me and mine sample their wares.

In particular I want to thank Alan, Chloe, Alexander, and Seiji for the countless hours they drove to and fro with me looking for the unusual, the exciting, and the memorable, or tiptoed past my office while I ignored everything but the screen glowing in the dark. Dana, Travis, and Bob Robinson cheerfully accompanied us on countless adventures and honestly shared their opinions. Thanks also, Dana, for sorting pictures while on your sickbed. Thank you James, Shawn, and Mark and Missy Ebbert for sharing your favorite family spots. Mariola O'Brien's sage and concise advice is gratefully acknowledged. Liza Conroy, Leslie DeVore, Sharon Chayra, and the Vince Sterns were friends indeed. Laurel and Winston MacDonald provided great company and excellent insight into the area. Thank you, Calvin, for keeping Seiji occupied while I completed my work. Joanne Lamb's artful editing and spontaneous laughter were a godsend when the manuscript was first completed, and I was in the throes of writer's panic. Thank you book-group friends for your thoughts.

Thanks also to all of the hardworking public-relations people who made sure that my information was as accurate and up to date as possible: Sue Bartling, Lynn Berk, Stephanie Bethal, Reggie Burton, Marsil Chaffee, Pat Dingle, Lani Doi, Stephanie Fosse, Alan Grant, Laura Herlovich, Lori Kennedy, Margaret Kurtz, Heidi Levy, Frank Lieberman, Andy Maiden, Dan Stan Moran, Ceres Morris, Sherry Pardoe, Ashley Rotondo, Kelly Schwarz, Paul Spiers, Tyri Squyres, Celia Thompson, Solveig Thorsrud, Madeleine Weekley, and Stephanie Wilson. Without your excellent work, this book would not have been possible; certainly, it would have been less pleasant to complete.

Finally, thanks to Lynn Zelem, my editor at The Globe Pequot Press, for her flexibility, good humor, and keen eye for detail. Her efforts have made the updated edition of the book even friendlier to traveling families.

Introduction

Traditionally, Las Vegas as the world knows it was built on gambling (locals prefer "gaming") dollars that covered the cost of free or low-cost rooms; complimentary tickets to see headliners such as Frank Sinatra, Wayne Newton, and Elvis Presley; and nearly free buffets that laid out copious amounts of average-tasting food to get gamers back to the tables as quickly as possible. The new Vegas paradigm considers gaming just one of many attractions that entice more than thirty-five million visitors here per year. In fact, during the past ten years, the "casino" has turned into the "casino/resort" with top-notch dining, elaborate production shows, kids' arcades, impressive swimming holes, and high-end shopping designed to lure the "high roller" to individual properties.

How do families fit in? In some cases, they don't. What seemed like a good idea in the early '90s (catering to the large family-travel market) turned into a nightmare for many facilities when irresponsible parents parked their children just outside of the age-restricted areas while they gambled the night away. With strollers blocking high-traffic areas, unsupervised children going back and forth through the casinos to the arcades, and finally the tragic murder of a child left unattended for hours as her father sat at a slot machine, many casinos struck back.

The Bellagio, for instance, does not allow children in the hotel at all, unless they are registered guests. The Mirage allows only registered guests to bring in strollers. Two of the newest hotels, Paris Las Vegas and the Aladdin, didn't include video arcades, especially elaborate pools, or family-friendly restaurants in their plans and make no special effort to accommodate children.

Still, families continue to visit in record numbers. Local residential areas swell with four-, five-, and six-bedroom homes as more families migrate here and those who already call Vegas "home" start or add to their families. One cannot go down to the Strip without seeing hordes of children with their parents. Young children adore the visual stimulation of just walking, driving, or being pushed down the Strip at night as lights flash, water dances, pirate ships sink, and volcanoes light up the sky. Older children are enchanted with the magic shows and state-of-the-art games. Those into thrill rides find more opportunities to drop at the speed of light than any place other than a major theme park. Special attractions and museums that are designed to attract adults are equally interesting to many older children.

Although the resorts on the Strip might not do much to cater specifically to those too young to gamble, as Vegas families continue to thrive and prosper in our relatively new community, a natural infrastructure is developing off the Strip that is beginning to provide the kinds of services and activities that families are accustomed to in other major metropolitan areas.

In addition, more and more families are coming to Vegas with no intention of visiting the Strip at all. Instead of man-made attractions, they seek the thrills that come with world-class outdoor opportunities, which many feel far surpass the much lauded glitter and glamour of the city. Just a hop, skip, and a jump away are areas as desolate and pristine as any on earth. The country's largest man-made lake offers a variety of water sports. Red rocks lure rock climbers and hikers. Hunters still come to shoot wild game, including bighorn sheep and mountain lion. Bird-watchers find the Western Flyway a seasonal paradise for catching a glimpse of rare and endangered birds. Historians love to explore former boomtowns that are now deserted, or stumble across ancient petroglyphs that sometimes cover whole canyon walls. Sand dunes, towering red cliffs, hot springs, wild sheep and horses, pristine waterfalls, and desert oases are simply the most obvious of the myriad sights and sounds that lie within a day's drive of our glamorous City of Lights.

And, we *still* have the pirate ships.

"You Mean People Live Here?"

When most people think about Vegas, they think about the south end of the Strip. Flying or driving in, visitors are astonished at the fields of pink stucco homes that cover the valley like gigantic wildflowers in bloom. Somehow, it seems strange to think that people really live here. But we do.

Once off the Strip, Las Vegas is still a town like no other. The last decade saw thousands of new hotel rooms built on and around the Strip. They say that as the hotel gears up, each room built creates five new jobs, requiring maids, cooks, and waitresses for the related restaurants, busboys, valets, front desk people, entertainers, janitors, and on and on. In turn, these employees need schools for their children, hospitals, grocery stores, homes, parks, movie theaters, and all the rest, just as in any other community.

Because Las Vegas is so new, a lot of those services are just beginning to appear. The services that are taken for granted in a mature town are often difficult to find here. Think of Las Vegas like a gangly teenager with all of the potential for a fully realized person, but still grappling for the kind of depth that allows him to be comfortable in his own skin. This lack of maturity is particularly felt in children's services. It may be difficult to find music lessons, for instance, close to home, or a choice of day-care options within easy reach.

As Las Vegas fills out, we can expect greater depth in children's services as well.

Deciding Where to Stay

Picking the right place to stay is half the battle when it comes to ensuring that a family has a great time in Vegas. To that end, consider whether you want to find an inexpensive base from which to explore, or whether you want to have a variety of entertainment options right outside of your room. The press tends to give a lot of coverage to the newest kids on the block, and most people naturally want to stay at the properties that they have read about. For families, that may not be such a great idea; the past five years have seen a shift in emphasis toward high-end luxury resorts with little or no special accommodations for kids.

Other cities expect many of their guests to bring along children. That isn't the case here. Because of that we've included more about accommodations than you'll find in most guidebooks, trying to provide a level of insight into how families would enjoy various properties. Although casino/resorts can't tell families *not* to come, they can choose to make things easier for guests with kids—or not. This guide will make an effort to let you know which properties are family friendly and why. Other properties may have attractions that you want to see, but may not always be the best choice at which to reside.

Of course, if you are Cher or Steven Spielberg, or are planning to lay down $100,000 a night at the gaming tables, forget about everything I just said. In that case, the resort will make your children feel like little princes and princesses if you bring them, along with comping you tickets to the hottest shows, offering you free dinners with their celebrity chefs, and providing no-cost suites that may be bigger than most of our entire neighborhoods. For the rest of us, read on.

Getting the Best Deal on Your Room

Getting a great room rate in Las Vegas is a bit like gambling. A lot depends on luck. Once you understand the underlying logic, however, your chances of getting a great deal increase dramatically. The first is that hotels want your gaming dollars. Everything they do is designed to get you onto the property so that the bright lights and happy sounds coming from the casinos entice you in. However, you have to be there to be enticed into the casino; therefore air/hotel packages are often some of the best buys around. Once you know you are going to Vegas, plan ahead and watch your local travel section for deals. They won't be there every week, but I promise you, if you watch it, they will come.

The second strategy, for those who are driving or want a specific hotel that isn't offering travel packages, is to book far, far in advance and to be flexible with your dates. Midweek can be half the price of weekend dates if a major convention is being held that weekend. Instead of seasonal rates, hotels in Vegas book much like airline tickets: As occupancy increases, so do the prices. The price ranges in this guide are *for the same base-level room with different arrival dates,* depending on whether the hotel is relatively empty or full and whether it expects high occupancy rates during that date because of a convention or special holiday.

December is often one of the slow times, except for New Year's Eve. Rooms that go for $400 to $500 per night during a convention can often be had for far less than $100 per night for those who plan properly. If you book in advance and maintain flexible dates, you can often stay in the most luxurious of hotels for the same price as last-minute lodging at a bargain motel.

So here is what you do:

- Plan your vacation far in advance.
- Check the hotel's Web site for special offers and promotions.

■   Call the top three properties of choice and ask, "What is your lowest rate and when is it available?" Some operators are more helpful than others. If you don't get satisfactory answers, call back later.

You might just save enough to pay for one of the top-rated shows for the entire family.

Dining with Kids

Trends come and go—in Vegas, faster than a quark—but what is very noticeable for people traveling with kids is that food has gotten very pricey here. In the newer, more prestigious resorts, one can find that all restaurants start their entrees at or above the $20 mark. For those of us who pay for three, four, or five entrees per meal, eating out can easily and unexpectedly eat up the entire vacation budget.

What happened? The newest resorts decided to forgo the family market and focus strictly on the "high rollers," those who come and can afford, without flinching, to throw down tens of thousands—sometimes a million dollars per night—on the gaming tables. To lure these select few patrons to their establishments, the resorts offer the best in high-end luxury, from spa treatments and Egyptian cotton sheets to designer shopping and world-famous chefs. Las Vegas now has more celebrity chefs than any other city in the world. While that may please the palate, it certainly doesn't please the pocketbook.

My kids like real food that includes pasta, chicken, steak, and seafood. Although they would prefer to dine at a "nice" restaurant every meal, frankly, that is out of our budget.

Happy Hour

Happy Hour is back with a vengeance at stand-alone restaurants throughout the valley. Although one wouldn't want to take kids to a bar for cheap drinks and food, it might make a nice afternoon getaway for Mom and Dad after a frazzling day in the video arcades. Consider a two-hour break while the kids have pizza and an in-house movie in the room.

McCormick & Schmick's. 335 Hughes Center Drive; (702) 836–9000. Weekdays 3:30–6:30 P.M. Appetizers, $1.95. Good food, good drinks. The real steal, however, is the 1¼-pound lobster for $11.95. Can't beat that.

Z-Tejas. 3824 Paradise Road; (702) 732–1660. Weekdays 3:00–7:00 P.M. If you are in the mood for some Southwestern grub, check out this place where much of the bar is half price.

Napoleon's. Paris Las Vegas, 3655 Las Vegas Boulevard South; (877) 796–2096. Weekdays 4:00–7:00 P.M. The chef will carve you a free gourmet sandwich when you buy a drink.

Adventurous eating is also one of the unique experiences of new locations. We keep within a budget—while still indulging ourselves—with these tricks.

Picnic in the Park. Adventurous diners like to eat out—on a swing set, that is. Grab a loaf of bread, some cheese, some pickles, some hard salami, an apple, and some grapes for an easy-to-eat treat on the run. You might find that this is a great way to introduce the kids to a new taste by bringing kalamata olives or an Irish cheese along. If you are still making the trek to Vegas, most small towns have a park in the center of town. If you are already here, Summerlin and Henderson are known for their lovely parks. You might just see some local color as well.

Ask about Portions. It is difficult when in a new restaurant to know how much food to order, particularly once kids are school-age and their appetites are no longer sated with Happy Meal–size portions. Even though you may not know how much to order, the waitress or waiter often will. Sometimes the children's hamburger is the same size as the full menu hamburger and can easily fill an active boy's growling belly. Other times the kids' portion is so small that a first grader remains hungry. As my children grew, we often found ourselves between the adult and kid-size portions, so I would order an appetizer and share a meal with my daughter, or perhaps two kids would want to share a pizza or other adult-size order.

Divide and Conquer. Once kids are old enough to be left in the room by themselves for an hour or so, they might love the chance to watch a video with pizza, popcorn, or room service. You and your spouse can indulge at one of the gourmet restaurants while the kids enjoy a little time on their own. They share secrets, tell jokes, and feel very independent. With cell phones, we are always reachable, in case something comes up. I love the special sibling bonding that this vacation from parents invariably seems to engender.

"Just Bessert!" When my oldest son was staying at his grandmother's house, she once asked him what he wanted for breakfast. "Just bessert!" he announced, decidedly, which isn't such a bad idea when it comes to getting a taste and the atmosphere of some of the finer restaurants for a fraction of the bill. Although dessert-only tables won't be welcome during peak seating times, most places will be happy to let you linger during the waning hours. That way you can enjoy a flaming dessert or gelato scooped from a frigid wall, complete with all of the full-dinner ambience.

Crowd Control

Although Vegas now has more hotel rooms than almost any city in the world, hotels are still booking at an incredible rate of more than 80 percent occupancy for much of the year. That means that at peak times—such as during Comdex, the annual computer convention, or during the National Finals Rodeo—not only are rooms packed, but the supporting facilities are overflowing as well. Restaurants, streets, attractions, shows—everything is crowded and, in my opinion, decidedly family unfriendly. I've noticed over the years that Vegas, like many big cities, tends to run over old people and children when overloaded. Grown men and women cut in line, push aside those pesky people with kids, and simply walk between mothers holding toddler's hands.

Advice then? Again, whether you are staying with friends, parking your RV, jetting in for a couple of days, or luxuriating at the swankest resort, check the dates and try to come when rates are lowest: that means when occupancy is expected to be slow and crowds minimal. Even for locals, checking any hotel's room rates might give you a better idea of when to spend the day at GameWorks or when to catch the pirate ship sinking. If possible, try to avoid weekends, when crowds are always thickest. Plan your driving trip to arrive on Monday, and leave by Friday to save beaucoup bucks in lodging and avoid potential headaches.

If you can't avoid peak times, or if you're coming because of a major event, think as if you are in Disneyland: Eat early or late; expect lines and bring a small deck of cards or hand toys to help pass the time; take public transportation or use the hotel service shuttles. Let the hotel concierge see to show, tour, and dinner reservations, and any other dirty details that you may be able to palm off—I mean get help with.

Freebies

Everyone knows that high rollers who can afford to throw down $10,000 at a crack get everything free, from gourmet dinners to 10,000-square-foot suites. But that doesn't mean that we low rollers don't deserve freebies, too—we just have to play the right games. If you plan to gamble at all, or even if you don't, sign up for the casino's slot club to learn about discounts, **free** tickets, and more perks offered to registered customers. Once on the list, you may get offers for everything from $20 worth of nickels for $10 to special room promotions and **free** meals.

Make sure that you show your club card before booking a room, eating at a casino restaurant, or using the child care center or spa. Often, just having the card will get you a discount on casino services, even if you haven't used the card in play. If you do play, make sure the casino knows it by using the card. As your play level increases (even if you are winning) the freebies will increase as well.

Another possibility for getting a **free** room is to sign up for a casino's credit card. Ask what benefits holding or using the card entitles you to; not all freebies are offered by all casinos.

Check out how to play the coupon game for fun and profit with the local expert on gaming and winning at www.lasvegasadvisor.com.

Show Me the Bargains

Periodically, one hears that Vegas has bargain ticket prices for those in the know. Unfortunately, I have yet to unearth any. A recent call to a handful of quality show venues that do not always sell out confirmed that the two-for-one ticket price (or any discount, for that matter) is rarer than a native white tiger. Occasionally, shows such as *Legends in Concert* at Imperial Palace offer guests discounts as a courtesy. Local **free** publications that offer coupons (*What's On, Where Las Vegas, The Best Read Guide Las Vegas,* and *View*) can be picked up at most tourist information booths, in hotels, and at attractions, and the entertainment section of the paper sometimes offers advertised discounts for some shows, attractions, and restaurants.

At publication time, however, no two-for-one ticket booth was planned; according to my sources, calling around for bargains would be time-consuming and fruitless. The only exceptions might be a new show hoping to get the word out, a dying show that may offer discounts as a form of artificial respiration, or targeted discounts aiming to expand a certain audience segment, such as seniors or twenty-somethings. Again, a good concierge or the ticketing agent should know.

Don't be taken in by those discount Web sites either. They claim to have the "lowest price in town," which is misleading, but not untrue. They really are offering the lowest price, but so is everybody else. Buying through these sites is fine as long as you don't pay a surcharge for the convenience. (To avoid the excessive Ticketmaster charges, book directly from the hotel if you can.)

Ticket brokers, those small booths inside of casinos, might be willing and able to offer a discount because they are paid a commission for the tickets they sell. If you are buying for a family, you may be able to negotiate a small break, although that certainly isn't standard.

Gamblers routinely get comped into afternoon shows, restaurants, and even rooms; if you plan to gamble, ask about the player's clubs in each casino.

How to Use This Book

Rates for places to stay and eat, as well as attraction admission prices, are represented with dollar signs and offer a sense of the price ranges at press time. Lodging rates are based on double occupancy and tend to increase seasonally depending on location; many establishments offer family rates and discounts.

Attractions and Activities

$	under $20
$$	$20 to $40
$$$	$40.01 to $70.00
$$$$	$70.01 to $100.00
$$$$$	over $100

Meals

$	most entrees under $10
$$	most $10 to $20
$$$	most $20.01 to $30.00
$$$$	most entrees over $30

Lodging

$	up to $75
$$	$76 to $149
$$$	$150 to $225
$$$$	over $225

Caution to Visitors
Watch Your Step

Unfortunately, one of Vegas's best-kept secrets is that each year many pedestrians on the Strip are injured or killed when struck by cars. Most accidents happen at the busiest intersections, such as Tropicana and the Strip. Much of the blame can be placed on gawking drivers, but more often than not, a large portion of the blame lies with the pedestrians themselves. They think they can save some footwork and beat oncoming traffic by skirting across the middle of the streets; they encroach into the street while waiting for the interminable lights to turn; or they ignore the walk signals altogether because they think they know better. The best way to keep safe is to cross at the street level as little as possible. When you do, play mother hen: Make sure that the brood is safely gathered and hustle everyone quickly across, resisting the urge to watch that pirate swing through the air.

Africanized Honeybees (Killer Bees)

Sometime during 1990, Africanized honeybees migrated into the United States. The bees don't look any different than the European honeybees that we have all encountered, but they do act differently. These bees aggressively protect their nests, attacking would-be intruders by the hundreds or even thousands. The late 1990s saw the bees extend their range into southern Nevada; since then, a small number of attacks on small animals and people have occurred.

Being stung by an individual "killer" bee is no more dangerous than any other type of honeybee—they aren't more poisonous, they don't have multiple stingers, they aren't larger than typical honeybees. Because they swarm en masse, however, they are much more dangerous. They are more aggressive when pursuing intruders, and so they pose a particular danger to small animals, children, and the elderly. Although a few serious attacks have occurred in southern Nevada, in all cases the people who received multiple stings survived. Now that the Africanized bees are here to stay, it is important to be aware of their behavior and know what to do if you encounter these bees in your yard or when out on an adventure. There are safety precautions that even the smallest children can take.

Report groups of bees to an adult. Typically, ten or so bees guard the nest, circling in the vicinity to keep an eye on possible intruders. If your children spot a small group of bees, have them tell you immediately, then avoid the area.

Leave the area. If you are hit or "bombed" by a single bee or more, back off. Most of the time the guard bees will try to intimidate an intruder before attacking. If you leave when the first bees dive-bomb you, the rest of the hive will remain happily ensconced in the nest.

Move inside. If bees are in your yard, avoid the area and call a professional to remove them immediately. (They love hollow trees, dead desert plants, and especially sprinkler boxes, where they can crawl into the small hole and build a nest in the dark interior.) DO NOT squirt them with a hose or try to remove them yourself. Authorities recommend leaving the bees alone, moving small children and pets inside, and calling an exterminator immediately.

Keep quiet. Humming noises such as lawn mowers and trimmers, and sharp noises such as barking dogs seem to agitate the colony. Bright flashing lights also seem to make the bees feel threatened.

Call an exterminator to remove a swarm. In the spring and fall when "homeless bees" swarm, looking for a new place to build a hive, you may encounter them hanging from tree branches, the sides of buildings, or other areas. Unless you attack them, they will leave you alone. If they are on your property, however, it is your responsibility to have them removed. Once the swarm finds a new location, it will build a nest and fill it with honey and its young. The natural behavior to protect home and young is what causes the bees to attack suspected predators.

Leave them alone. Bees gathering pollen are not in the attack mode and will leave you alone if you leave them alone.

Call 911 immediately if you witness an attack. If you see the bees attacking an animal or person, call for help immediately. If you scream or wave your arms in agitation, the bees will attack you as well. Once the person is immobile, the bees will probably leave, but if you try to help, they will attack you.

If you are being attacked, run into a shelter as fast as you can. Most people, even children, can outrun the bees. Try to cover your face with your hands. Plunging into water is not a good idea, because the bees will wait for you to come up for air.

If you have been stung more than ten times or already know that you are allergic to bee stings, call 911 immediately. Bee stings can be life threatening. Dizziness, difficulty breathing, and blue lips or fingernails are all signs of an allergic reaction and require immediate medical attention.

Call the City of Las Vegas Africanized Honeybee Information Hotline, (702) 229–2000, for more information. For a list of recommended pest control companies, call (702) 385–5853.

For More Information

Las Vegas Convention and Visitors Bureau. 3150 Paradise Road, Las Vegas, Nevada 89109; (702) 892–7575 or (800) 332–5333.

Las Vegas Welcome Center. 3333 South Maryland Parkway, Suite 11, Las Vegas, Nevada 89109; (702) 451–7648 or (800) 821–6624.

Las Vegas Chamber of Commerce. 3720 Howard Hughes Parkway, Las Vegas, Nevada 89109-0320; (702) 735–1616. The chamber is accessible via e-mail at info@lvchamber or on the Web at www.lvchamber.com.

Attractions Key

The following is a key to the icons found throughout the text.

SWIMMING		**FOOD**	
BOATING / BOAT TOUR		**LODGING**	
HISTORIC SITE		**CAMPING**	
HIKING / WALKING		**MUSEUMS**	
FISHING		**PERFORMING ARTS**	
BIKING		**SPORTS / ATHLETIC**	
AMUSEMENT PARK		**PICNICKING**	
HORSEBACK RIDING		**PLAYGROUND**	
SKIING / WINTER SPORTS		**SHOPPING**	
PARK		**PLANTS / GARDENS / NATURE TRAILS**	
ANIMAL VIEWING		**FARMS**	

The New Strip

For most of the world, the Strip *is* Las Vegas. The glittering lights, the neon signs, the roaring volcano, the black pyramid, and the many other images that televise so gorgeously all lie in a row on Las Vegas Boulevard, most clustered as close together and as orderly as peas in a pod. However, these are very big peas. Since the family-friendly days of the 1990s, a new style of resort has taken over the south end of the Strip. These resorts are primarily huge, upscale, adult oriented, and full of high-priced restaurants. (One notable family resort, the MGM Grand, has even gone so far as to close its theme park to all but group sales.) Nonetheless, supervised children are welcome. With the size of the Las Vegas resorts, it simply isn't safe to leave them any other way.

Many small towns have fewer people, fewer attractions, and fewer places to eat than you'll find at a single resort/casino. It is utterly possible to spend an entire vacation without leaving the property at which you are staying. In other words, if you want to see more than your home hotel, bring your tennies, because otherwise you will spend your second day just soaking your feet.

Unlike most cities, in which hotels are built to accommodate people who are drawn to an area because of its lovely beaches, historical areas, or other intrinsic attractions, Las

Scenic Byway

The 4.3-mile stretch of the Strip from Russell Road to Sahara Avenue is now listed as the eighty-third National Scenic Byway. Scenic Byways are chosen for their scenic, historic, recreational, cultural, or natural beauty. The Las Vegas Strip is indeed scenic, historic, recreational, and cultural, and anything but natural. The Strip has long been regarded as unique, rivaling that other "City of Lights" for nighttime splendor, but now the whole world knows what showgirls have always known: You don't necessarily have to be born beautiful.

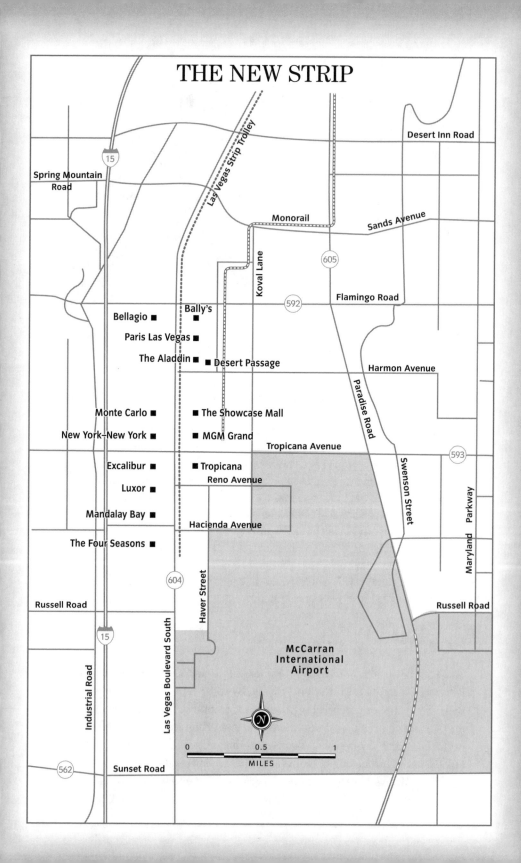

Planning Is Everything

A wise option for families is to pick sight-seeing battles up-front, realizing that one can't see everything. During the year that I aggressively researched Vegas (and I live here), I still was unable to experience everything. Most of the attractions are inside the hotels, usually at the end of a long and winding road. Although they may be worth seeing, it is difficult to hit a series of hotel attractions in a time-effective manner. Instead, as in any successful vacation with kids, aim for two, possibly three attractions in a half day. Spend the other half relaxing at one of the great pools or visiting one of the wonderful outdoor recreational areas that lie nearby. You may not see everything, but that only leaves more reason to come again.

Vegas hotels *are* the attraction. Most tourists come here to gamble in the hotel casinos, shop in the hotel stores, ride the hotel rides, swim in the hotel pools, visit the hotel museums and attractions, or see the hotel shows. More than hotels, the larger properties are closer to all-inclusive resorts.

The Four Seasons Hotel Las Vegas

3960 Las Vegas Boulevard South; (702) 632–5000 or (877) 632–5200. $$$–$$$$

As pricey as some rooms have gotten in Vegas, you may find staying in the only AAA five-star hotel in Nevada a real bargain. You won't find any children's arcades or thrill rides to lure families, but treats like cookies and milk on arrival; a children's menu for every restaurant, even the most exclusive; childproofing your room upon request; a complimentary basket of baby essentials, including diapers; and tub toys in the bathrooms say it all: Kids are invited guests here. This is one place, however, that uses traditional "seasons" to set prices and forgoes the confusing range of prices based on occupancy.

Although relatively compact, through a unique partnership with the adjacent Mandalay Bay, the rooms sport fantastic thirty-five-story views looking out over the Strip and the nearby Red Rock Canyon mountains. For a mere $4,000 per night, stay in one of the presidential suites that has more square footage than most homes. The bargain rooms lack the spectacular views of the Strip, facing the mountains instead. Nonetheless, they sport all the luxuries and services of the rest of this world-class hotel.

The Four Seasons' manageable size and quiet ambience are a wonderful relief from the gargantuan alternatives close by. But the biggest sell to families, in my mind, is that because this is a nongaming hotel, you won't have to worry about dragging the kids through the casinos when going to and fro. Considered a boutique hotel by Vegas standards, there are only 424 rooms, including 86 suites, which allows the staff to cater to your every need. Put the award-winning concierge team to the test by asking for anything from kids' toothpaste to birthday candles. Their goal is to have the requested item delivered to your room on a silver platter within fifteen minutes.

The little things are what make staying at the Four Seasons such a pleasure. Put out the shoes and they come back all polished. Order breakfast while sipping coffee and lounging in the hotel's lush terry bathrobes, and read the complimentary morning paper while the kids play with some of the hotel's toys. When you are ready to explore, borrow a stroller. The best part, however, just may be the soothing quiet on your return, a sharp contrast to the jangling, hustling bustle of the rest of the Strip.

The Pool and Spa (all ages)

Although not the largest or the most elaborate, again, it may be the little things that make swimming here such a treat, things like cold cucumber slices for the eyes, complimentary cabanas, and **free** ice-cold fruit. For a little more excitement, take advantage of the pass to the Mandalay Beach, right next door. Parents can take advantage of the **free** spa area, another novelty in Vegas, where access to spa facilities is often $25 or more.

The Goyas'
TopPicks for fun on the new Strip

1. Climbing the world's tallest freestanding climbing wall at GameWorks

2. Drinking an icy glass-bottled Coke at Everything Coca-Cola

3. Buying a magic trick from Houdini's Magic Shop at New York–New York

4. Keeping your dinner in on the Manhattan Express Roller Coaster at New York–New York

5. Wandering through King Tut's Tomb at the Luxor

6. Watching the water dance in front of Bellagio

7. Searching for the Obelisk at the Luxor

8. Having lunch in the Veranda at the Four Seasons

9. Walking under the lions at the MGM

10. Sharing bread pudding at the Brewery in the Monte Carlo

Where to Eat

Veranda. Steak, seafood, pasta; breakfast 6:30–11:00 A.M.; lunch 11:00 A.M.–4:00 P.M.; high tea 2:00–5:00 P.M.; dinner 5:00–10:00 P.M. Ever since my daughter was very small, we would periodically put on our best dresses and hats (the hats were essential) and go out for a "lady's lunch." We would go to a nice restaurant with white linens and more glasses than we knew what to do with and practice our manners, including holding polite conversation with our hands folded discreetly on our laps. The sign of a fabulous restaurant was one in which the waiter or waitress noticed that there were two people at the table and treated the one who needed the booster seat with as much consideration as the one who did not. Despite the fancy fare at many of Vegas's pricey restaurants, children are, at best, an afterthought—at worst, an unwelcome one. The Veranda is a charming exception.

"How could you *not* have fun, there?" my six-year-old volunteered after dining at the Veranda. He was laden with little things to keep him occupied while he waited for the food, asked personally for his food preferences, and offered adventurous tidbits with the adults, yet comforted with standard kid food on the children's menu—and the food was excellent. If you are looking for an elegant evening to remember, consider dining here. $$–$$$

Mandalay Bay

3950 Las Vegas Boulevard South; (877) 632–7000 or (702) 632–7777; www.mandalaybay .com. $$–$$$$

Generally regarded as having the best pool facility in town, this 3,700-room behemoth was named one of the thirty-six best new hotels in the world in *Condé Nast Traveler*'s May 2000 issue. Situated next to the Luxor and the Excalibur, both with large children's arcade and entertainment areas, Mandalay Bay has refrained from adding a children's area of its own.

Secret **Entrance**

Although valet parking is always available, Mandalay Bay's back entrance is the fastest way to get inside. Take Las Vegas Boulevard to Russell Road, turning toward the freeway (from I–15 take the Russell Road exit). Turn at the only stoplight in between to wind around behind the megaresort. The first parking entrance past the convention center parking structure is unmarked, but clearly a parking garage. Not only does this avoid a left turn on a busy section of Las Vegas Boulevard, you can often find parking right next to the elevators, which take you to the heart of the entertainment and food options, letting you avoid the casinos entirely. If you still want to valet it, just go to the first floor where valet parking is almost always quick.

Mandalay Bay has three major showrooms that often offer patrons the chance to see some of show business's greatest legends and hottest new stars. We have seen Ricky Martin swivel those hips, Bill Cosby highlight the trials and tribulations of growing older, and the Three Tenors compete for most impressive lung control. Although some events may not be appropriate for children, this upscale resort caters to the classiest acts around. What?! You mean we might find some culture in Vegas?

Mandalay Beach (all ages)
For guests only. Free.

Staying with the theme of a tropical island paradise, Mandalay Bay has imported 1,700 tons of sand to surround the three swimming pools, nine private bungalows, sixteen cabanas, and the lazy river ride. The wave pool varies the size of the waves up to 6 feet and is great for splashing or mock body surfing (which results mostly in getting rolled around). Lifeguards are always present, as are hordes of fellow sun-lovers. Winter nights here can bring a crisp frost, but daytime temperatures are often very comfortable for reading in the sun, even during our darkest days. For those who wish to lounge poolside, at least one pool is open year-round, with all pool facilities open during the heavy bathing season.

Tropical Aquarium (all ages)

If you like to snorkel without getting wet, glide by the 12,000 gallons of natural seawater in the registration lobby. A 14-foot-tall glass wall shields beautiful coral reefs that flourish in the Indo-Pacific region and the South Pacific. Pacific blacktip sharks, soldierfish, angelfish, puffers, and butterfly fish swim within.

Valley of the Waterfalls (all ages)

Seen from the street, the sweeping waterfalls and breathtaking firepots are something to gawk at for **free,** but when wandering within, under stately palms, lush landscaping, and mystical architecture, this really is a unique view of Vegas. Just bring your earplugs to tune out the romantic rush of nearby traffic. The easiest access is near the valet parking area.

Shark Reef at Mandalay Bay (all ages)
(702) 632–7580; 10:00 A.M.–11:00 P.M. with the last ticket sold at 10:30 P.M., 4 and under free. $

Spend an hour exploring an ancient temple that has been slowly claimed by the sea—Las Vegas style, that is. We like water exhibits in the desert; they make us feel less parched. One of the city's newest aquatic attractions contains nearly 2,000 dangerous and unusual tropical creatures including one hundred species of tropical and freshwater fish, reptiles, marine invertebrates, rays, and twelve species of sharks. The largest is a 12-foot-long nurse shark swimming over, under, around, and through the exhibit.

Mariola's **Monorail** Guide

My friend Mariola is one of the most efficient and thoughtful people I know. When she has out-of-town visitors, she provides them with this little itinerary to make the most of their time and energy (in other words, how to see the most attractions with the least amount of legwork—an important consideration when dealing with kids). The tram rides themselves are not scenic; they primarily go through parking garages and they don't cover the whole Scenic Byway. But, the trams will save time and energy when taking in the newer Strip section (the South end). You can fill in the blanks later.

1. From the Four Seasons or Mandalay Bay, walk over to the Luxor to see the Sphinx and the megawatt light.

2. Catch the monorail at the Luxor to Excalibur.

3. Walk across Tropicana to check out New York–New York, then cross the Strip to the MGM.

   Optional detour: From the MGM you can take a brief walking detour to see GameWorks, the World of Coca-Cola, and M&M World.

4. Catch the monorail at the MGM to Bally's.

   Optional detour: At least take a pause to see the Eiffel Tower and the lighted balloon at Paris, as well as Aladdin and the water ballet at Bellagio. There is a good view of all from the second-story balcony at Bellagio at the end of the overhead crosswalk.

5. Cross the street to Caesar's outdoor promenade through lighted statuary and fountains and then meander inside to see the Forum's neon sky.

6. From the Forum, head toward the volcano at the Mirage to catch another monorail to Treasure Island and the Pirate Show.

7. Walk across the street to the Fashion Mall.

8. Cross again to walk into the Venetian.

9. Circle back and reverse course, catching the tram at the Bellagio and ending up at the Monte Carlo on the way back.

Monorail Extension. The Las Vegas Monorail system is a 3.9-mile dual-beam line that connects the MGM Grand with the Sahara Hotel and Casino to the north. Stations are located along the route at Bally's/Paris, Flamingo Hilton, Harrah's/Imperial Palace, and the Las Vegas Convention Center. The system is built to carry up to 5,000 passengers per hour in each direction. Officials estimate that it will lighten traffic along the Las Vegas Strip by 4.4 million trips annually and prevent 135 tons of carbon monoxide emissions per year.

Although the petting area and the tunnel through the aquarium are fun, we loved the cool golden crocodile that just sat there staring at us. My six-year-old prized the walk over a clear plastic floor that made him think he was walking on water; my eleven-year-old loved the otherworldly jellyfish. The attraction can get a little crowded during the midday; try to visit in the early morning or late afternoon. At $10 a crack, though, the exhibit is rather pricey.

Mamma Mia! (ages 5 and up)

Mandalay Bay Theatre; (702) 632–7580; www.mandalaybay.com or mamamia.com. Wednesday, Thursday, and Sunday at 7:00 P.M. and Friday at 8:00 P.M. Saturday and Monday performances at 7:00 P.M. and 10:30 P.M. $$$–$$$$.

After huge successes in London, on Broadway, and during its national tour, this box-office bonanza is a natural for Vegas. Based on twenty-two songs from the Swedish group, ABBA, the story revolves around a young bride's upcoming wedding. There is just one problem: With three potential fathers, who does she ask to give her away?

Using a sadly common theme, the search for an unknown father, the play hints at some of the downside of the sexual revolution. But, no fear: True love and upbeat songs always win in the end.

House of Blues (age appropriateness varies)

Mandalay Bay, next to the Sportsbook Bar on the Casino level; (702) 632-7607. Sunday through Thursday 8:00 P.M.–midnight, Friday and Saturday 8:00 P.M.–1:00 A.M.; "Acoustic Night," Sunday 8:00–11:00 P.M.

The House of Blues is second to the pool as a must-see destination for kids at Mandalay Bay. The outside is covered with glittering, very cool mosaics made from broken pottery, bottle caps, and various junk that can be either broken, painted, or torched to create an impressionist image. Found-materials artist Gregory Warmack recently completed a 120-foot wall embedded with more than 50,000 bottle caps.

The nightclub features many performers that older kids either could see or should see. Jazz legends like Etta James and B. B. King are often seen here, as are those who can only hope to reach this kind of stature, such as the Goo Goo Dolls and Juice Newton. Ask if the venue is appropriate for kids. Teens and preteens will think it way cool to see a favorite band up close, particularly in such an intimate yet rad setting. Check out the Sunday Gospel Brunch to "Praise the Lord and pass the biscuits." Rousing gospel groups keep things lively.

Where to Eat

House of Blues. (702) 632–7406. Daily 8:00 A.M.–midnight, Friday until 1:00 A.M., Saturday until 2:00 A.M. Loud vintage and contemporary rock, blues, and soul music accompanies Southern-style food. It's pretty hard to carry on a conversation; however, with the visual and audio overload, no one will mind if the kids get a little squirrely in the booths. As for the food, the ribs are a real treat, and I love having a hearty serving of greens with my meal. The fish is excellent, and the key lime pie is delightfully tangy. $$

The Noodle Shop. (702) 632–7406. Daily 11:00 A.M.–3:00 A.M. This traditional Cantonese noodle kitchen is nestled within Raffles Café and serves a wide range of noodle items, congee, rice, and barbecue dishes. $–$$

Raffles Café. (702) 632–7406. Daily twenty-four hours. This upscale cafe overlooking the tropical gardens and pools offers a wide range of dishes from fluffy Spanish omelets to decadent desserts. $–$$

Trattoria del Lupo. (702) 740–5522. Sunday through Thursday 5:00–10:00 P.M., Friday and Saturday 5:00–11:00 P.M. This elegant Italian restaurant has a large selection of pizzas, a children's menu, and lovely original seafood dishes. Kids who find dips irresistible will appreciate the daily special dip (Chloe couldn't resist asking for a second dipping cup of the bean soup) as well as a staff that caters to little ones' every culinary whim, whether on or off the menu. $$–$$$

Family **Climbing** Fun

I talked with *Southern Nevada Family Magazine* Executive Editor David Clark when he was at Duck Creek's spray park with his six-year-old. "We have just started climbing together and my sons, ages six and eight, have really taken to that," he says. Climbing families love the tight bonding that comes with climbing and the thrill of tackling a new wall and getting to the top. Although climbing is an individual effort, few sports insist on the teamwork and communication skills that successful climbing requires.

GameWorks. Showcase Mall, 3785 Las Vegas Boulevard South; (702) 432–4263. Daily 10:00 A.M.–10:00 P.M. Friday and Saturday until midnight. "It is $10 per climb, and at a gym you can climb all day for that price, but the wall is a lot of fun for a special day."

Nevada Climbing Center. 3065 East Patrick Lane; (702) 898–8192. Monday, Wednesday, and Friday 11:00 A.M.–9:00 P.M.; Tuesday through Thursday 11:00 A.M.–10:00 P.M.; Saturday 9:00 A.M.–9:00 P.M., Sunday 11:00 A.M.–7:00 P.M. "This gym offers twenty different ropes for all levels with all levels of difficulty." Weekday daypass $10.00, weekends $12.00, gear $8.00.

Powerhouse Indoor Climbing Center. 8201 West Charleston Boulevard; (702) 254–5604. Monday through Thursday 11:00 A.M.–10:00 P.M.; Friday 11:00 A.M.–8:00 P.M.; Saturday and Sunday 10:00 A.M.–8:00 P.M. "The climbing center features indoor rock climbing, which is great for a hot or windy day." Shoes and harness $8.00, climbing fee $14.00.

Luxor Hotel and Casino

3900 Las Vegas Boulevard South; (702) 262–4000 and (800) 288–1000. $–$$$$

Luxor's great, onyx-hued pyramid rises 350 feet to its apex where, at night, the world's brightest beam of light (forty billion times more candlepower than a strong search-light) shoots out to the stars. The place is just so unusual that both kids and grown-ups adore it (it was recently voted one of the top fifty resorts in the United States by *Gourmet* magazine readers), from the Sphinx who guards the entrance to the authentic Egyptian ornamentation inside.

It is hard to describe how visually rich this place is and how fun kids find it. Once inside, visitors are greeted by a life-size replica of the Great Temple of Ramses II, which rises 35 feet into the towering atrium. For those who choose to stay here, the 4,467 rooms and suites are accessed via the "inclinator," an incline elevator that slides up the sloped edge of the pyramid—truly a unique experience.

At the Pharaoh's Pavilion in the center of the great pyramid, an entire floor is devoted to extracurricular activities that children can enjoy, including an IMAX Theatre, shopping, a food court, a museum, an arcade, and more. Best of all, there are no one-armed bandits in sight.

Kids will adore the Karnak Kiosk. At this unique souvenir shop, they can have their names embroidered in Egyptian hieroglyphics on a hat or a T-shirt.

Oasis Pool and Spa (all ages)

Five swimming pools with four Jacuzzis lie within the outside pool area. Small "islands" are scattered throughout the pools as waterfalls cascade over faux rocks surrounded by plenty of lifeguards. For the ultimate in pampering, a full-service health spa offers frazzled parents twenty-four-hour access.

Giza Gallery (all ages)

There is something very mysterious about the Egyptian era. This shopping area, reminiscent of an ancient Egyptian bazaar, offers a variety of stores in which to sample that time. Located on the main level of the East Tower, elegant fountains, exotic statues, and stone walkways greet visitors. Artifacts, authentically crafted Egyptian vases, body oils reminiscent of Nefertiti's legendary beauty regimen, fine clothing, and a children's shop are all represented. Then, of course, we must have the $5.00 replica of the Las Vegas pyramid to take home.

Kids who love to shop love to shop here, where everything is slightly historical and kitschy. What kid doesn't love the mystery and magic of pyramids? Here are two of our favorites. **The Pyramid Shop** features every-

thing you ever wanted to discover about these ancient shapes. Do take the time to look at the real things, some dating back to 2400 B.C., that are on display and for sale at **Treasure Chamber.** Some items are surprisingly affordable.

Blue Man Group: Live at Luxor (ages 6 and up)
(702) 262–4400. Wednesday through Saturday 7:00 and 10:00 P.M., Sunday and Monday 7:00 P.M. Saturday matinee at 4:00 P.M. $$$.

The electric blue faces that mutely promote Intel on television commercials are a definite draw for kids, who will adore sitting in the front rows. (Be sure to plan for a bath afterward.) The silly antics, rhythmic drum beat, otherworldly faces, and feigned or real innocence of the performers will definitely strike another chord. Parents will admit they have never seen anything like it as these three stooges make fun of magic acts, music, light, sound, the universe, personal self-importance, and plumbing. Plumbing as a metaphor for life will be a sure fire hit with kids (although, when we were there, the grown-ups were nearly hysterical with laughter) and the plumbing-as-music is as innovative as anything I've ever seen on stage. We won't give away the finale, but let's just say that it keeps coming, and coming, and coming and involves virtually everyone in the audience. Since nary a word passes between the people on stage, you don't have to worry that it will be over anyone's head—figuratively, that is.

King Tut's Tomb and Museum (all ages)
Pharaoh's Pavilion; (702) 262–4555. Daily 10:00 A.M.–11:00 P.M. $5.95 per person.

"I see wonderful things!" archaeologist Howard Carter breathed when he first peered into King Tut's tomb. That discovery is legendary, and this full-scale authentic reproduction of the tomb effectively captures the feeling that the exploration team must have felt when wandering through the priceless treasures that became one of the greatest archaeological finds of all time.

The museum contains replicas of items originally found in King Tutankhamen's tomb. Each of the handcrafted replicas was reproduced in Egypt using the same gold leaf and linens, precious pigments, tools, and 3,300-year-old artisan methods of the originals. Once completed, the pieces were brought to Las Vegas and faithfully positioned as they were originally discovered. Treasures are scattered across floors; rooms reveal piles of priceless artifacts and stone guardians. The fifteen-minute self-guided audio tour is about the right length for children, who may become surprisingly knowledgeable about Egyptian history. My crew found the whole thing fascinating.

Games of the Gods (age appropriateness of games varies)
Pharaoh's Pavilion. Prices vary.

This Sega Virtualand Arcade has 18,000 square feet of video arcade that includes movies, Virtual Formula Race Cars, and an F-16 Flight Simulator. With unique video games and attractions, this is one of the most fun and least crowded arcades in town. Experience the thrill of fast cars, battle villains, race, and even ski in a near virtual-reality setting. What's more, kids can make their own MTV–style video at the Karaoke Recording Studio.

IMAX Theatre (all ages)
Pharaoh's Pavilion; (702) 262–4555. $.

If you have never been to an IMAX theater, you're in for a treat, whatever the subject. The screen is nearly seven stories high, capturing film frames that are ten times the size of conventional film. Almost like in a planetarium, one just sits back and enjoys being immersed in the experience.

In Search of the Obelisk (all ages)
Pharaoh's Pavilion. Daily 9:00 A.M.–11:00 P.M. $.

In this motion-based simulator ride, kids can visit the dig site of a spectacular subterranean civilization. Board a levitating vehicle to participate in a fast-paced chase that includes battling bad guys and chasing a mysterious crystal obelisk—campy, but fun.

Mysteries of Egypt (all ages)
Pharaoh's Pavilion. Daily 9:00 A.M.–5:00 P.M. $.

This short A&E documentary explores the ancient history and mystery of Egypt's legendary leaders, including a pharaoh who had more than twenty children by the age of twenty-five, the scandalous behavior of Cleopatra, and insights into the greatest tombs of all time.

Where to Eat

Gourmet magazine readers, of course, like to eat and have found a host of quality eateries here ranging from formal restaurants to casual cafes and delis. Their responses ranked the Luxor among the top five destinations in the Pacific Northwest and Mountain states region. Thousands of subscribers named their favorite hotels and then rated them according to fifteen criteria, four of which were food related. Families will also enjoy the dining options. Those with older children may want to order room service for the kids while escaping to a romantic rendezvous at one of the top-of-the-line dining rooms.

Isis. (702) 262–4773. Friday through Tuesday 5:30–11:00 P.M. Open for dinner only, Isis was named one of the top ten gourmet rooms in the United States by the *Best of the Best* restaurant guide. An intimate colonnade walk of caryatid statues takes you through glass doors with gold-embossed "Wings of Isis" into a canopy of indoor stars where patrons overlook the Luxor casino. This gourmet menu may be too adventurous for some, but the magnificent flambé desserts appeal to everyone, kids included. $$$$

Nile Deli. 7:00 A.M.–10:00 P.M. Get your fill of kosher-style deli foods in this New York–themed eatery. The menu includes New York favorites such as potato pancakes, potato knishes, blintzes, chopped chicken liver, and triple-decker sandwiches. $

Papyrus. (702) 262–4774. 5:00–11:00 P.M.; closed Tuesday and Wednesday. Kids will love the Otemanu Hot Rock Sampler, Luxor's version of Pacific Rim hot rock grilling at your table. The Asian-style food runs from Cantonese and Szechuan to Polynesian and Pacific Rim specialties. $$–$$$

Pyramid Cafe. Open twenty-four hours. The Pyramid Cafe offers a wide range of breakfast, lunch, and dinner selections, whether your family is in the mood for scrambled eggs or prime rib. Images of ancient Egyptian gods and goddesses line the walls, a grove of palm trees flanks the island booths, and special column treatments replicate those found at the Temple of Luxor in Egypt. The menu also features a number of calorie-conscious selections. $–$$

Sacred Sea Room. (702) 262–4772. Daily 5:00–11:00 P.M. (reservations recommended). Award-winning cuisine offers a variety of seafood that is shipped in fresh daily. Murals and hieroglyphic reproductions of fishing on the Nile line the walls, and a wavelike blue ceiling mosaic provides a cozy dining experience. A favorite is the stuffed prawns of Aswan, filled with Gruyère cheese and herbs. This is a "Best of the Best" award winner from the American Academy of Restaurants and Hospitality Sciences. $$$–$$$$

Excalibur

3850 Las Vegas Boulevard South; (702) 597–7777. $–$$$$

Kids love the white castle with the colorful spires that was redecorated in 1999. At night, Merlin beckons from the tower, and a rather hokey dragon fight occurs in the moat at the castle's front entrance every hour on the hour from dusk until midnight. The casinos are a perpetual hazard when entering and leaving the hotel rooms, which is the rule rather than the exception in Las Vegas. Nonetheless, Excalibur's relative small scale, proximity to the major kid attractions, attractive room rates, and family-friendly staff make it a preferred place to stay as well as visit.

Excalibur Pool (all ages)

The pool area comfortably holds 800 guests and features two heated pools, a twenty-five-seat spa, waterfalls, water slides, a large deck, and a shaded dining area. A snack bar and a cocktail bar are open daily.

The Medieval Village (all ages)

10:00 A.M.–10:00 P.M. The Spirit Shop has sundries and stays open twenty-four hours.

Here you'll find dozens of shops, four restaurants, a village pub, a food court, and strolling entertainers. The princess hats, plastic swords, costumed ladies, and performers make this more than just a shopping area.

I'd hold hands while visiting the Dragon's Lair (breakable seems to be the byword here), but definitely do stop in if you want a cool souvenir. Little boys especially love the crystal and pewter dragons. But big boys—dads, for instance—can't help but be impressed with the cool swords and armor that grace the walls. Highly polished swords in a variety of styles make moms glad that we've passed the days when people actually used them.

Tournament of Kings (all ages)

(702) 597–7600. Dinner/performances daily at 6:00 and 8:30 P.M. $$$. Children under 3 may share your seat and meal for free.

Okay, this dinner show is hokey, like the moat dragon, but it sure is fun, especially for boys. I thought my twelve-year-old might find the whole knights-in-armor thing too silly, but as the show progressed, so did his grin. The concept is simply this: We are all celebrating with King Arthur and the Knights of the Roundtable, so we eat with our hands, drink watery cola, bang on the table, and shout cheers to our King while he jousts (Yes! They really joust!) atop his thundering, glorious steed. There are sword fights and various other forms of battle, first in a games atmosphere, then for "real" when the green knight appears and challenges King Arthur in a fight to the death. Silly? Yeah. Isn't it great?

Court Jester's Stage (all ages)

The Medieval Village. Daily 11:00 A.M.–7:30 P.M. Free.

Jugglers, singers, puppeteers, and other performers appear throughout the day in medieval costume at this free stage show.

Fantasy Faire (all ages)

Some height restrictions apply.

Carnival-style games take up the entire lower level. Most games cost $1.00 or less. The Magic Motion Machine theater shows various heart-racing films such as the runaway alpine train or dune buggy thrills in the desert. This seems to be one of the best arcades in town for kids to actually win prizes, at least in our experience.

Merlin's Magic Motion Machines (42 inches and taller)

Daily 10:00 A.M.–11:00 P.M. $ per ride.

These rides are more whimsical than wild, but they are still a lot of fun. In our favorite, the Kid Coaster, the riders turn into toys and hop aboard a toy train track—but boy, what a track! Like the old game Mousetrap, one thing leads to another as we careen around a toy-filled room. Desert Duel takes riders on an off-road truck race, and in Glacier Run your car accidentally runs off the track, taking you on a series of near collisions before you arrive safely at your destination.

Where to Eat

Cold Stone Creamery. (702) 597–7690. Food Court. 9:00 A.M.–11:00 P.M. Another of our favorite interactive desserts, this ice cream is so fun you could eat it twice. The "cold stone" is an icy slab that probably once was stone, but is now stainless steel. Once the customer selects an ice cream (usually vanilla, chocolate, mint, strawberry, French vanilla, or frozen yogurt) a lavish scoop is placed on the stone. Then, one must select one or more of the mix-ins (chocolate chips, various fruits, cookies, chopped candies, gummy bears, fresh brownies, etc.) that are hand pummeled into the cream. Customer favorite combinations are posted on the wall, and you can fill out a card with your own concoction. At least one of us always goes with our favorite: French vanilla with fresh brownies and raspberries. Ummm! (Excuse me while I make a quick trip to the ice cream store.) $

Krispy Kreme Doughnuts. (702) 597–7777. Food Court; www.krispykreme .com/krispykr. Open twenty-four hours. If you haven't ever eaten Krispy Kremes, you are in for a real treat. These sweet confections are melt-in-your-mouth good. And, somehow, it is simply fascinating to watch through the viewing window as donuts are plopped into hot oil, flipped, covered with a sheet of hot white glaze, then packaged right before your very eyes. $

Regale Italian Eatery. (702) 597–7777. Daily 5:00–10:00 P.M., until 11:00 P.M. Friday and Saturday. Italian cuisine served in an Italian village setting. With a full menu of pizzas, families can find anything from the classic cheese to a broccoli, cauliflower, and carrot pizza. $$

Sherwood Forest Cafe. (702) 597–7777. Open twenty-four hours. Enjoy sandwiches and other diner-style menu items like spaghetti or meat loaf. $$

Sir Galahad's Prime Rib House. (702) 597–7777. Daily 5:00–10:00 P.M., until 11:00 P.M. Friday and Saturday. This Tudor-style steak house features prime rib carved tableside for a fun adventure in eating. Kids can enjoy a creamy baked macaroni and cheese. $$

Tropicana

3801 Las Vegas Boulevard South; (702) 739–2222; www.tropicanalv.com. $–$$$

Almost everyone has seen a televised image of a Las Vegas casino implosion. From the famous to the infamous, out-of-date casinos quickly turn into dust, but a few stand tall. The Tropicana has charmed guests for more than fifty years now, with its relatively small size and comfortable atmosphere. With fewer than 2,000 guest rooms and suites, it is one of the smaller local resorts, but it still has a variety of adult and G-rated entertainment options, a large water playground, and reasonably priced fine-dining establishments. Formerly located "Where Las Vegas Begins," it now sits in relative quiet among the cacophony of the Luxor, the Excalibur, New York–New York, and the MGM Grand. Although not family-appropriate entertainment, the Comedy Stop at the Trop brings in some of the best stand-up comedians in the country; the Celebration Lounge features live nightly entertainment for after the kids are in bed.

Pool (all ages)

Between the hotel's twin towers are five acres of tropically landscaped grounds, pools, lagoons, bridges, and waterfalls, creating a garden setting for one of the world's largest indoor/outdoor swimming pools. The large main pool is open seasonally; the indoor portion is separated by glass doors and heated in the winter for year-round swimming. Three relaxing spas, cascading waterfalls, two lagoons, and the lagoon pool are surrounded by lush tropical plants to complete this desert paradise. Parents can try their hand at the world-famous swim-up blackjack tables at the pool during the summer months, complete with a special waterproof layout and money dryers. Don't look for the Wildlife Walk, though; it has been closed.

Tropicana Bird Show (all ages)

Tropicana Lounge. Daily 11:00 A.M., 12:30, and 2:00 P.M. Free.

Join a flight of feathered friends as Tiana Carrol leads her avian friends through an amazing array of behaviors, including singing, dancing, riding a bicycle, juggling, and flying through hoops. The audience participation makes this a kids' favorite.

Illusionary Magic of Rick Thomas (all ages)

Tiffany Theatre; (702) 739–2411. Saturday through Thursday 2:00 and 4:00 P.M.; dark Friday. $ (table), $$ (booth).

Crowned Stage Magician of the year at the recent World Magic Awards, Thomas weaves music, magic, dance, and exotic animals into a mystical spectacle. An imposing figure, the 6'4" magician might be one of the most graceful of the town's illusionists. (He won the Amateur United States Ballroom Dancing Champion title during his teens.) With some deft comedy thrown into the mix of disappearing tigers, levitation, floating dancers, and incorporeal bodies, Thomas's act becomes one of the bargains in Vegas.

The Best of Folies Bergere (ages 5 and up)

Tiffany Theatre; (702) 739–2411. Monday through Saturday 7:30 P.M. (covered) and 10:00 P.M. (topless, adult only); dark Thursday. $$$.

For more than forty years, the Folies have paid musical tribute to the Parisian cabaret. With today's sensibilities, the show is relatively tame, other than the bare-breasted beauties who parade through the late show. Only two "Las Vegas showgirl"–type production shows are left on the Strip, with magic, Broadway, and high-end production numbers pulling in the crowds. Of the two, Jubilee has the best headdresses, but the Folies seems to have better dancers, choreography, and a general sense of fun. The classic cancan may be the most enjoyable number in the show, with acrobatic as well as comedic touches. Basically a variety show, the Folies signed Wally Eastwood, a talented juggler/comedian who combines broad physical comedy with dexterous juggling. At one point he plays a rapid-fire song on a keyboard, using tennis balls to strike the keys. Pretty impressive.

Where to Eat

Calypso's. Open twenty-four hours. More than a coffee shop, Calypso's serves everything from breakfast specials to Caribbean delicacies. The hot items, though, are the steak and crab leg dinner, or the late-night T-bone steak and eggs. There's a children's menu for those ages eight and younger. $$

Java Java. Two locations: Main floor by the Celebration Lounge, 6:00 A.M.–11:00 P.M., and in the convention area, 6:00 A.M.–9:00 P.M. Take an afternoon break with the kids at this not-Starbucks-or-Jitters coffee shop. Supplied by the Northwest's premier coffee roaster, the Boyd Coffee Company, the menu offers a variety of hot and cold coffees, fruit smoothies, and pastries. $

Legend's Deli. Daily 7:00 A.M.–9:00 P.M. A deli is a deli, except when it has locals' favorites on the menu, such as Elvis's notorious sandwich made with white toast, grilled banana, peanut butter, and grape jelly. You can't come to town without trying that. Aside from celebrity-named sandwiches, the deli offers breakfast items, appetizers, salads, cheese and fruit plates, and desserts. $–$$

Mizuno's Japanese Steak House. (702) 739–2713. Daily 5:00–10:45 P.M. Reservations recommended. If you have never eaten Teppan, you have to try it with the kids. Talented Mizuno chefs toss shrimp into their pockets, shake seasonings under a strobe light, and use cooking utensils as musical instruments. Serving everything from chicken to sushi to lobster tail, Mizuno's was voted the best Asian restaurant for the year 2000 by the Southern Nevada Hotel Concierge Association. $$–$$$

Pietro's. (702) 739–2341. Daily 5:00–11:00 P.M. Reservations required. Ranked one of America's top one hundred restaurants of the twentieth century and one of the top ten gourmet rooms in the United States by the International Restaurant and Hospitality Rating Bureau, among other awards, this place is one of the best restaurant bargains in town. With tableside cooking, hand-tossed Caesar salads, and flaming deserts, it is also a lot of fun. $$

Savanna. (702) 739–2222. Daily 5:00–11:00 P.M. Reservations required. The Trop still remembers the days when fine dining and cheap prices were part of the Las Vegas experience. The Savanna features dinner specials; pasta, chicken, or beef entrees; or more exotic selections such as fire-roasted sea scallops and tiger prawns. Families will love the "Hakuna Matata" (No Worry) Savanna dessert sampler with Ivory Coast tiramisu, Tanzania caramel custard, or other chef's favorites. There's no children's menu, but chefs will meet kids' requests. $$–$$$

New York–New York

3790 Las Vegas Boulevard South; (702) 740–6969. $–$$

At the height of that building period in Las Vegas when everything had to be a mini something else, this hotel took a bite from the Big Apple. Truly one of Vegas's most recognizable landmarks, the facade re-creates the Brooklyn Bridge, the Statue of Liberty, and a host of skyscrapers. Inside, a meandering stream directs guests to the food court and entertainment area. Interestingly, the grime of an older city was also re-created, with graffiti, old signs, and a general gritty patina coating everything.

Rita Rudner (ages 7 and up)

Cabaret Theatre; (702) 740–6815; www.ritafunny.com. Monday through Friday at 8:00 P.M. and Saturday at 7:00 P.M. and 9:00 P.M. $$$.

Rudner's wildly wicked wit is very womanly and never cheesy. Dressed in to-die-for gowns, her routines routinely harpoon marriage, shopping, men, women, shopping, fingernails, shopping, and other feminine topics of interest. Most boys probably won't think this is too funny, but inviting a shop-a-holic daughter to see Miss Rudner could be a whole lot of fun. Then go out and have your fingernails done.

Manhattan Express Roller Coaster (54 inches or taller)

(702) 740–6969 or (800) 693–6763. Daily 10:00 A.M.–11:00 P.M. and Saturday until 11:30 P.M. $ per ride.

Generally considered one of the best coasters around, this 203-foot Coney Island–style thrill ride speeds around the New York facade and lets riders experience a 180-degree "heart line" roll with drops of up to 144 feet at speeds up to 67 mph. Set in the heart of the Strip, this is a sight-seeing wonder, both night and day. During daylight hours, you get to see the tiny ants on the street gaping in awe as you skyrocket around the Statue of Liberty. At night you get one of the most fabulous views of the Strip—if you can open your eyes, that is. Take your choice.

Coney Island Emporium (all ages)

(702) 740–6969 or (888) 696–9887. Open twenty-four hours, but maintains city curfew hours for unaccompanied minors: 10:00 P.M. on school nights, midnight on weekend and holiday nights. Cost varies by activity.

This arcade contains an interactive laser tag game, virtual reality games, a shooting gallery, bumper cars, and more. Compared to some of the other arcades, though, my kids ran out of activities relatively early.

Houdini's Magic Shop (all ages)

(702) 740–6418. 9:00 A.M.–1:00 A.M. daily.

Near the second-floor entrance coming from the MGM, our favorite magic shop contains a little bit of history, as well as some of the best magic shop magicians in town. The Great Houdini's handcuffs are for sale here, as well as other memorabilia from him and other renowned magicians. Since many of the other magic shops are specifically geared toward supporting their namesake's star, they are more prone to pitch his or her stuff. This casino has no magic show, so it banks on the classic names to lend mystery and awe.

There's **Magic** in the Air

I don't know of anywhere else in the world where magic is so accessible. Not only does Las Vegas have more world-class magicians presenting world-class shows, the area is rife with talented newcomers vying for their own place on the Strip. Unknowns will astound you at the magic shops that can be found at many local resorts. Part of these magicians' jobs is to demonstrate and sell magic tricks. The easiest way to do that is to ask some kid to help out by holding a string, loaning a card, or looking inside of a box. Soon, a small crowd has gathered and business is booming. There are tricks for around $5.00 that are wonderful souvenirs to remember Vegas by, particularly if your kids have become inspired after attending one of the many magic shows that are in town. Anyone buying a trick gets to enter a secret chamber with the magician for a free demonstration. Although the rooms are small, all five of our family members crowd in to witness the magic charm in action.

Where to Eat

America. (702) 740–6451. Open twenty-four hours. A clever idea with dependable food that kids always eat (hamburgers are a specialty; naturally, they offer pizza), this restaurant gives kids a new way to see our country. Overhead hangs a huge relief map of the good old U.S.A., built at the Brooklyn Navy Yard by fifty different artists, with appropriate and sometimes puzzling icons that depict key elements of each state. Of course, we had to check out our favorite states and debate whether the map was appropriately sensitive or blatantly stereotypical in its choice of symbols, but that was half the pleasure and hatched a fun and sometimes funny discussion of varying family views of our country. One wall is covered with quotes from letters home, perhaps inspiring a nighttime postcard to Grandma from your own brood. The menu tries to stay with the theme of something from each area, but mostly just renames standard choices. It's surprisingly good, however, with large servings. You may want to share a meal to save room for dessert at the bakery next door. Avoid the macaroni. $–$$

Il Fornaio. (702) 740–6403. Daily 8:30 A.M.–midnight, Friday and Saturday 8:30 A.M.–1:00 A.M. Il Fornaio presents award-winning Italian cuisine made from authentic regional recipes featuring house-made pastas, rotisserie meats, mesquite-grilled fish, wood-fired pizzas, and hearth breads. $$–$$$

Il Fornaio Panetteria. (702) 740–2425. Daily 7:00 A.M.–9:30 P.M., Friday and Saturday 7:00 A.M.–11:30 P.M. Well, the secret's out. My family has a real sweet tooth, but with discrimination. My daughter bakes the world's best cookies (according to her little brother), and my son makes a killer tapioca pudding. So, although we have a penchant for sweets, just anything won't do. This place will do, and so will its bread. Part of a fairly large regional chain of restaurants and bakeries located primarily throughout California, this is Nevada's only location.

Mae West's Powder Room

Before you eat, make a special trip to wash your hands and see a powder room tribute to that American icon, Mae West, whose loungey photos decorate the walls. Faux velvet-painted curtains adorn the doors, and pink sinks with elaborate brass faucets are framed by Frank Lloyd Wright wallpaper borders and filigreed lighting sconces. The pink rose theme throughout is topped by the wrought-iron roses framing all the mirrors and the stained-glass roses on the far wall. My daughter thought this was the most amazing restroom she had ever seen. (Restrooms out here deserve their own book.)

With gourmet coffees and breakfast pastries, salads, and lunchtime sandwiches made with their own fresh breads, it is an enjoyable way to start the day or savor a mid-day retreat. For a snack, though, the pastries are gorgeous—the kind that intricately layer cake and cream, then wrap it all in a chocolate box—and reasonable. The chewy breads, high-end extra-virgin Italian olive oils, and balsamic vinegars make you want to create a romantic moment in your room after the little ones are asleep. Can't you just see the two of you sitting at that tiny table in the corner, dipping little chunks of bread and gazing into each other's eyes? $

Nine Fine Irishmen. The top chefs in Ireland contributed their favorite recipes to this new pub to showcase the diversity and freshness of authentic Irish cuisine. Set in a bona fide Irish pub hauled directly from the Emerald Isle and filled with a variety of stouts, lagers, ales, and festivities, dining here offers a chance to share Irish ballads and storytelling with your own wee bairnes. $$

The Village Eateries. This is one of the better food courts with nine small restaurants serving New York–style grub like deli sandwiches with sauerkraut, pizzas, and more in a faux–New York neighborhood. Divided into small courtyards, the atmosphere is intimate and fun. The roller coaster provides a trainlike atmosphere as it periodically whizzes by overhead. All of the food is reasonably priced and each restaurant sets its own hours. Something should be available from 7:00 A.M. to 3:00 A.M., with America, next door, providing food coverage for the missing hours. $

Monte Carlo

3770 Las Vegas Boulevard South; (702) 730–7777 or (800) 311–8999. $–$$$$

Opened in 1996, this $344 million full-service resort is now one of the classic hotels on the Strip, although it never seems to get the recognition that it deserves. With more than 3,000 rooms and 250 luxury suites, it is low-key and elegant. Because of the Monte Carlo's fantastic swimming area and one of the family-friendliest entertainers in town, my family gives it our own five-star rating, maybe because it feels like an elegant hotel first instead of a large casino with rooms.

Holiday **Lights**

I have a secret confession: I love glitter and sparkling lights, and so do my kids. Christmas lets us indulge in public. Here are some of our favorite places to sparkle.

Ethel M. Chocolates "Light the Night." 1 Sunset Way; (702) 433–2500. After dark. Wander at your leisure through the more than 300 species of plants in this cactus garden, all covered in strands of Christmas lights. My daughter feels sorry for the people who have to put those lights up. Before you leave, just try to resist stopping in for a free chocolate.

Festival of Trees and Lights. Bally's, 3645 Las Vegas Boulevard South; (702) 648–1990. $. For one week during the holiday season, Bally's overflows with trees, wreaths, centerpieces, Hanukkah decorations, and gingerbread houses. The items are later auctioned off to the public with proceeds going to the Down's Syndrome Organization of Southern Nevada, the same organization that sponsors it. Thanksgiving Day is free.

The Gift of Lights. Sunset Park, 2601 East Sunset Road; (702) 451–1641. November–January. Drive down Winter Wonderland Way, turn on Toyland Crossing, and continue to Once Upon a Time Land. No, this isn't Disneyland. It's Sunset Park's "The Gift of Lights," which is full of splendor and has more than a hundred lighting displays, music, and holiday cheer. The cost is $10.00 per vehicle; special price $8.00 if you donate a bag of slightly used clothing to any Goodwill center in Las Vegas or Henderson or on-site at the event.

Opportunity Village's Magical Forest. 6300 West Oakey Boulevard; (702) 259–3700. Daily 5:00–10:00 P.M. $. The village is lit up with more than three million lights, 15-foot candy canes, and animated characters. Trains take you around the village to the carousel, the Magic Castle, and the food court. Train and carousel ride passes cost $10 for children and $12 for adults. Come to Santa's Gazebo; every so often Santa drops by for a quick visit.

Pool (all ages)

We had a blast lounging and playing in this series of pools. With a wave pool, a lazy river, an enclosed children's pool, and a sunbathing pool, families have a variety of choices on how to splash the day away. Rafts and some water toys can be rented.

Tennis Courts (all ages)

(702) 730–7777 or (800) 311–8999. Tennis shop open 9:00 A.M.–5:00 P.M.; courts open until midnight. Racket rental $. Daily clinics 10:00–11:30 A.M., $$; just show up.

What better way to break a sweat than hitting some balls with your kids? The four lighted tennis courts are usually available (after dark, you need a receipt from the pro shop to show security guards). The daily clinics offer a chance to work with a pro or meet some good competition, for either one-on-one or doubles play. One of the best family deals is to hire the pro for an hour (at $75 per hour) and let him or her work with the whole family. Because the fee is per hour, not per person, everyone can get some tips.

Golf (ages 8 and up)

(702) 730–7777 or (800) 311–8999. Individual play at the various courses $$$$–$$$$$.

The Monte Carlo was the first resort in Las Vegas to have an in-house golf division that offers play on twenty-two of the most desirable courses in Vegas, including Wild Horse, TPC Senior Canyon Course, and Stallion Mountain. Now that Vegas is increasingly known as a top golfing destination, the courses have seemed to breed like rabbits. Monte Carlo can set up play at Walter's courses, the critically acclaimed Paiute course, and the Balihai, the only golf course on the Strip with PGA Bermuda-style play complete with tropical trees and white sand beaches. The Monte Carlo has a full-service pro shop where a golf concierge can fully equip interested golfers. The concierge can also schedule same-day play or make reservations up to thirty days in advance. Lessons for kids, parents, or a combination of both can be scheduled at six of the courses. Lessons are $110 for one hour or $300 for three hours with a master instructor and $150 for one hour or $425 for three hours with Mike Davis; children under 17 receive a 25 percent discount. For a group of three or more (including children) the resort can arrange custom play at the Royal Links Golf Club with Davis as the instructor for $175 per person for three hours of play.

Lance Burton, Master Magician (all ages)

(702) 730–7160 or (800) 311–8999. Tuesday through Saturday 7:00 and 10:00 P.M. $$$.

Burton always starts his show with the routine that made him the first American to win the Grand Prix at the Federation Internationale des Societes Magique, earning him the title "World Champion Magician." The ease with which birds, candles, coins, and even a car come and go makes conjuring in his accomplished hands appear as commonplace as rolling out pie dough. His blend of first-year enthusiasm and, dare we say, modesty makes him unique in this town of false fronts and over-the-top production numbers. His obvious love of children makes kids respond in kind, particularly when he calls them up to help out with a trick. We barely left the showroom before my youngest was begging to go back.

Burton's natural affinity for children makes this one of the best children's shows in town. His excellence in his field makes him second to none in wizardry. A gentleman at heart, he usually showcases another talent while he takes a brief break during the middle of the show. We first saw Mac King on his stage. King has gone on to his own place on the Strip, but Burton continues to include other talented magicians, jugglers, and specialty acts.

Where to Eat

Andre's at the Monte Carlo. (702) 730–7955. Reservations recommended. Daily 5:30–9:30 P.M. When locals want a romantic dinner for two, this is the place that has been on the top of the list for years, despite the influx of trendy restaurants. Chef Andre presents extraordinary French cuisine that can be complemented by a selection from the restaurant's world-class wine cellar. $$$

Dragon Noodle Company. (702) 730–7965. Sunday through Thursday 11:00 A.M.–10:00 P.M., until 11:00 P.M. on weekends. Choose from a wide selection of delicious noodle dishes, roasted meats, uniquely prepared chicken, and fresh seafood at this Asian food and tea emporium. $–$$

Market City Caffe. (702) 730–7966. Daily 11:00 A.M.–11:00 P.M., until midnight on weekends. Enjoy the authenticity of this warm, inviting trattoria. Generous portions of Italian fare, including an antipasto bar, homemade pastas, pizzas, and grilled entrees are served at inviting prices. This is the kind of place where you might consider sharing a meal with a loved one. After all, we're all family. $–$$

Monte Carlo Pub & Brewery. (702) 730–7777. Daily 11:00 A.M.–3:00 A.M., until 4:00 A.M. on weekends. Enjoy a microbrew in this sports authority kind of pub with lots of TVs featuring the latest sporting event. Boys love the atmosphere, and the whole family enjoys the surprisingly good food. Because the whole place is rather cacophonic already, there is no need to worry that little Sally is too loud. Share a bucket of mussels or a rack of baby back ribs, but be sure to save room for the delectable bread pudding. $–$$

MGM Grand

3799 Las Vegas Boulevard South; (702) 891–1111 or (800) 646–7787; www.mgmgrand .com. $–$$$$

The MGM Grand was one of the first newer resorts to go after the family market, and it did it with a vengeance, spending $1 billion to create a 115-acre, 5,000-room resort that had it all. The movie-themed hotel caters to families with family-friendly entertainment, a large swimming hole, child care facilities, an arcade, and an on-site medical clinic for guests and employees. Because it is so large, it is able to offer satellite registration/hotel check-in at McCarran Airport, and American Airlines AAdvantage miles for overnight stays, entertainment tickets, and slot and video play.

It is huge, however, and an adventure in itself just to get to your room or from your room to a restaurant. It also seems to be changing its attitude toward families. Although its main show is very appropriate for kids, it now seems to be going after the high-roller market, along with everyone else, dropping the attractions and services that made it one of the first places one thought as a family-friendly resort.

Grand Pool Complex (all ages)

Designed for never-ending fun, this 6.6-acre complex features five swimming pools, three large whirlpools, a relaxing river, lush tropical landscaping, bridges, fountains, and waterfalls. Families can rent private cabanas to give little ones a break from the Nevada sun.

Arcade Center (all ages)

Games of skill and the latest video arcade and high-tech virtual reality games are available at the 11,400-square-foot center.

Youth Activity Center (ages 3 to 12, out of diapers and pull-ups)

(702) 891–3200. Sunday through Thursday 11:00 A.M.–11:00 P.M., Friday and Saturday until midnight. Two-hour minimum stay per day, five-hour maximum. $ per hour, meals and snacks extra.

Supervised by professionally trained youth counselors, this self-contained facility is available for children of hotel guests and Las Vegas visitors. The facility features an arts and crafts room, Super Nintendo, lounge area, table tennis, mini pool tables, hockey and basketball group activities, movies, and board games as well as a complete preschool room. Licensing restricts attendance to five hours at a time; if children take a two-hour break, they can return for an additional five hours.

Business with Kids

Increasingly, older kids are accompanying parents on business trips. Who better to relax with after-hours than your own sweet one? A number of local hotels have recognized this trend and provide quality day-care facilities for guests and nonguests. These facilities have small adult-to-child ratios, a wide variety of activities, colorful play areas, and seasoned, licensed staff. Parents have invariably been impressed with the quality of the attention, and their kids have been happy to return. Licensing agreements often limit the number of hours that a child can spend at the facility, however, so that it remains a drop-off center rather than a full-day child care center.

Currently, the MGM Grand, the Goldcoast, and Sunset Station all offer quality drop-off facilities. You don't have to be a guest to take advantage of the service, although guests do pay less than nonguests. This benefit allows a working parent the flexibility to turn a business trip into a special outing with a favorite sidekick.

CBS Television City (age appropriateness varies)
Studio Walk; (702) 891–5752. Daily 10:00 A.M.–9:00 P.M. Free.

CBS Television's research center for TV pilots becomes an interactive experience for the rest of us. Check out the video wall
featuring entertainment programs or the theater-style screen-
ing rooms. Two focus-group rooms are available to get
your feedback on upcoming programming. Most
programs are for ages ten and up, although pilots
for small children's programming also come through.
Call before coming to verify which pilots are currently being screened. Once there, ask at
the front desk for free tickets to see the pilot. To further influence CBS programming,
sign up to become part of the entertainment panel. You will receive regular surveys in the
mail that scope out your television preferences.

The retail shop stocks VH-1, MTV, Nickelodeon, and CBS show merchandise. Look for
Survivor T-shirts. Want state-of-the-art TV for yourself? Sony and Blockbuster present the
newest in digital home theater, and then some.

The Lion Habitat (all ages)
Open 24 hours. Free.

Not the largest exhibit ever seen, but there's a lot of bang for the buck here. In a unique
exhibition area, transparent walls surround the "cage" and feature a clear tunnel that lets
viewers walk through and beneath the center of the exhibit. The naturalistic enclosure
mimics an open savannah, with three levels of rock outcroppings, four separate waterfalls,
a pond, and acacia trees. Trainers regularly get inside to toss tidbits of food next to the
glass so that the lions and the humans are separated by less than a few inches. These are
truly impressive creatures, and you can stare right into their pale eyes. I never realized
just how *huge* these animals were until I stood within a couple of feet of one. Critics con-
tend that the enclosure is too up-close and personal, with the human hordes in constant
proximity to these inherently wild beings, but I suppose that could be said about most
zoolike exhibitions. Crowds always seem present, so try to go early in the day or during
afternoon tea times, when crowds generally thin. The adjacent shop donates part of its
profits to animal preservation.

Where to Eat

**Emeril Lagasse's New Orleans Fish
House.** (702) 891–7374. Daily 11:00
A.M.–2:30 P.M. and 5:30–10:30 P.M. Winner of
Wine Spectator's 1999 "Best of Award of
Excellence," as well as other accolades, this
brick-and-wood-walled dining room with an
indoor patio and an oval seafood bar features
Emeril's signature blend of modern
Creole/Cajun cooking. Adventurous kids may
enjoy the New Orleans BBQ shrimp. After the
crowd thins out, stop by for a late-night
banana cream pie with banana crust and
caramel drizzles. $$$$

**Mark Miller's Coyote Cafe and Grill
Room.** (702) 891–7349. Daily 8:30
A.M.–10:30 P.M. Chef Miller won the presti-
gious James Beard "Best Chef in the South-

west" award. He oversees both the cafe and the grill room, so families can sample his cuisine at the cafe or splurge at the grill. Hand-painted coyotes, lizards, and other southwestern motifs enchant kids. The grill has an elegant, rich feel reminiscent of Santa Fe. Try the "Cowboy" rib steak at the grill room or a breakfast of blue corn pancakes, portabello mushroom tamales, or pear cajeta gingerbread with vanilla ice cream. Cafe, $$; Grill Room, $$$$

Rainforest Cafe. (702) 891–8580. Sunday through Thursday 8:00 A.M.–11:00 P.M., until midnight on weekends. This is the place where people are encouraged to take their kids for pasta, salads, and sandwiches. The 10,000-gallon walk-through saltwater aquarium at the entrance features more than twenty-two species of fish from around the world. Kids like that. Trumpeting animatronic elephants, simulated tropical rainstorms (complete with thunder and lightning), and the animated animals and birds on the walls seem especially kid friendly, but I couldn't help wondering when was the last time those things were washed. Using Disneyland technology, there is a definite Disney feel to the place. Delicious smoothies are a hit with kids, as were the dinosaur-shaped chicken nuggets with my littlest one. Clever names like Gorillas in the Mist Cheesecake try to stay with the theme. Somehow, however, the unimpressive food didn't really appeal to the older kids and, as my logical one commented dryly, "There aren't *really* any dinosaurs in a rain forest." $$

Ricardo's Mexican Restaurant. (702) 736–4970. Sunday through Thursday 11:00 A.M.–11:00 P.M., weekends until 1:00 A.M. For more traditional Mexican fare and a lively, festive atmosphere, try this family-friendly restaurant. Most kids love the bean burritos, older kids enjoy making their own fajitas. There is also a walk-up margarita bar, and an exhibition palapa taco bar. Live Latin music comes from the adjacent cantina. Locals recently voted it the best Mexican restaurant in Vegas. $$

Wolfgang Puck Cafe. (702) 891–1111. Daily 11:00 A.M.–11:00 P.M. With the colorful tile booths surrounding the open kitchenette, kids can order a classic pizza while parents taste dishes like Wiener schnitzel, a crispy veal cutlet with warm potato salad, or zwiebelrostbraten, a marinated and herb-buttered rib eye served with onions and garlic potatoes. Dine early or late, if you can, as there is usually a line to get in. $$

The Showcase Mall

3785 Las Vegas Boulevard South; (702) 597–3122.

This whole place is geared toward kids who love a place that doesn't offer anything good for them, but is pure, sugary, adrenaline-pumping fun.

M&M's World (all ages)

(702) 597–3122. Daily 10:00 A.M.–midnight, Friday and Saturday until 1:00 A.M.

Wander through 26,000 square feet of M&M's fun, from crystal M&M's evening bags to bright red calculators with M&M's keys. (All right, we had to have one. But it *is* educational!) You will find more M&M's colors than you can imagine, and pins, pens, purses, and paraphernalia galore, all related to those little round candies. At Colorworks, a rainbow of M&M's is displayed in individual bins. Kids can make their own color mix to take home to Grandma. What could be sweeter than that?

Pet-Friendly Hotels

Sometimes your pets just can't stand to be without you, and after all, how can you leave them behind while you and your family go have fun? Unfortunately, not all hotels are agreeable to your desire to bring along the family dog. Here are some "pet-friendly" hotels that will accept both you and your furry friends.

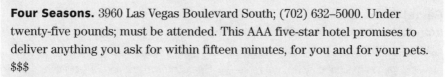

Four Seasons. 3960 Las Vegas Boulevard South; (702) 632–5000. Under twenty-five pounds; must be attended. This AAA five-star hotel promises to deliver anything you ask for within fifteen minutes, for you and for your pets. $$$

Glass Pool Inn. 4613 Las Vegas Boulevard South; (702) 739–6636 or (800) 527–7118. This forty-six-room motel has survived since the 1950s, primarily on this location and due to the fact that its twenty-four-hour heated pool has cool windows that let a swimmer look out onto the Strip. It also offers a lounge with food, beverages, and gaming; kitchens; a Laundromat; HBO and ESPN; and it lets you bring along Fido, with a deposit. $

Hawthorn Suites. 5051 Duke Ellington Way; (702) 739–7000. Just minutes away from the Strip, this is one of the rare pet-friendly hotels. Comfortable and with good service, the hotel offers accommodations for both families and Fido. $

Holiday Inn Express Suites. 8669 West Sahara Avenue; (702) 256–3766. $20 fee; up to fifty pounds. The hotel offers a walk area out back for pets; just make sure they are on a leash. $

La Quinta Inn & Suites NW. 7101 Cascade Valley Court; (866) 824–9330. Up to twenty-five pounds maximum. The hotel welcomes both you and your pets. The weight limit is not strictly enforced. $–$$

Everything Coca-Cola Las Vegas (all ages) 🔵 🍴
(702) 270–5965 or (800) 720–COKE. Daily 10:00 A.M.–11:00 P.M.

It is hard to miss the giant 100-foot Coke bottle elevator that faces the Strip. The 28,000-square-foot attraction that lies within contains everything you could ever imagine about Coke and allows you to purchase everything you could imagine shaped like a Coke bottle. As you are lifted in the dual elevators, the sound of Coke pouring over ice creates obvious connections that prepare visitors to buy, buy, buy the small glass-bottled Cokes from the many vending machines inside and the host of other Coke paraphernalia.

Renovations have canned the upstairs museum, but families can take a load off at an old-fashioned soda fountain that specializes in—are we surprised here?—Coke floats; cherry, lemon, chocolate, and vanilla Cokes; and other soda fountain specialties. A small theater area shows old-time favorite Coke commercials and gives visitors a history of Coke. The white polar bear featured in recent years comes alive throughout the day to let little ones receive an old-fashioned bear hug. Our favorite part, though, may be just gazing out the front windows at the glittering lights of the Strip where, ironically, New York–New York sports a huge flashing sign that says PEPSI-COLA. Now how did that get there?

GameWorks (all ages)
(702) 432–4263. Daily 10:00 A.M.–midnight, Friday and Saturday until 2:00 A.M. $–$$.

Steven Spielberg was the mastermind behind this gamer's paradise. With a batch of one-of-a-kind games designed by DreamWorks SKG, Sega Enterprises, and Universal Studios to thrill the most savvy of game players, families can find just about everything here. The exclusive Drive Power Sled, one of only three in the world, lets kids feel what it is like in a bobsled as it powers down a run. Wild River is a simulated white-water rafting experience. Most locals feel this is the best arcade in town, with restaurants, bars (adult only, of course), and video game attractions grouped in several themed zones. There are plenty of old-fashioned video games, like PacMan and pinball machines, as well as specially designed games for younger folk so that little ones also have a lot to choose from. The 75-foot-tall freestanding climbing wall is fun to watch, as well as try (kids must have consent from a *parent*, not just an adult, to climb).

To its credit, GameWorks has responded to the outcry against gory video play by implementing a special V Card for those under sixteen. The card restricts access to the 15 percent or so of games that have "mature" themes. Parents can purchase standard Smart-Cards at their own discretion, but staff will only sell V Cards to gamers who are not yet sixteen.

Prices for games range from 50 cents to $3.00 each, $20 Smartcards get $25 worth of play, $25 Smartcards get $35 worth of play. For the first or last two hours of operation, $20 per person gets unlimited play. Rock climbing wall, $10, but must weigh at least eighty pounds.

Where to Eat

GameWorks Grill. (702) 432–4263. Daily 11:00 A.M.–midnight, weekends until 1:00 A.M. Take a break from your virtual fun to grab pizza, pasta, appetizers, or sundry other menu items. $–$$

Harley-Davidson Cafe. Next door to Showcase Mall; (702) 740–4555. Daily 11:00 A.M.–11:00 P.M., Friday and Saturday until midnight. The usual burgers, salads, chicken, and steak fare, but what a wild setting! Expect a Harley-Davidson kind of crowd, only now those longhairs have law and medical degrees. One thing that hasn't changed, though, is the love of black leather outfits and those monster motorcycles. $–$$

Desert **Passage**

The main attraction at Desert Passage, located behind the new Aladdin, is its shopping center. More than 135 stores lie within this unique 500,000-square-foot shopping "adventure." Along the cobblestone street, the shops wind from Spain to North Africa to Old India. Antiques and antique reproductions add an air of authenticity. At one point a summer storm rains on a ship in harbor. Street performers sing, dance, and play along the way. You can even have someone pull you around in a cart.

Our favorite wing is one that seems filled with children's shops, including **GAP for Kids** and **Desert Brats. Build a Bear Workshop** lets kids pick an unstuffed bear and dress it with any of the hundreds of costumes and accessories within the shop. Then the bear is stuffed to your child's desired cushiness.

Two places of note are the Anasazi and Commander's Palace. At the **Anasazi,** cowboys and Indians finally come together in this mix of Native American and Northern New Mexico dishes that made this restaurant a recipient of the distinguished AAA Four Diamond Award. **Commander's Palace** has been a Louisiana landmark since 1880, winning the prestigious James Beard Best Restaurant in America Award, with its cutting-edge New Orleans food. House specialties include the seared jumbo crab cake served over fire-roasted corn. Kids, however, won't want to leave until they get their fill of the Bananas Foster.

Paris Las Vegas

3655 Las Vegas Boulevard South; (702) 946–7000. $$–$$$$

If you can't make it to the real thing, this place is a pretty good second. With incredible attention to detail, some of Paris's more notable landmarks have been re-created here. Inside, however, it is confusing, and may be a place that you just want to visit.

The Pool (all ages)

The rooftop swimming pool rests among two acres of manicured French gardens, complete with flower beds and sculpted hedges.

Golf, Tennis, and Jogging (all ages)

Guests can enjoy an array of outdoor activities, including golf at nearby courses, on-site tennis, and jogging.

The Eiffel Tower (all ages)

(702) 946–7000. Daily 10:00 A.M.–midnight, weekends until 1:00 A.M. $, under 5 free.

The hotel's signature landmark was designed from Gustav Eiffel's original drawings, complete with the original lighting design. This half-scale replica is complete with a 350-foot-per-minute glass elevator trip to the top. A better view-from-the-top experience can be had at the Stratosphere, because this small observation deck is often too crowded to enjoy.

L'Arc de Triomphe (all ages)

(702) 946–7000. Free.

Located just outside of the entrance to Paris Las Vegas, this fountain is a two-thirds replica of the original, which opened in 1805 as a monument to the soldiers who fought in the battle of Austerlitz. The names and dates of Napoleon's victories are inscribed on it.

The Louvre

Free.

The Louvre facade houses the Mon Ami Gabi cafe on the Las Vegas Strip. The original structure in Paris, which opened in 1793, is now the richest museum in the world. The five statues atop both the original and this replica depict famous French historical figures.

Re Society Gallery and Atelier (all ages)

(702) 946–7000. Daily 10:00 A.M.–8:00 P.M. Free.

Just to the right of the Strip-side casino entrance, guests can gaze through a plateglass window to watch artisans printing large-scale reproductions of famous cinema and art posters from the Golden Age of Posters. In this century-old process, kids will see a rare French lithography press in action. The eight-ton Marinono Voirin editioning press is the same kind used by print masters Toulouse-Lautrec and Cassandre. Viewers can get their

The **Goyas'** Top Ten Family Shows

We love shows, theater, magic, and everything Vegas. (Well, not *everything*.) Take advantage of the entertainment options and see a good show while you're here. Watch for your favorite band or singer, who probably will grace the stage at one time or another, but the permanent shows are also a real treat. Here are our family favorites.

• Mac King (Harrah's)

• Lance Burton (Monte Carlo)

• Clint Holmes (Harrah's)

• Legends in Concert (Imperial Palace)

• Tournament of Kings (Excalibur)

• *Mystère* (Treasure Island)

• *"O"* (Bellagio)

• Blue Man Group (Luxor)

• V–Ultimate Variety Show (Venetian)

• Rick Thomas (Tropicana)

If either Jerry Lewis or the Smothers Brothers are in town, don't miss out on their classy, classic acts.

pictures taken in front of the press as a poster is being printed, then have the finished print shipped to their home.

If you prefer to choose a print to match a favorite theme or color scheme, the gallery is right next door. Magnificent, vibrant full-scale posters fill the gallery. The haunting sepia-toned poster for the classic silent film *Metropolis* and the fetching *King Kong* are both kid pleasers. Remastered vintage art nouveau posters by Alphonse Mucha, bold geometric art deco posters, and classic Hollywood film posters are also featured. Rounding out the gallery's collection is a line of Picasso ceramics, a selection of antique posters, and the society's exclusive collection of vibrant lithographs and paintings of Peanuts characters by contemporary artist Tom Everhart. Most Re pieces are priced at about $400 and are hand-pulled, hand-signed, and numbered.

Ohh, La La, **Check Out** the Best

Local resorts and restaurants love to tout their recognition from magazines, consumer groups, and their own peers, but one of the oldest and most consistently recognized awards is the AAA diamond rating. Many feel that AAA's is the most comprehensive hotel and restaurant survey in the world. Only one Las Vegas establishment, the Four Seasons, has garnered the elite five-diamond ratings; a mere eight can claim membership in the four-diamond club. Of the thousands of international hotels rated, only 3 percent make it to the four-diamond level, deemed to be excellent properties that display a high level of service and hospitality and a wide variety of amenities and upscale facilities in the rooms, on the grounds, and in public areas.

As of 2001, these eight Las Vegas properties had achieved the four-diamond level: Bellagio, the Golden Nugget, the Las Vegas Hilton, the Mirage, Treasure Island, the Venetian, Paris Las Vegas, and Mandalay Bay. No local restaurant has achieved a five-diamond rating; the following rate four diamonds: Aureole at Mandalay Bay, the Eiffel Tower Restaurant at Paris Las Vegas, Michael's at the Barbary Coast, and Renoir at the Mirage.

Where to Eat

Eiffel Tower Restaurant. (702) 946–7000 or (702) 948–6937. Daily 5:30–10:00 P.M., Friday and Saturday until 10:30 P.M.; bar 5:00 P.M.–midnight. Serving classic French cuisine, this restaurant is located on the eleventh floor of the fifty-story Eiffel Tower replica. The restaurant offers a breathtaking view of the Strip, accompanied by classical piano music, and diners enjoy gourmet French dishes tailored for the American palate as well as daily specials. $$$–$$$$

JJ's Boulangerie. (702) 946–3280. Daily 6:30–11:00 P.M., Friday and Saturday until 2:00 A.M. If you've had enough of sidewalk dining, sit in the middle of a working bakery to watch bakers knead dough, create French pastries, and remove racks of baguettes from the oven. Take your time sampling the sand-wiches, soups, and salads. The fast service outlet also offers croissants with assorted fillings served fresh from the oven. $

Le Café Ile St. Louis. (702) 946–7000. Open twenty-four hours. Parents will appreciate resting in this quaint boutique coffee shop set amid the cobblestone streets and winding alleyways of Paris's shopping district. From French breakfast pastries to luxurious chocolates to petite cakes, deciding what to indulge in is the real challenge for families. Don't miss the freshly baked croissants, the apple turnovers, and the brioche. This is a perfect place to supply your midday picnic in the park. $

Le Provençal. (702) 946–7000. Daily 11:30 A.M.–2:30 P.M. and 5:30–10:30 P.M. Le Provençal serves French-Italian food native to the Provence region. The open kitchen helps re-create the festive, merry atmosphere of an old European village. Wearing traditional French peasant garb, the wait staff sings and interacts with guests for a lively evening of fun. $$–$$$

Mon Ami Gabi. (702) 946–7000. Daily 11:00 A.M.–10:00 P.M. If you love French onion soup, quiche, and innovative sandwiches, this is the place to be for lunch. Ask to dine on the patio (it's our very, very favorite people-watching spot). At night the patio is the perfect place to view Bellagio's dancing fountains. Chef Gabino Sotelino, recipient of the James Beard Foundation's Perrier-Jouet Chef award, offers everything from steak frites to fruits de mer. $–$$$

Polo Towers, Inc.

3745 Las Vegas Boulevard South; (800) 935–2233 x1089. $$

Set in the heart of the Strip, these time-share apartments can also be leased by the day or week. For less than $200 per day, a family can enjoy a two-bedroom suite with a fully appointed kitchen, televisions in each bedroom, and private balconies. Kids are welcome guests here with treats like weekly pizza parties, bingo, barbeques by the pool, and discounts to places like Wet 'n' Wild and Scandia Adventures.

The family friendly Hawaiian Marketplace, in front of Polo Towers, is an 80,000-square-foot shopping center that has the feel of an outdoor market. Designed to attract the average tourist, it bucks Vegas' current addiction to high-end everything. Built with a man-made banyon tree as the mall's centerpiece, the open-air facility will try to re-create the feel of the International Marketplace in Honolulu with meandering walks, places to sit, and a low-key, friendly atmosphere.

Bellagio

3600 Las Vegas Boulevard South; (888) 987–7111 or (702) 693–7111; www.bellagio.com. $$$–$$$$

This luxurious hotel boasts high-end shopping, world-class chefs, a stunning production show, and the only Picasso in town. Children are not allowed in the hotel unless they are guests, have tickets to "O," or reservations at one of the restaurants. Security guards at the entrances ensure that no one brings children onto the property without the preceding "tickets" of admission. And although the guards are courteous, they are definitely firm about the no children rule. If you are admitted, however, make sure that you stop in and see the garden; it is delightful. Most restaurants are very exclusive, very pricey, and not particularly suitable for children, although we had a lovely time at **Noodles,** where the kids were treated *very* well.

The Pool (all ages)

Open year-round.

Heated to 85 degrees, this series of five sparkling pools is styled in classic Mediterranean elegance, surrounded by tropical trees and white columns.

The Fountains of Bellagio (all ages)

Daily every thirty minutes from 5:00 P.M. (dusk) until midnight, Saturday from 2:00 P.M. until midnight. Free.

This elaborate laser fountain display is choreographed to an array of music that changes from one watery symphony to the next. More than a thousand fountains dance in front of the hotel, enhanced by music and light. The display spans more than 1,000 feet, with water soaring as high as 240 feet into the air. One of the most enchanting places from which to watch the display is the outside terrace adjacent to Prime, the steak house. The Mediterranean-style patio has the same dress code as the restaurant (no tennis shoes, shorts, or T-shirts) and is often a quiet retreat. Order a drink or a cup of hot tea and a hot chocolate for the kids while watching the water dance. From Pavarotti to Sinatra, you never know what you will hear or how high the water will fly.

Conservatory and Botanical Garden (all ages)

Children are allowed only if they are registered guests or have tickets to "O" or reservations at one of the restaurants. Free.

This free exhibit is a garden fantasy of seasonal themes. Floral and topiary displays surround a series of elegant reflection pools spotlighting a gazebo as fanciful as anything described in a fairy tale. Often used as a backdrop for photographing newly married couples, anyone is allowed to snap a quick picture in this flowery bower. Look up, look down, and look all around to see floating swags, innovative topiaries, and (our favorite) the tiled pathway that meanders throughout the conservatory. Inspired by Mediterranean mosaics, the whimsical paths are inlaid with butterflies, twisting vines, flowers, and crawling insects.

Wander outside toward the lobby and look up. A handblown glass garden of poppies floats overhead, suspended from the 18-foot ceiling. Called *Firori di Como* by glass sculptor Dale Chihuly, whose work has been exhibited in major museums throughout the world, the flower petals tumble over one another and appear lit from within. Actually, they're lit from above, and this subtle lighting simply seems to enhance the rich calliope of color.

Cirque du Soleil

If there is a quintessential "Vegas Show," it isn't topless girls in forty-pound headdresses; it is the internationally acclaimed athleticism of Cirque du Soleil. *Mystère* started it all; *"O"* creates a world-class splash; Celine flies in *A New Day;* and *Zumanity* (for adults only) gets up close and extremely personal. It is expected that Cirque shows will replace Siegfried and Roy, open at the MGM, and be featured at Steve Winn's new resort.

Because Cirque du Soleil productions present a world of pure sight and sound, parents don't have to worry that children will be left behind—even my six-year-old loved *Mystère* and *"O"*. But at these prices, you may not feel it is worth taking very young children, even if you can get tickets. Those with younger children may prefer the two classics: *Mystère* and *"O"*. *Mystère's* prices are lower, the lines shorter, and the imagery more upbeat. The performers are equally enthralling, although *"O"* has been acclaimed by a loud chorus of critics and peers as the most innovative and breathtaking show in the world and perhaps the best theatrical performance ever staged. If you do decide on *"O"*, don't expect to get in at the last minute unless you are a high roller or a movie star. This show consistently sells out, with three- to four-hour waits for we mortals who are hoping to get in through other's cancellations. Either book ahead of time (up to three months in advance) or get to the waiting line by 5:30 P.M. for the 7:30 show. If you do get in, make sure that you are seated, with your popcorn in hand, by 7:15 when audience members are whimsically entertained with an appropriately circuslike preshow.

"O" (ages 5 and up) (♫)

(702) 693–7722. Wednesday through Sunday 7:30 and 10:30 P.M. $$$$–$$$$$.

If these people were human, we would be astounded at the sheer physical prowess they exhibit, but obviously, they are the inhabitants of another world that is much more watery, more exotic, more colorful, and absolutely more fun than ours. Like *Mystère*, this is a Cirque du Soleil production, but this one exists in a slightly more dangerous world. Despite one's best efforts, an occasional gasp will escape as the performers fearlessly accomplish feats that no mere mortal would dare. In fact, there is a haunting feel to *"O"* in its strong use of black and white costumes, the water that mysteriously appears and disappears, the love and death symbolism, and the death-defying acts. Less intrinsically beautiful than *Mystère*, it is ultimately more enigmatic; in fact, it is as unfathomable as life, love, and risk themselves.

Tours

Sundance Helicopters (all ages)

265 East Tropicana Avenue, Suite 130; (702) 736–0606 or (800) 653–1881. $$$$–$$$$$ per person.

Fly in an air-conditioned, jet-powered helicopter into the depths of the Grand Canyon or over the bright lights of the city Strip. Custom tours are also available to destinations as varied as Hoover Dam or Mt. Charleston.

Lake Mead Cruises (all ages)

Lake Mead Marina; (702) 293–6180; www.lakemeadcruises.com. $$–$$$$ per person, $ ages 2–11, children under 2 **free.**

Don't leave Vegas without seeing the water-with-all that makes our desert oasis possible. Lake Mead Cruises offers midday paddleboat excursions to Hoover Dam, dinner and music cruises, and a quick trip up the river to the grand Canyon. You'll be surprised by the colorful canyon walls and the crystalline blue water, but not by the friendly staff.

Rebel Adventure Tours (ages 5 and up)

713 East Ogden Avenue; (702) 380–6969; www.rebeladventuretours.com. $$$$$ per person, half price for ages 5–12.

Those bright yellow desert Hummers that you see cruising around town are a one-way ticket to adventure. Tours include hotel pickup, lunch, and a variety of excursions, including horseback riding through the Spring Mountains; ATVing in the Valley of Fire, where Captain Kirk kicked the bucket (ages 16 and up); exploring a lost gold mine; white-water rafting through the Grand Canyon; and more. If you're lucky, Ron, the owner and an old explorer with the gift for gab, will be your guide. I promise you, you won't be bored.

The Classic Strip

The classic casinos between Flamingo and Sahara offer some of the best sightseeing on the Strip. Nothing can compare with the fabulous entry to Caesar's Palace. The Mirage is one of the most elegant facades man ever made, and when the volcano blows, the heat reaches all the way out to the street. The giant neon pink flamingos speak for themselves. The Venetian's richly textured artwork is, well, like something out of Venice.

None of these hotels particularly caters to kids. Nevertheless, this area holds some of my favorite places for families to stay. I don't agree that kids only want burgers and video arcades. Frankly, they get tired of the same old, same old. Hotels like Caesar's and the Venetian offer so many things to do, aside from gaming, that adults and kids will fall in bed exhausted and happy.

More people come here for entertainment now than for gaming, as reported by the Las Vegas Visitors and Convention Bureau. "There are things for people of all ages to do," a *Review-Journal* article said. "Certainly, Las Vegas has become more of a family destination, but it's a fact of what the destination has become that people can find plenty of things to do," said Richelle Thomson, spokeswoman for the Las Vegas Convention and Visitors Authority. Children do visit, however, and in increasing numbers. About 10 to 12 percent of the thirty-four million visitors to Las Vegas each year are under the age of twenty-one. Las Vegas also has one of the fastest-growing school districts in the nation. As long as kids stay out of the casinos—as they should—this is a fabulous place for families to come.

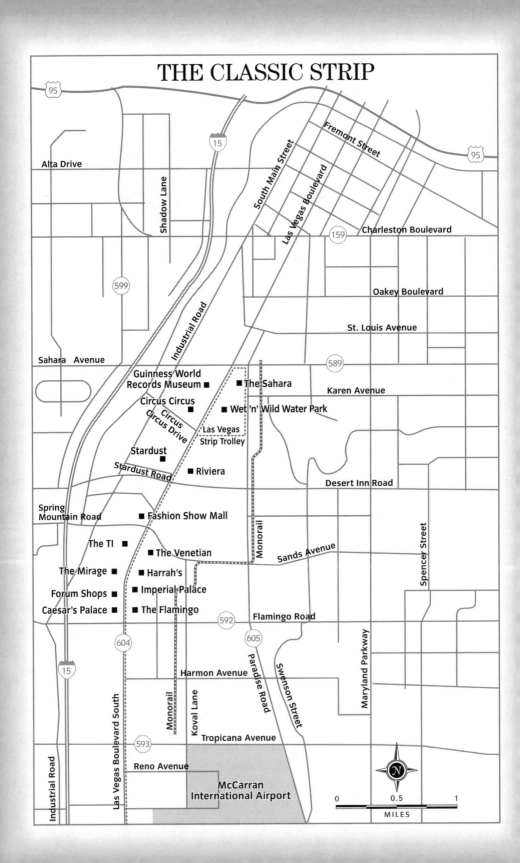

THE CLASSIC STRIP

Caesar's Palace Las Vegas

3570 Las Vegas Boulevard South; (702) 731–7110; www.caesars.com. $$–$$$$

Awarded four diamonds by AAA for more than twenty years, Caesar's has long been considered one of the most elegant places to stay on the Strip. The eighty acres of fountains, glowing marble statuary, and classic architecture attract both tourists and art lovers. Here you'll find full-size replicas of some of the most famous statuary in the world, including the *Rape of the Sabines, Victory at Samothrace*, Michelangelo's *David* and *Bacchus,* and the Brahma Shrine, a monument to the Hindu God of Good Fortune.

Nineteen restaurants offer a variety of dining options, from the casual snack food near the pool to a six-course Roman feast at the Bacchanal or dinner at the Palace Court, a French restaurant that is consistently voted one of the top restaurants in the country. For an extra special night, visit the mysterious catacombs that lie within the Magical Empire.

The Garden of the Gods Pool (all ages)

The Garden of the Gods pool area includes three large swimming pools and two outdoor whirlpool spas amid towering pines, cypress trees, and elegant landscaping. An adjacent spa area offers quality pampering for Mom while Dad takes the kids for a swim. Families

The Goyas'
TopPicks for fun on the classic Strip

1. Getting a picture with Elvis at Madame Tussaud's

2. Touring the underground workings of the Aquarium at the Forum Shops

3. Going to see Mac King's latest magic trick at Harrah's

4. Riding the lazy river at Wet 'n' Wild

5. Seeing the dolphins flip at the Mirage

6. Discovering an ibis, a koi, and a penguin at the Wildlife Habitat at the Flamingo

7. Watching the dominoes fall at the Guinness Book of World Records Museum

8. Riding the flume at Adventuredome

9. Watching colorful street performers while riding a gondola at the Venetian

10. Racing for Atlantis at the Forum Shops

can rent shady poolside cabanas at the Venus Pool, each equipped with a television, table for beverage and snack service, and an upholstered lounge chair. The pools are no more than 4 feet deep and lifeguards are on duty, so parents can supervise children with relative ease. Nearby are the fitness center and three lighted tennis courts.

Celine Dion: A New Day (ages 5 and up)
The Colosseum, (702) 866–1400. Wednesday through Sunday at 8:30 P.M. $$$$–$$$$$.

A lot is riding on Celine Dion's show. With a $100 million theater and a cast of fifty-eight, this show casts a spell that we, here in town, are hoping will hit over the stadium wall. We'll try to forget that even Babe Ruth missed more often than he hit.

Forum Shops (all ages)
(702) 731–7110. Daily 10:00 A.M.–11:00 P.M., Friday and Saturday until midnight.

This is the first Vegas shopping center to be completely enclosed with a Day-Glow ceiling that simulates a full day's skyscape in a matter of minutes. More than 50,000 people traipse through here daily, 70,000 during holidays! The shops are built to look like an ancient Roman streetscape, with immense columns and arches, ornate fountains, massive piazzas and classic statuary, and kids think it very cool to go into a shop at sunset and emerge in the middle of the night.

Two concierge centers, one at the People Mover entrance and one by the Fountain of the Gods, are there to offer **free** wheelchairs, stroller rentals, tours, show tickets, and car rentals. This place is larger than you'd imagine, so think about the stroller if you have a little one. The shops still have their reputation for being pricey, but with stiffer competition in the local upscale shopping market, the Forum prices don't seem as astronomical as they once did. If you keep your eyes open, you're bound to see someone famous.

People-watching

This is one of the best people-watching spots in the city. Here kids can eavesdrop on conversations in every language imaginable. It isn't just regular people, showgirls, and exotic foreign millionaires who pass by. Because the Forum has been a must-see spot since it opened, it attracts many of the rich and famous who are visiting or headlining on the Strip. People spotters have seen Mike Tyson, Andre Agassi, Robert DeNiro, Celine Dion, David Copperfield, and more. Usually it's no big deal to see a celebrity, but we have seen too-friendly fans swarm like killer bees. Teach your kids that it is cool to be respectful and to allow the celebrity to shop or dine in peace. A friendly smile and a quick hi! or a wave are always appropriate though.

Talking Heads (all ages)

Forum Shops. Shows on the hour, 10:00 A.M.–11:00 P.M.

You must see the talking statues at the Festival Fountain. At the top of each hour, Bacchus himself comes to life amid laser lights, computerized dancing waters, and a mock thunderstorm.

A second **free** robotic statue show is featured hourly in the west corridor with Neptune and his feuding children reenacting the tragic story of Atlantis.

Aquarium (all ages)

Forum Shops. Lectures at 3:15 P.M. and 7:15 P.M. daily. Free.

While you are waiting to see Atlantis, don't miss the 50,000-gallon aquarium with species of fish from twenty-five different fish families. Or do it all, with Atlantis at 3:00 or 7:00 P.M., followed by the 3:15 or 7:15 lecture at which a marine biologist, assisted by a scuba-diving aquarist, feeds the fish and points out interesting facts about the marine life. This is the best chance to see the more timid species that hide amid the coral reefs between feedings.

If your kids are more engineers than scientists, take advantage of the **free** below-the-scenes guided tours of the support facilities of the aquarium (Monday through Friday at 1:15 and 5:15 P.M.). Just show up at the aquarium to see the show, then wait by the sign for the tour guide. The tour includes visits to underground tanks that house new or sick fish, as well as a peek at some of the elaborate hydraulic gear that is needed to stage the aboveground Atlantis exhibit.

Fountain of the Gods (all ages)

Forum Shops. Free.

If you can't make it to Rome, Hercules and Xena fans of all ages must see the Fountain of the Gods. Lying within the apex of the L-shaped facility under a rotunda measuring 62 feet

Forum **Favorites**

Wandering through **FAO Schwarz** may be free, but only if you can get out of there without buying any of the cuddly stuffed animals, the state-of-the-art electronics, the entire section of Barbies, or any of the other wall-to-wall toys. Our favorite stop is at the store's Monopoly Cafe or Star Wars Cantina, where you can grab a snack or a leisurely cola as you watch starry-eyed children shop til they drop.

Immediately adjacent to the Festival Fountains, **Antiquities** is full of movie star memorabilia, Elvis posters, and autographed pictures. Almost any movie fan will find something to see. We took home a Marilyn magnet, but we had our choice of stars.

high, this simply magnificent re-creation of one of the most famous and beautiful sculptures in the world will impress even the most anti-art kid critic. Surrounded by cascading water, Jupiter rules from Mt. Olympus with Pegasus, the winged horse, Mars, Venus, Neptune, and Diana. Stop at the nearby Virgin Books and pick up a mythology book to read about these gods and their great adventures.

Race for Atlantis (42 inches and taller)
Forum Shops; (702) 733–9000. Daily 10:00 A.M.–11:00 P.M., Friday and Saturday until midnight. $.

Kids will enjoy the IMAX 3-D motion simulator adventure ride, a multisensory chariot race through the legendary kingdom where fog machines, an E3-D electronic headset, and state-of-the-art sound combine to make you feel as if you're really racing the gods.

Caesar's Garden of Games (all ages)
Forum Shops. Daily 10:00 A.M.–11:00 P.M., Friday and Saturday until midnight. $.

Caesar's Garden has T-ball, Tom & Jerry and Jetsons motion rides, and a video arcade and fun center. Most games cost $1.00 or less.

Cinema Ride (42 inches and taller)
Forum Shops; (702) 389–4008. Daily 10:00 A.M.–11:00 P.M., Friday and Saturday until midnight. $.

These 3-D motion simulator rides use real military-quality flight simulators in the following rides that rotate throughout the year: Galactic Flight, the Atlantis Submarine Race, the Coaster Crazy, Warren Miller's Ski Ride, Haunted Graveyard Run, and Runaway Coasters. The cost is $15 per ride or with Forum shop coupon four rides for $20, six rides for $25.

Where to Eat

Bertolini's. (702) 869–1540. Daily 11:00 A.M.–11:00 P.M. The food is pricey, and you have to look to find great kids' food, but if it isn't crowded and you can get a table outside, do it. This is one of those places where if you just sit still, everyone in the world will walk by. Located beside the Fountain of the Gods, you will see people of every culture, every country, every socioeconomic status, and every race. It is simply fascinating. Order a pizza and a gelato, then linger over your coffee as the whole world parades before you. What an education! $–$$

Chinois. (702) 737–9700. Daily 11:30 A.M.–9:30 P.M. Wolfgang Puck's Chinese restaurant offers plenty of vegetarian fare along with imaginative pairings of fresh vegetables and exotic meals. $$–$$$

Planet Hollywood. (702) 791–STAR. Daily 11:00 A.M.–11:00 P.M., Friday and Saturday until midnight. Reservations suggested. This place really gets hoppin' when the town is busy. The famous name is part of it, but the food is also family friendly, if not absolutely wonderful. Take a long walk to the powder room to see costumes, memorabilia, and props from some of your favorite movies. $–$$

Spago. Caesar's Palace, (702) 369–6300. Café opens daily at 11:00 A.M., dining room opens at 6:00 P.M. California-style cuisine features daily specials including a variety of fish, pasta, and salads such as roasted red snapper with lobster triangles, artichokes, zucchini, and glazed shallots. Try a California-type pizza, but let the kids experiment with bread. $$

The Flamingo Las Vegas

3555 Las Vegas Boulevard South; (702) 733–3111. $$–$$$$

We all know that Bugsy built this place, although the original hotel is long gone. Unlike Bugsy, though, the flamboyant pink Flamingo remains at top form. Truly a resort, it offers enough kinds of on-site recreation to keep a family happily entertained, despite the adult-themed shows. Located in the heart of the Strip, it is also a perfect place to embark on the mandatory walk to see what the other resorts have to offer. Relatively inexpensive by today's luxury resort standards, you might go home feeling as if you have spent a weekend by a lake, complete with all of those syrupy memories that we all cherish.

Ask the golf concierge to schedule tee times at a wide variety of local courses, including Angel Park Mountain, Royal Links, Desert Pines, Stallion Mountain, and Siena Golf Club. Grab a few tennis balls to hit with the kids on the hotel tennis courts.

The Pool (all ages)

It doesn't have wave machines or a "lazy river," but this elaborately landscaped resort does have spouting flamingos. With five pools, some that are connected by elaborate water slides and others with bridges, kids will take days to decide which is the most fun. For classic elegance, take the time to sunbathe around the pool encircled by flamingo fountains. Then play hide-and-seek in the cave hidden behind a waterfall. Next, play follow-the-leader down the series of water slides. For those with ones too little to swim, a separate baby pool provides relative privacy. Kids will love to explore until they find the biggest surprise of all, real pink flamingos and Chilean penguins.

The Flamingo Las Vegas Wildlife Habitat (all ages)

This is a lush garden area that kids will love. Look for the secret koi pond or a discover a penguin wandering among the palm fronds. The habitat also contains Mandarin ducks, African penguins, other exotic birds, and a three-story waterfall. This area is not restricted to guests.

Gladys Knight (ages 5 and up)

(702) 733–3111. Tuesday through Friday at 8:30 P.M. and Saturday at 7:30 P.M. $$$–$$$$.

If your family likes soulfully sung tunes with a lot of heart, join the "Queen of Hearts" on the Strip. She was inducted into both the Rhythm & Blues and the Rock & Roll Hall of Fame in 2002, a good year for this seasoned songstress. In Salt Lake City, she sang in the Olympic torch with her original composition, "Light Up the Land," grabbed a Grammy for *At Last,* and was declared the number one show in Vegas by the *Las Vegas Review-Journal.*

Full of memorable R&B tunes and a nice retrospective of the Motown years, Knight's night is easygoing, amusing, and full of family charm. She shares the stage with her older brother, a former Pip who tries to steal the show and succeeded in keeping my littlest laughing all the way home.

The Second City (ages 10 and up)
Bugsy's Celebrity Theater; (702) 733–3333. Tuesday, Friday, and Saturday 8:00 and 10:30 P.M. and Sunday and Monday 8:00 P.M. $$.

Use your discretion here, as comedy clubs are notoriously lowbrow. Every time we've been there, the cast made a decided effort to keep it clean. The quick wit, inanity, and twisted view of the world sometimes surprises, often amuses, and occasionally results in gales of laughter. Since improv depends on audience participation, there isn't a whole lot the cast can do to totally eliminate potty-language requests from the audience. If your kids enjoy *Saturday Night Live* and you can tolerate the skits there, you have nothing to fear from this thoroughly entertaining troupe.

Where to Eat

Baywatch Beach Club Café. (702) 733–3111. Daily 10:30 A.M.–10:00 P.M. Jump into this hot TV-themed restaurant for a bit of low-concept fun and high-concept food. Featuring a wide range of fare from sandwiches to pizza to grilled lobster tails and oven-roasted chicken with a sweet and spicy sauce, this poolside lark is designed to put you in the middle of the Baywatch lifestyle. Enjoy live entertainment Wednesday through Sunday with weekday happy hours from 4:00 to 7:00 P.M. $–$$

Bugsy's Bagel Company. (702) 733–3111. Daily 6:00 A.M.–6:00 P.M., Friday and Saturday until 11:00 P.M. Freshly prepared burgers, salads, sandwiches, and other delicatessen favorites can be eaten here or taken for a picnic. $–$$

Cafe Flamingo. (702) 733–3111. Daily 5:00 A.M.–8:00 P.M. Enjoy traditional American fare at this coffee shop. $–$$

Hamada of Japan. (702) 733–3455. Daily 6:00–10:30 A.M., 11:00 A.M.–2:30 P.M., and 5:00 P.M.–12:30 A.M. This highly reputed Japanese restaurant prepares steak, seafood, and other delicacies in the traditional Teppan style—right in front of your very eyes. $$–$$$

Lindy's. (702) 733–3111. Open twenty-four hours. Be treated like the royalty you are at this coffeehouse with everything from sandwiches and salads to steak and a good reputation, too. $–$$

Harrah's

3475 Las Vegas Boulevard South; (702) 369–5000 or (800) HARRAHS. $–$$$

This is one of the classic casinos. If you're looking for a nice place to stay that is centrally located, Harrah's might be your best bet. It doesn't have an elaborate swimming pool or a fantastic attraction; what it does have is location, location, location. With recently renovated rooms, some that overlook Caesar's and the Mirage's volcano, the rock-bottom prices may be all that you need. Without a lot for kids, you won't be spending a lot of time in the hotel, but because it is in the heart of the Strip, walking is easy and fun. Be sure to catch the sly sculpture on the main walkway going from the restaurants to the outdoor entertainment complex. It features a middle-aged couple who has apparently just won a jackpot, money and tummies trying to escape their gaudy clothes. If you can't turn that into a lesson, you don't deserve to be called a parent. Besides, it's really funny.

Clint Holmes (ages 5 and up)
Harrah's, 3475 Las Vegas Boulevard South; (702) 369–5111. Monday through Friday 7:30 P.M., Thursday and Saturday 7:30 and 10:00 P.M. $$$.

If Sinatra were alive, this is the kind of show that he would give: a quality live band complete with a five-piece horn section, and a mixture of music, from Samba to classic to jazz, with a few witty and moving stories thrown in. Well, Sinatra may have left the Strip, but charismatic Clint Holmes hasn't. A relative unknown outside of Vegas, he is poised to make a name for himself with Harrah's backing. This isn't a "kids' show," but it is a wonderful way to introduce your family to live music that you can all enjoy in a truly Las Vegas setting.

Mac King's Comedy Magic (ages 5 and up)
(702) 369–5111. Tuesday through Saturday 1:00 and 3:00 P.M. $.

If a six-year-old could do magic, he'd have a show like this one. One of the most charming things about Mac King is his innocence. Like an excited kid, he seems just as surprised as we are when his magic tricks work. We laughed for days over his secret cloak of invisibility, then puzzled over how he pulled a live goldfish out of thin air. If you are looking for sophisticated humor, don't look here. (About his loud plaid outfit he says, "Do you like this suit? It was my father's. Before that it was my mother's couch.") But if you enjoy good-humored silliness, you can't find a better way to spend an afternoon. King has already been featured on a number of television specials. We think his show is an amazing bargain—catch it while you can afford it.

Where to Eat

Asia. (702) 369–5084. Friday through Tuesday 5:30–11:00 P.M. Reservations suggested. A favorite with local writers, this lovely restaurant will expand your palate in one of the most serene settings on the Strip. $$–$$$

Carnaval Court. This outside courtyard has it all: a chocolate shop, a hot dog stand, shops, live music in the evening, and a lot

Mac King's **Favorite** Family Day

Working two afternoon shows per day leaves a lot of family time for this masterful magician. That means lots of playtime with his young daughter. A perfect day might revolve around simple pleasures made special by a young child's delight.

The favorite day might go something like this:

Early morning means an excursion to **Star Nursery,** 8725 South Eastern, (702) 361–5202, to buy a pallet of plants and a bucket of ladybugs. "Every time my wife and daughter go, they come back with fifteen hundred lady bugs. When you release them in your garden they go everywhere, and my daughter goes wild picking them up and letting them crawl on her. It is a feast for her, she is so delighted with that many ladybugs all at once. It is euphoria."

After a morning in the garden, late morning might mean a quick trip to the new family center off Green Valley Parkway where Mac's daughter is learning to swim.

Then, while Elizabeth naps, Mac is off to work making a packed house roar with laughter at his silly, wonderful magic.

Back home, there is still time for a vicious evening game of croquet in the backyard before heading to a favorite restaurant, like **Carrabba's,** where Elizabeth is entertained with a piece of raw dough that she can knead into her own magical shape before it is taken back to the kitchen to bake.

more. A great spot to people-watch, there isn't a whole lot of seating. But the center court often has a great band, and because the whole thing is outside, it has a unique feel that nothing else in the area matches.

Carnaval Court Bar & Grill. (702) 369–5000. Daily 11:00 A.M.–9:30 P.M. After 9:30 patrons must be 21 or older. Take in the **free** bands at this outdoor stage and eating area. Hot dogs are served from a stand, and other foods can be ordered from a menu. The real attraction is the festive street-party atmosphere. $

Garden Café. (702) 369–5000. Open twenty-four hours. A local favorite, this clas-

sic coffee shop offers a variety of menu items for the whole family. $

Ghirardelli Chocolate Company. (702) 369–5000. Daily 10:00 A.M.–10:00 P.M. Delectable ice cream, shakes, sundaes, premium chocolates, coffees, and gift items are sold in this shop located in the Carnaval Courtyard. $

The Range Steakhouse. (702) 369–5084. Daily 5:30–10:30 P.M. Reservations suggested. Steaks, seafood, prime rib, and chicken entrees are served along with one of the best views on the Strip at this award-winning steak house. $$–$$$

Common Sense and the Law

You aren't in Kansas anymore. The following policy is enforced by all casino/hotels in the area and is quoted from Harrah's Web site. Be aware that it is not appropriate for children to wander casino properties on their own.

"Parents are warned through signage and brochures about our policies, and employees are asked to keep an eye out and call security for any child that does not know his or her parents' whereabouts. Upon catching a minor trying to gamble through false identification, or finding any child left willfully unattended by a guardian, our security officers will intervene and may contact outside law enforcement."

The Mirage

3400 Las Vegas Boulevard South; (702) 791–7111 or (800) 929–1111; www.mirage.com. $–$$$$

Another AAA four-diamond resort, the 3,044-room Mirage was designed with the tropics in mind. Its lush foliage, waterfalls, and lagoons provide Mirage guests with a serene atmosphere despite the clanging gaming machines. The indoor tropical rain forest was one of the first of its kind, with misters, life-size trees, and a bridge that crosses a rushing stream. Rich tropical colors and carved teakwood add graceful touches throughout the hotel. The entrance and check-in area has one of our favorite sculptures, a pair of life-size bronze mermaids rising out of the sea. It also features a colorful 20,000-gallon saltwater aquarium behind the front desk. With more than ninety species of tropical fish, including leopard, white, and blacktip sharks, puffers, and surgeonfish, as well as vibrantly colored coral, kids will enjoy a virtual hide-and-seek game with the inhabitants.

For the truly indulgent, the Mirage features six opulent lanai bungalows, each with a private garden and pool. Or go all out and stay at one of the eight extraordinary two- and three-bedroom private residences.

The Pool (all ages)

Waterfalls, lush foliage, and private cabanas surround two outdoor tropical pools and three spas designed to resemble a series of wandering, interconnected lagoons linked by two palm-tree-lined islands. Kids can walk or swim to either of the islands to play beneath the cliffs, where water streams into deep grottoes. Cabanas surround the pool area and can be rented to provide shade for little ones. You can relax the whole day away while the kids wear themselves out, and then eat poolside. Tropical drinks and sandwiches can be found at the Paradise Cafe and the Dolphin Bar.

Secret Garden of Siegfried and Roy and the Dolphin Habitat

(all ages) 🐘

(702) 791-7111. Daily 11:00 A.M.–5:00 P.M., until 7:00 P.M. on weekends. Admittance to both exhibits, $. Children under 10 are free.

Home to six rare animal breeds, including the white tigers of Timbavati and Siegfried and Roy's Royal White Tigers of Nevada, the exhibit is part of the magic couple's effort to increase public awareness of the plight of all endangered animals and to foster dialogue about the world's rarest breeds. This $15 million, two-and-a-half-acre natural habitat also includes Bengal tigers, panthers, snow leopards, and an Asian elephant.

Dolphins are longtime residents of the Mirage. Sculpted dolphins surround the waterfall volcano out front and can be seen live in action at the Dolphin Habitat.

Seiji's Favorite **Ice-Cream** Shops

Danielle's. 6394 West Sahara Avenue; (702) 259–7616. Monday through Thursday 10:00 A.M.–9:00 P.M., Friday through Saturday 10:00 A.M.–11:00 P.M. Closed Sunday. Old-fashioned, homemade goodness in this soda shop that serves hand-dipped candies, floats, and sweet frozen creams. $

Coconut's. Mirage, 3400 Las Vegas Boulevard South; (702) 791–7111. Daily 11:00 A.M.–11:00 P.M. Generous servings of not-too-sweet ice cream in a variety of luscious flavors. Try the coconut, coffee, and chocolate—three of our favorites—especially in a banana split. $

Luv-It Frozen Custard. 502 East Oakey Boulevard; (702) 384–6452. Weekdays 11:00 A.M.–10:00 P.M.; until 11:00 P.M. on Friday; Saturday noon–11:00 P.M.; Sunday 1:00–10:00 P.M. This family-owned and operated business has been around for more than twenty-five years. One taste of the ice cream tells you why. $

Grandma Daisy's Candy & Ice Cream Parlor. 501A Hotel Plaza, Boulder City; (702) 294–6639. Daily noon–10:00 P.M. Winter hours vary. Some traditions can't be improved upon, and the candy shop is one of them. Hand-dipped chocolate strawberries and cherries, gummy everything, and ice cream by the scoop is timeless. $

The Mirage Volcano (all ages)

Erupts every fifteen minutes from 6:00 P.M. to midnight. Free.

One of the easiest to see and most spectacular attractions on the Strip is the Mirage's volcano. (One of the best places from which to view it is the valet area while you are waiting for your car.) The night sky lights up when this volcano shoots into action. Flames split the air as fire shoots 100 feet above the 50-foot volcano. More than 3,000 computerized lights simulate the flowing lava pouring into a three-acre lagoon. Las Vegas seems to adore the myriad ways to play with fire, and visitors seem to love this exhibit.

Royal White Tigers Habitat (all ages)

Open twenty-four hours. Free.

A separate specially designed habitat serves as home to Siegfried and Roy's Royal White Tigers, also known as the Royal White Tigers of Nevada. Set near the walkway entrance on the south side of the Mirage, the habitat was created to allow guests to see these magnificent animals roaming in a natural setting. It is the rare person who isn't taken with these creatures when up-close and personal. While the magic men call these animals an endangered species, that isn't technically true. They do not occur naturally in the wild. But then, neither do poodles.

Danny Gans (ages 5 and up)

(702) 792–7777 or (800) 374–9000. Tuesday through Thursday, Saturday, and Sunday 8:00 P.M. Tickets may be purchased ninety days in advance. $$$$.

His clean, good-natured portrayal of top country, pop, rock, and classic stars is mixed with impressions of our most recent presidents, including Bush, Reagan, and Clinton. Part improvisation, part impressions, and part Vegas-style singing/dancing, Gans's performances have consistently sold out for a number of years now. The Mirage theater, built especially for this show, jazzes up the act with bigger special effects, but the real crowd pleaser is the man himself.

Where to Eat

The California Pizza Kitchen. Daily 11:00 A.M.–midnight, Friday and Saturday until 2:00 A.M. Gourmet wood-fired pizzas are all the rage in California, and now here. When isn't pizza a hit? Parents may want to become more adventurous with the Thai pizza or the variety of pastas. $$

Caribe Cafe. Open twenty-four hours. Many menu items have a Caribbean flair, but more staid diners (and kids) will appreciate the classic salads, sandwiches, and all-American breakfasts. $–$$

Noodle Kitchen. Daily 11:00 A.M.–2:00 A.M. Set within the tropical environment of the Caribe Cafe, the Noodle Kitchen features a variety of soups, braised noodles, barbecue, rice, and congees. $–$$

Onda. (702) 791–7223 or (888) 777–7552. Daily 5:30–11:00 P.M. Reservations suggested. Features the classic regional dishes of Italy as well as New American cuisine; my kids love the homemade pasta and fresh breads. $$–$$$

Samba Brazilian Steakhouse. Daily 5:30–11:00 P.M. Reservations suggested. Brazilian "Rodizio" cuisine features a variety of skewered rotisserie meats that are carved tableside to the entertainment of all. Adventurous kids will enjoy the black beans, rice, and fried plantains served with all meals. $$–$$$$

The TI

3300 Las Vegas Boulevard South; (702) 894–7111 or (800) 944–7444; www.treasure island.com. $–$$$$

TI's $65 million renovation resulted in a coveted AAA four-diamond award for the property. As guests approach, they find themselves transported to a bustling eighteenth-century hamlet. Many people bring their families here, but since they took out the large pool slide, I'd prefer to stay somewhere else.

The Pool (all ages)

This modest pool is surrounded by shady awnings, brightly colored flowers, and leafy greens. Cabana rentals are available for full and half days and include bottled water, juices, sodas, cable television, telephone, rafts, and a changing room. A half day will probably be plenty, since most of the area is taken up with wall-to-wall lounge chairs.

Sirens of TI (all ages, sort of)

Daily 7:00, 8:30, 10:00, 11:30 P.M. (Shows may be canceled due to high winds.) Free.

Scantily clad women battle and seduce equally scantily clad sailors in this updated naval battle. You won't see anything racier than on TV, but this show isn't geared toward small kids. The modern rock music and dance should be fun for teens and preteens, however.

Mystère (all ages)

(800) 392–1999 or (702) 796–9999. Wednesday through Sunday 7:30 and 10:30 P.M. $$$$.

Cirque du Soleil scours the world to find and then refine acts that might once have been in a circus or flying across a gym floor or simply flying. Kids are as entranced as adults when the unbelievable, the incredibly beautiful, and the daring all combine to make you leave the theater truly feeling as if you have been in another world. *Mystère* and *"O"* are the two best Cirque du Soleil shows in Las Vegas for kids. *Mystère* has exotic birdlike costumes and is a little lighter in tone. It has more of a three-ring feeling as events, activities, and actors appear from everywhere: smoothly crawling down walls, descending from above, and playing jokes in the midst of the audience. But the sheer physical beauty of the performers as they effortlessly execute feats of strength and agility with godlike detachment make these shows like nothing you have ever seen before. This is truly an extraordinary show.

Where to Eat

Buccaneer Bay Restaurant. (800) 944–3777 or (702) 894–7223. Daily 5:00–10:30 P.M. No children under 5 allowed. Take a private elevator to this restaurant that overlooks the Buccaneer Bay Village and the fierce sea battle. While you are there, enjoy excellent a la carte prawns, lobster, seared tuna, Chilean sea bass, and scallops as well as lamb, duck, and a variety of steaks. The five-course tasting menu is usually a real hit. $$$–$$$$

The Venetian

3355 Las Vegas Boulevard South; (702) 414–1000; www.venetian.com. $$–$$$$

Re-creating Venice might seem inappropriate in any other place, but here, it fits right in with the general atmosphere. After all, we already have Monte Carlo, a small Italian village, an emperor's palace, and a miniature Big Apple. This hotel's construction beat out the Bellagio for the world's most expensive hotel, costing $1.5 billion. A bevy of artisans painstakingly copied, modified, and re-created Venice from photos of the real thing, resulting in a richly detailed artistic experience for the guest. Graceful arched bridges, flowing canals, and stone walkways leading to a vibrant piazza capture the spirit of Venice and lead visitors to the central St. Mark's Square where strolling minstrels are often found serenading the guests.

The Venetian also holds the record for the largest standard room in the world, which is a plus for families. At an average size of 700 square feet, the standard room is nearly twice the size of the typical Las Vegas hotel room and features a private bed chamber, a sunken living room, an in-room bar, and two TVs.

The Pool (all ages)

Daily 9:00 A.M.–8:00 P.M., Saturday and Sunday until 9:00 P.M.

Five swimming pools cover one quarter the size of a football field and are sprinkled throughout the rooftop garden. With more than five acres on the fourth level overlooking the Las Vegas Strip, this year-round heated pool complex has plenty to occupy active kids. Cabanas rent for $50 to $150 per day, depending on hotel occupancy. The world-famous Canyon Ranch SpaClub is also located around the pool complex, so a harried parent can pop inside for premier pampering.

Golf Concierge (ages 5 and up)
(702) 414–3707 or (888) 446–5330.

The Venetian golf concierge can schedule tee times at the Stallion Mountain Country Club, the Royal Links Golf Club, and the Desert Pines Golf Club for interested family members.

Artiste del Arte (all ages)
Daily starting at noon. Free.

As part of the festive ambience of the Venetian's public spaces, guests are entertained by singers, dancers, jugglers, a stilt walker, and other performers dressed in full Renaissance regalia. Costumed characters include real-life and fantasy notables, from Casanova to Doge.

Gondola Rides (all ages) ⬆
St. Mark's Square. Same day reservations must be made in person at the loading dock. $.

Guests can float through the canals on a full-size replica of an Italian gondola, complete with traditionally garbed singing gondoliers. A private gondola costs $50.

Madame Tussaud's Celebrity Encounter (all ages)
(702) 414–1000; www.madame-tussauds.com. Daily 10:00 A.M.–10:00 P.M. $, under 5 free.

More than a hundred celebrities are waxing warm for you and your family at this campy museum. From Whoopi Goldberg to Siegfried and Roy, these headliners are just waiting for you to come up and see them sometime. Film, sports, and entertainment giants gather in themed settings. *The Big Night* shows Goldberg, Brad Pitt, Jerry Springer, and Oprah chatting it up. What better souvenir than a photo of you with Babe Ruth or Muhammad Ali? There's also a behind-the-scenes tour of the process that creates these wax portraits.

Lasting Memories

Chloe, now a teen, has a special travel journal that she has kept since she could write. Each night, only while on vacation, she writes a couple of sentences or draws a picture of the day's activities. It is hard to express how precious the two diaries are to her and to us. This year, Seiji will start his first vacation book. Now that scrapbooks are so popular, I might consider creating one so that ticket stubs, postcards, bird feathers, sugar packets, or travel brochures might also fit.

For three-dimensional memories, we tote along a small vial to fill with a tiny portion of local dirt. Once we get home, I find an antique or colorful jar, fill it with all of our special finds, write a brief note describing our adventures, and then stick it on a shelf with the rest of our past vacation memories.

Guggenheim-Hermitage Museum (all ages)
(702) 414–2440. Daily 9:30 A.M.–8:30 P.M. $, under 6 free.

Some of the most prestigious museums in the world have too much art. Too bad. This collaboration between the Venetian, the Guggenheim in New York, and the Hermitage Museum in St. Petersburg, Russia, is definitely a coup for Las Vegas and its visitors. It allows works of art that may not have seen the light of day for years to be exhibited in a setting that befits them. With 7,660 square feet of exhibition space, the museum houses fine works of art ranging from the late nineteenth century to the present, focusing on impressionism, postimpressionism, and early modernism. The rotating exhibit, featuring forty original masterpieces from artists such as Cézanne, Picasso, Matisse, Monet, and Renoir, is valued in the billions.

Michael Flatley's Lord of the Dance (ages 5 and up)
(702) 740–6815. Daily at 8:00 P.M. and Tuesday, Wednesday, and Saturday at 10:15 P.M. $$$$.

Loosely based on an old Irish legend pitting good against evil, Michael Flatley's Celtic ballet depicts the epic battle between the Dark Lord, Don Dorcha, and the Lord of the Dance. If we never quite figure out what they are battling over, who the characters are, or what is ultimately won, it isn't that much different than waking up from one of those really nice dreams that just won't quite come to the surface. It's not about understanding the plot; ultimately, it's about images, feelings, and passion—and those are clearly understood. What kids and adults adore is the pyrotechnic footwork shown in the commercials. It is simply primal and blood-stirring when the company pounds the microphoned floorboards. The dance-to-the-death between the Dark Lord's and the Lord of the Dance's battling forces may even make your little boy think dance lessons aren't just for girls. It did mine.

V–Ultimate Variety Show (ages 5 and up)
The Venetian Showroom; (702) 992–7970 or (866) 80–SHOWS. Daily at 6:00 P.M., Monday at 8:00 P.M. $$–$$$.

Although there is a little off-color humor, this fast-paced variety show has a little bit of everything. The show we saw had a flying duo, jugglers, pole climbers, a balancing act, a magician, and an I-don't-know-what who kept us in stitches while he flipped on and off about one hundred costumes and lip-synched (lipsank?) to at least that many song fragments.

Time Traveler: The Ride (height restrictions)
Grand Canal Shoppes Food Court. Daily 10:00 A.M.–11:00 P.M., until midnight on weekends. $.

As these motion machines continue to get more lifelike, they also get longer and more exciting. The Venetian offers five different 3-D motion rides in two theaters, including the wide screen Titan Theater. Ask which rides are appropriate for your group (some jerk more than others). Blue Magic! takes you to the Bahamas and is appropriate for Grandma, pregnant women, and small children. Single tickets are $7.00 or $9.00, a two-ride package costs $12.00, a four-ride package costs $18.00.

Houdini Museum (all ages)

Adjacent to Houdini's Magic Shop on the second level in the Grand Canal Shops; (702) 796–0301; www.houdini.com. Daily 9:00 A.M.–11:00 P.M., Friday and Saturday until midnight. $.

Still considered one of the greatest magicians of all time, Harry Houdini continues to attract the curious and the mystical. Artifacts and documents from his heyday line the small showcase and include Houdini's straitjacket, his famous Pillory Escape, the spare glass for the original Water Torture Cell, and hundreds of other items.

Where to Eat

Grand Lux Cafe. (702) 414–1000. Open twenty-four hours. This cafe presents an extensive menu of well-crafted dishes and desserts by the wildly successful Cheesecake Factory. $–$$

Noodle Asia. (702) 414–3000. Daily 11:00 A.M.–3:00 A.M. Open for lunch, dinner, and late night dining, this restaurant features large portions of noodle dishes, vegetarian specialties, rice, and soups. $$

Tsunami Asian Grill. (702) 414–1980. Sunday through Thursday 11:00 A.M.–11:00 P.M., Friday and Saturday until midnight. Very fresh vegetables generously proportioned, along with rich, flavorful sauces and lean meat make you feel as if you can indulge in one of Tsunami's superb desserts. Before that, though, try a little adventure. Enchanted by the name, *unagi Q,* Seiji ordered the eel rolls and to my astonishment loved them. Alex tried *pad thai* for the first time and was equally—well, almost equally—charmed. We all felt very Japanese and Seiji loved that he had found something that I wouldn't try, despite his most earnest urgings. Ah, the table has turned. We found that no one needed urging to indulge in the sampler dessert tray, which may contain two of the best desserts in town. $–$$

Valentino. (702) 414–3000. Grill: daily 11:30 A.M.–10:00 P.M. Dining room: daily 5:30–10:00 P.M. Reservations suggested. Piero Selvaggio's famed restaurant serves Italian regional dishes in a casual or a fine-dining setting. The original Los Angeles–based restaurant was lauded not only as one of the city's top tables, but also as one of the best Italian restaurants in the nation, as well as making *Bon Appetit*'s "America's Top 10 Tried and True Restaurants." $$–$$$$

Fashion Show Mall

3200 Las Vegas Boulevard South; (702) 369–0704. Hours vary seasonally but generally are daily 10:00 A.M.–9:00 P.M., Saturday until 7:00 P.M., and Sunday noon–6:00 P.M.

The $1 billion expansion of this classy mall makes it one of the premier shopping destinations in the world. Going after the high-end shopper, this mall features most of the top names in retail including Neiman Marcus, Saks Fifth Avenue, Macy's, Dillard's, Robinson-May, Bloomingdale's Home, Nordstrom, and Lord & Taylor.

I suspect the mall may make some customers feel as if they stepped into the futuristic movie, *Minority Report,* as larger-than-life indoor and outdoor videos, audio and print advertisements mingle with living signs to encourage customers to "see, touch, and buy."

Floating over the entrance, a "state-of-the-art cloud" (who realized there was such a thing?) performs a variety of light, sound, and other multimedia presentations to capture any wayward tourists who might otherwise plan to forgo this experience.

Inside, the Great Hall may well be the centerpiece with an elevated stage, runway, and the ability to back up its fashion shows with multimedia glitz on multiple screens.

Circus Circus

2880 Las Vegas Boulevard South; (800) 444–2472; www.circuscircus.com. $$

Considered the first family-friendly hotel, the theme itself is one that kids will enjoy. Because it is no longer located in the heart of the Strip, the more famous attractions are not within walking distance, which, in my mind, makes the property less family friendly than it used to be. It does have four large pools that make up for other shortcomings.

Circusland RV Park (all ages)
(877) 224–7287. $.

Circusland RV Park offers 384 spaces with full hookups. The entertainment options at the hotel are available to all guests, and there are special conveniences on the RV park grounds, including a twenty-four-hour convenience store, arcade, Laundromat, playground, pet runs, and a disposal station. It even has its own pool! Spaces with grass are available, but must be specifically requested. AARP and AAA discounts are available.

Carnival Midway (all ages)
Daily 10:00 A.M.–midnight. $.

Many of the larger hotels offer an area of games for children. Circus Circus has one of the best, with a large midway of arcade and various carnival games of chance for kids. Most of these games are similar to those found at your local fair, with prizes that often relate to the hotel theme. Right next to the Midway is a state-of-the-art video arcade with almost 200 games. Whether or not you are interested in playing the games here, check it out any-

Problem **Gambling**

There is nothing less appealing than a child waiting in a crowded walkway for a parent to finish gambling, or sleeping in a hallway because the room is locked and the parents can't be found. Unfortunately, this does happen. I know families who have lost their homes because of a parent who gambled everything away. Living in Vegas, you can't help but hear stories of tragic dimensions, but one doesn't have to live here to lose control.

Most adults gamble when they come to Las Vegas. According to the National Council on Problem Gambling hotline, addictive personalities can quickly find that their betting has gotten out of control. "I just went crazy," is a common comment. The following questions are from the National Council on Problem Gambling.

1. Have you often gambled longer than you had planned?

2. Have you often gambled until your last dollar was gone?

3. Have thoughts of gambling caused you to lose sleep?

4. Have you used your income or savings to gamble while letting bills go unpaid?

5. Have you made repeated, unsuccessful attempts to stop gambling?

6. Have you broken the law or considered breaking the law to finance your gambling?

7. Have you borrowed money to finance your gambling?

8. Have you felt depressed or suicidal because of your gambling losses?

9. Have you been remorseful after gambling?

10. Have you gambled to get money to meet your financial obligations?

If you find that you or your spouse answers yes to these questions, contact the national hotline at (800) 522–4700.

---

way for the **free** live circus acts in the center ring. Performers from around the globe make it the world's largest permanent circus and include aerialists, trapeze artists, and clown shows. Most games are $1.00 or less.

The Adventuredome Theme Park (all ages)

(702) 794–3939. Sunday through Thursday 10:00 A.M.–6:00 P.M.; Friday, Saturday, and certain holidays 10:00 A.M.–midnight. **Free** admission. Rides cost $.

When the sidewalk outside gets hot enough to fry an egg, this enclosed, air-conditioned theme park may be just the way to cool off rising tempers. Freebies like the robotic dinosaurs and the 140-foot waterfall make the place a kick. Adventuredome kicks back with nineteen attractions spread over five acres with rides like the Canyon Blaster, the only indoor double-loop double-corkscrew roller coaster in the world, and the Rim Runner, a water flume ride with a 60-foot plunge. That still leaves time for laser tag, bumper cars, and bungee jumping. Variety acts play throughout the day, with slapstick humor and clowns being the premier attractions. Grand Slam Canyon also boasts **free** clown shows, a carousel, and a generous area for those with smaller kids. All-day wristbands available for unlimited rides: 48″ and taller $19.95; 33″ to under 48″ $12.95; under 3 years or 33″ **free.** Nevada residents receive a $3.00 discount Monday through Friday. Log onto www.adventuredome.com for discount coupons and upcoming events.

Thrill Rides

The excitement at the Adventuredome includes several white-knuckle rides.

IMAX ride/film *ReBoot: The Ride* and Fun House Express (must be 42 inches tall). In *ReBoot*, created completely with computer generated images, an Internet virus threatens to destroy the world. You are the good guy, however, and must fight virus with virus. The Fun House Express begins when an amusement park cart runs amok and crashes into the clown's house.

Canyon Blaster (must be 48 inches tall). Parents will want the all-day pass for their kids, once they ride this one. At one minute and forty seconds, this ride is short but sweet, careening in and out of caves and interacting with the Rim Runner.

Rim Runner (must be 48 inches tall). Prepare to get wet in this three-and-a-half-minute water flume ride with a 60-foot plunge. You might want to save this one for last because the inside of the Adventuredome is air-conditioned.

Inverter (must be 48 inches tall). Hanging upside down in midair might not seem like a great idea, but kids can't seem to get enough. The subsequent plunge is smooth and welcome.

Chaos (must be 48 inches tall). Adventuredome's newest ride flings you around like a bug on a Frisbee. Hold on tight.

Where to Eat

Blue Iguana Las Vegas. (702) 794–3767. Daily 5:00–10:30 P.M., Friday and Saturday until 11:30 P.M. The festive atmosphere and the hot bean dip served with chips were real hits with my crew. With a slightly different take on traditional Mexican dishes, it almost seemed adventurous eating here. Try the sampler appetizer plate, with a little bit for everyone's taste. $$–$$$

The Pink Pony Cafe. Open twenty-four hours. For reasonable food at reasonable prices, this is one of our favorite stops with small children. The large circus murals on the wall can keep the kids entertained until the food comes, and the service is always friendly. You can get prime rib for lunch for less than ten bucks or share some chow mein after 5:00 P.M. when it switches to Asian cuisine. $–$$

The Steak House. (702) 794–3767. Reservations recommended. Daily 5:00–11:00 P.M., Saturday until midnight. The price you have to pay for food on the Strip becomes a bargain here when you realize that this is not only one of the top restaurants in town, but in the country. For eleven years in a row, locals have voted it Best Steak House; for the past three years, the prestigious *Zagat Survey* agreed, naming it Top Steak House against competitors such as Morton's in Chicago and The Palm. *Zagat* also named it one of the top five restaurants in Las Vegas, regardless of cuisine. There is no children's menu, but little ones who enjoy a fine-dining experience can share. Another option is to sneak in a romantic evening while the kids get room service and a movie (one of our favorite ways for both kids and parents to rejuvenate during a family vacation). $$–$$$

The Sahara

2535 Las Vegas Boulevard South; (702) 737–2111, (888) 696–2121, or (800) 634–6666. $–$$

Crowned "The Jewel of the Desert" when it opened in 1952, the recent $100 million renovation has allowed it to keep up with the pack. Although remodeled, the 1,720-room hotel has stayed with its Moroccan theme.

The Pool (all ages)

Open daily in summer only 8:00 A.M.–8:00 P.M.; spa open daily year-round 9:00 A.M.–5:00 P.M.

A 5,000-square-foot pool area nests in the heart of the property, surrounded by thirteen cabanas, circular fountains, and a gazebo-covered spa.

Las Vegas Cyber Speedway (54 inches and taller)

(702) 737–2887 or (888) 696–2121. Riders must be 54 inches tall. $.

Race cars, ⅞ the size of actual stock cars, speed after a checkered flag on a track modeled after the Las Vegas Motor Speedway. Drivers can bark at the pit crew as they fly at speeds of up to 220 mph in this race against up to eight other drivers in virtual cars. If you note each other's numbers, you can keep track of each other as you, or they, speed by.

What about **Grandma** and **Grandpa?**

Just as weddings are happening in Vegas in increasing numbers, so are family reunions, and for the same reasons. The "host" can just relax while the guests pick from the huge array of entertainment options, dining choices, and indoor/outdoor preferences. Banquet facilities in all price ranges can easily accommodate the main event, while a typical 10 percent discount for blocks of ten or more rooms can be found to fit all price ranges. Those who want to go white-water rafting at the Grand Canyon can fit that in while Comedy Central addicts can hop over to the Improv to catch a favorite comedian. Young cousins and siblings can splash all day at the hotel pool or take turns slipping down the water slide off a family-size houseboat as the family cruises Lake Mead. Best of all, airfare is often the biggest bargain of all, with frequent discounts offered in the paper or through your travel agent.

On the third Monday of each month, a $10 fee lets you compete against other drivers in the Cyber Speedway's racing series. Warm-ups begin at 7:00 P.M., with races beginning at 8:00. Win or lose, participants get unlimited passes to Speed—The Ride, the stock car simulators, and the 3-D theaters.

Speed—The Ride (54 inches and taller)
NASCAR Cafe. Daily 10:00 A.M.–10:00 P.M. $.

This state-of-the-art roller coaster uses electromagnetic force to launch the coaster from 1 to 35 mph in two seconds. After you pass through a disorienting tunnel complete with mist, the coaster jacks up to 70 mph in another two seconds. The ride takes you through the Sahara's marquee and up a 224-foot pole where, for a brief eternity, you get to stare straight into the blue sky before plummeting back down. Most people think the wait for the front row is worth it, but it's up to you to decide your thrill level.

The Platters, The Coasters, and The Drifters (ages 5 and up)
Sahara Congo Room; (702) 737–2515. Daily 8:00 P.M. $$–$$$.

These R&B bands from the '50s and '60s had thirty-three top-twenty hits among them and can still sing impressive blues.

Where to Eat

NASCAR Cafe. (702) 737–2111. Monday through Thursday 11:00 A.M.–10:00 P.M., Friday 11:00 A.M.–11:00 P.M., Saturday 9:00 A.M.–11:00 P.M., Sunday 9:00 A.M.–1:00 P.M. Enjoy solid American burgers and sandwiches in this themed restaurant. Just make sure you ride Speed before you eat, not after. Not the best food in town, but you'll want to take your time playing here, so this is a good pit stop. $–$$

Other Shows and Attractions

Like a lot of locals, going down to the Strip was not something I looked forward to until I became an entertainment correspondent for a major Web site. The casinos, the crowds, and the congestion were not terribly appealing, so I made the trek only when friends or family visited. As I became more familiar with the entertainment options available here, the scales fell from my eyes and I now love going to the Strip. I discovered that entertainment here is plentiful, varied, high quality, and often very reasonable.

Because entertainment brings people in, the tickets are often underwritten by the casinos. That means that you can often see major names for the cost of a dinner out. Tickets for the very hottest stars will not be a bargain, but often for $25—sometimes even less—you can see entertainers with recognizable names but who no longer or have yet to top the charts. The Orleans, Sunset Station, and the Stardust offer family-friendly performers at surprisingly affordable prices. This is a fun way of introducing older children to the pleasure of live entertainment.

The three mainstays in entertainment here are music, comedians, and magic. Music and magic are rarely inappropriate for children; you do have to be careful when going to see a comedian. Don't even try the comedy clubs. The Smothers Brothers, Jerry Lewis, Howie Mandel, Danny Gans, Rita Rudner, and others present clean shows. Ask the box office if a comedian is appropriate for children.

G-rated **Vegas**

Most attractions can be divided into a few categories. To cater to "families," most casino/resorts have some kind of arcade where kids can play an assortment of games for amusement and prizes. Some offer thrill rides that compete to claim the biggest drop, the longest plunge, the highest-fastest-longest-deepest-scariest sensation to be found. Circus Circus is the only resort with a Disneyland-style park that has an assortment of rides and games. A newer trend uses 3-D experiences and moving chairs to place you in virtual situations. More recently, a flurry of bowling alleys has sprouted up in a number of casinos.

But it is hard to beat the Strip itself as **free** virtual entertainment. There really is nothing like the Strip at night, with giant volcanoes erupting, pirate ships sinking amid the blaze of cannon and fire, water dancing, and much, much, much more. All of which doesn't mean that you should miss the classic old facades. Our favorites continue to be Bally's glowing colored columns, the giant pink neon flamingo of the Flamingo Hotel, and the just plain classy glittering lights that make up the Stardust sign.

Because Vegas is a major entertainment booking opportunity, many acts play here repeatedly throughout the year. The following are either permanent shows or attractions that are appropriate for kids (although they may be the only family-friendly attraction at that location), or they are headliners who offer a show that you can feel comfortable bringing your kids to.

Legends in Concert (all ages)

Imperial Palace, 3535 Las Vegas Boulevard South; (702) 794–3261 or (888) 777–7664. Monday through Saturday 7:30 and 10:30 P.M. $$, under 2 free.

A live band, dead stars, great music, and lots of heart make this one of the most entertaining shows in town. Kids feel very sophisticated in this G-rated nightclub atmosphere. Ask for a booth, if possible, where you can sip your two free drinks in quiet seclusion as this high-energy variety show explodes on stage. For almost twenty years, local entertainers, backed by a top-notch band and versatile dancers, have re-created legendary performers, from Liberace to Marilyn Monroe. While Vegas is known for its impressions of major stars, especially Elvis, this show is consistently one of the best. An added attraction is that the acts are from a variety of musical styles, including jazz, rock 'n' roll, and country. Anyone might be there: Expect the likes of the Blues Brothers, Kenny Rogers, Dolly Parton, Michael Jackson, Cher, the Righteous Brothers, Buddy Holly, John Lennon, Elton John, and more. It always ends with Elvis though. I must credit this show with making my six-year-old an Elvis fan, even to the point of slicking back his baby hair while leaving one lone curl to grace his forehead. Impressionists are born young, I guess.

The Auto Collections (all ages)

Imperial Palace's fifth floor parking garage, 3535 Las Vegas Boulevard South; (702) 731–3311 or (800) 634–6441. Daily 9:30 A.M.–9:30 P.M. $.

Little boys and their sons will love the dream machines showcased in this rotating collection that features 350 classic cars from the beginning of the century to the present. Hold on to the pocketbook because, unlike most collections, these are all for sale, from $20,000 up to a cool $1.5 million. Racing, muscle, roadsters, Cadillacs, and a 1933 silver Pierce Arrow are just some of the beauties here. Elvis's 1976 Cadillac Eldorado may still be displayed, if no one has snapped it up yet. Delivery and insurance are available. Just hope the willpower isn't running on empty.

Once you get tired of car-gazing, check out the bronzes, statues, and antique furniture also for sale, or visit the Franklin Mint store.

Guinness World Records Museum (all ages)

2780 Las Vegas Boulevard South; (702) 792–3766. Daily 9:00 A.M.–8:00 P.M. June through August, until 5:30 P.M. September through May. $, 4 and under free.

Hidden behind Arby's, a quarter of a block north of Circus Circus, this museum seems strangely appropriate in Vegas, the world capital of biggest, grandest, most expensive, and just plain most. Still, the things people will do to set a record . . . like the man covered with bees, the most bodies stuffed in a VW bug, the largest collection of airplane vomit bags. It kinda makes you wonder. Some of the exhibits are just plain gross; others, however, are curiously poignant, like the story behind the world's largest man. With more than 5,200 square feet of exhibitions, collections, hands-on displays, and life-size replicas, everyone will find something to shout about. While not the weirdest, our favorite exhibit was actually a video of the 1998 domino competition in the Netherlands, in which students used 2.3 million dominoes to create calculated destruction. Once felled, the dominoes produced elaborate pictures of everything from a space shuttle launch to the American flag. Stand up and cheer.

Wet 'n' Wild Water Park (all ages)

2601 Las Vegas Boulevard South; (702) 871–7811. Open late April through September: 10:00 A.M.–6:00 P.M. in spring and fall, 10:00 A.M.–8:00 P.M. in summer, until 10:00 P.M. on summer weekends. Admission varies by height. $$, children under 2 free. Season passes and senior discounts are available. Coupons are almost always available; call to find out where you can pick one up.

In the heat of summer, it is easy to spend a whole day at this fifteen-acre water park. With a variety of rides, it pleases thrill-lovers of all levels. We've spent the day there with teens, grandmothers, mothers, and little babies, all of whom took advantage of the rides, slides, chutes, floats, and flumes. For the little ones, a special big-kids-prohibited area is filled with small slides, big squirt guns, and lots of shallow splashing room. Bigger kids will enjoy low-speed shallow water and moderate rides. Daredevils (over 48 inches tall) can fall, twist, and twirl to their hearts' content on a variety of heart-thumping thrill rides. Shaded picnic areas surround the pool complex. The park has food courts, but many people bring a cooler stocked with drinks (in unbreakable containers) and snacks. Don't forget your water shoes: During the hottest summer months, little feet can burn while walking from ride to ride.

Downtown

Although "The Strip" ends at Sahara Avenue, Las Vegas Boulevard continues on for miles. Just kitty-corner from the Sahara is a local landmark, the Bonanza Gift and Souvenir Shop, at least in my family's minds. The good news is that north of Sahara, prices drop dramatically, both for food and for rooms. Hotels aren't as fancy-dancy and certainly not as large as the resorts on the South end of the Strip, but at these rock-bottom prices, they're sending you their siren song, hoping to lure your gaming dollars their way.

If there is an "old section" of Vegas, this is it. This is where the first small public buildings appeared, catering to the wandering traveler or the desire to break out after a week of backbreaking work constructing Hoover Dam. From its beginning, Vegas lured the rich and the infamous. (Clark Gable's wife put in her six weeks here, giving Gable the freedom to marry Carole Lombard.) Although those buildings have long since been displaced, there is a less frenetic atmosphere downtown. Good food can be had at rock-bottom prices, and crowds are less dense here. This is also where our oldest residential neighborhoods are, and many of our museums and historical sites.

As of press time, the city was deciding what to do with a huge tract of land downtown that has become available for renovation. Existing businesses are being provided funds for face-lifts, and two of our most exciting coming attractions are being lauded locally, even as they attract visitors from around the world.

The Las Vegas Springs Preserve and the Neon Museum Boneyard and Visitor's Center highlight dramatically different parts of local history. The preserve will save and showcase a unique, pristine wilderness; the Neon Museum will save and showcase the bones of our gaudiest times past. Local supporters know that there is glory, tradition, and excitement in both, and that it just may be the placement of a giant silver slipper less than a mile away from a home for the only native tree fox on the continent that shows most clearly the Vegas of today.

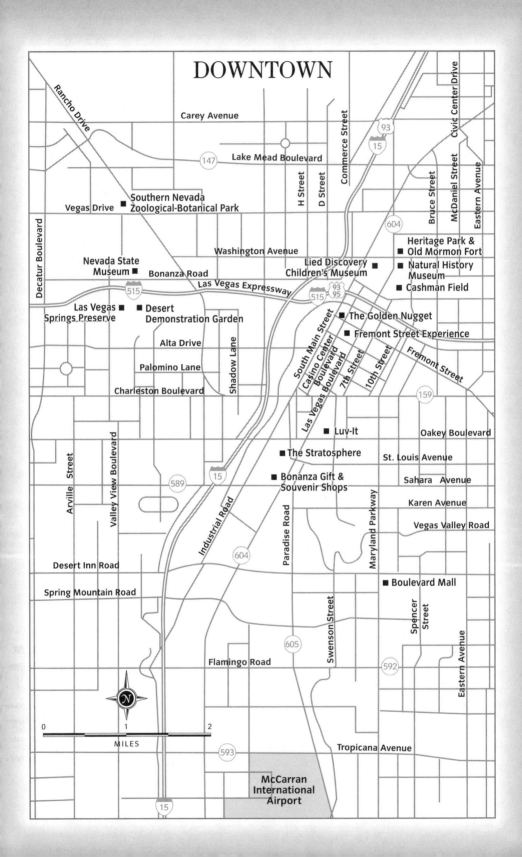

Take the Trolley

Even people who are taking advantage of the cheaper hotel rates downtown still want to see the Strip. Eight trolleys run between Mandalay Bay and the Stratosphere Tower, offering a range of stops along the way. If your hotel doesn't offer a shuttle, this is a low-cost alternative. Also consider using the trolley just to gawk. It takes about two hours to make a complete round, which takes you past all of the major neon and outdoor Strip attractions. (You'll see a lot more back doors than you knew existed.) The windows are large and the trolley is air-conditioned, so this might just be one of the best bargains in town.

The circle: South Stratosphere Tower to Circus Circus, Stardust, Fashion Show Mall, Caesar's Palace, Jockey Club; New York–New York; Excalibur, and Mandalay Bay, then north to Tropicana, MGM Grand, Bally's, Harrah's, Fashion Show Mall, DFS, Riviera, Wet 'n' Wild, Sahara, Hilton Las Vegas, and Stratosphere Tower.

The trolley runs daily, about every fifteen minutes from 9:30 A.M.–1:30 A.M. The fare is $1.50 (exact change required). Ages four and younger ride **free.**

The Stratosphere

2000 Las Vegas Boulevard South; (702) 380–7777 or (800) 998–6937; www.stratlv.com. $–$$$$

That needlelike tower you see from any vantage point in Vegas is the Stratosphere. It has been trying hard to keep up with the big guys since it opened and hopes to up the ante with its $75 million expansion.

The Pool (all ages)

The pool area was recently renovated and now showcases a 67,000-square-foot pool with waterfalls, cabanas, and food service on the recreation deck.

Outdoor Amphitheater (age appropriateness varies)

When this 3,700-seat outdoor amphitheater opened in 2001, the Beach Boys were the main attraction.

Tower (all ages)

Open daily 10:00 A.M.–1:00 A.M.; Friday, Saturday, and holidays until 2:00 A.M. $, rides and games extra.

This is the best place to see the Strip and all of Vegas in its full nightly regalia. The tower

The Goyas'
TopPicks for fun Downtown

1. Watching the lights come on over the Strip at sunset from the observation deck of the Stratosphere

2. Imagining discovering the world's largest gold nugget, the Hand of Faith, at the Golden Nugget

3. Browsing through Albion Books

4. Experiencing the Fremont Experience

5. Finding all of the signs restored by the Neon Museum

6. Hearing the speed of sound at Lied's Discovery Museum

7. Attending the Young Poet's Corner at the West Las Vegas Arts Center

8. Wandering the Mystic Falls Park then bowling at midnight at Sam's Town

9. Seeing one of the rarest birds in the world at the Southern Nevada Zoological-Botanical Park

10. Enjoying a cup of vanilla frozen custard at Luv-It

features a **free** nightly light show designed to be visible throughout the Las Vegas Valley. X-Scream, the Strip's newest ride, is an eight-passenger teeter-totter that takes guests over the edge of the tower, then flicks them back. The High Roller, the world's highest roller coaster, wraps around the crown of the tallest building west of the Mississippi. The ride starts at 909 feet above ground and whips you around the perimeter of the tower. Although it doesn't have the longest drop or the steepest descent, its sheer height and 32-degree angles literally take you over the edge. As for the Big Shot ride, let's put it this way: Once you are at the top of the tallest building this side of the Mississippi, get yourself strapped into a tiny, itty-bitty contraption to shoot up 160 feet to the 1,081-foot level before plunging back down. Those still sane say it's a blast.

For the less daring, there is the Strat-o-Fair midway attraction, featuring a renovated Ferris wheel circa 1958, and a child-size Little Shot. The decor is a '60s view of the future and is complete with 3-D Hyper Bowl, midway games, and two food outlets. For my money, the open observation deck on the 109th floor is plenty scary. Those more cautious may stay behind glass.

Up, Down, and All Around

Thrill rides to (almost) die for, or at least to have that predeath flashback that coaster riders love, are one of the area's major family attractions. We're talking roller coasters here, and not just rinky-dink ones. Most have height limits that riders must meet, meaning that little kids are not allowed. For bigger kids, however, including dads and moms who like the feel of an adrenaline rush, Las Vegas competes with the big guys for a collection of the best rides in the country, maybe the world. Details about each ride are given under the casino that sponsors it, but here is a quick list to check off as you exit on your adrenaline-shaky legs.

- Manhattan Express at New York–New York
- Canyon Blaster, Chaos, and the Flume at Circus Circus
- Desperado at Buffalo Bill's, Primm
- High Roller and Big Shot at Stratosphere
- Speed—the Ride at the Sahara
- Water rides at Wet 'n' Wild
- X-Scream at Stratosphere

Viva Las Vegas (ages 5 and up, minors only with adult supervision)
Broadway Showroom; (702) 380–7711. Daily except Sunday, 2:00 and 4:00 P.M. $.

Not a bad way to spend the afternoon, this low-budget Vegas-style production offers an inexpensive variety show.

American Superstars (ages 5 and up)
Broadway Showroom; (702) 380–7711. Sunday through Tuesday at 7:00 P.M.; Wednesday, Friday, and Saturday at 7:00 and 10:00 P.M. $$.

American Superstars and Legends in Concert vie for the best tribute shows in town. The Superstars band is hot, hot, hot as it supports impressions of singers like Michael Jackson, Charlie Daniels, and Madonna.

Where to Eat

Roxy's Diner. (702) 380–7777. Daily 11:00 A.M.–10:00 P.M., weekends until 11:00 P.M.

Enjoy **free** entertainment as singing waiters and waitresses serve you '50s-style food. $–$$

The Golden Nugget

129 East Fremont Street; (800) 634–3454 or (702) 385–7111; www.goldennugget.com. $–$$

The Golden Nugget Hotel and Casino has long been a favorite vacation destination for travelers from around the world. Just outside the front door, guests can enjoy the world-famous Fremont Street Experience with **free** shows nightly, and a "Celestial Canopy" with 2.1 million lights, comprising the venue for spectacular light and sound shows. A lavish $36 million remodel has enhanced the Golden Nugget's reputation as one of Las Vegas's truly first-class hotels.

The Pool (all ages)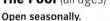
Open seasonally.

Dip into an Olympic-size pool amid the shade of palm trees and an outdoor misting system. White alabaster swan statues, bronze fish sculptures, and verdant landscaping add a touch of elegance to the pool terrace. Unwind in the whirlpool spa or simply bask in the sun while sipping an exotic cocktail. Pool attendants are happy to provide you with complimentary lounge chairs and towels. Cocktail service, snack bar, and pool products such as tanning oil, sunglasses, and visors are also available.

Hand of Faith (all ages)

You may not be able to take it home, but you can see it for **free.** The Hand of Faith is the world's largest gold nugget, weighing sixty-one pounds, eleven ounces. It's on display just off the coolly elegant lobby. Found in the mid-1980s with a metal detector, it was just 6 inches underground.

Where to Eat

Carson Street Cafe. (702) 385–7111. Daily twenty-four hours. Dine in a European-style sidewalk cafe next to the pool with torch lighting, fringed awnings, and latticework. Serving American food, health-conscious items, and ethnic offerings, this small cafe offers one of the largest menus in Las Vegas along with a variety of bottled wines. $–$$

Lillie Langtry's. (702) 385–7111. Tuesday through Saturday 5:00–10:30 P.M. Reservations suggested. East meets West with traditional Szechwan and Cantonese cuisine.

Langtry's offers a soft and surreal setting in which to enjoy the aromas of ancient Chinese delicacies including Mongolian beef, lobster Cantonese, stir-fried lobster, and prime mesquite broiled steaks. $–$$$

ZAX. (702) 385–7111. Weekdays 11:00 A.M.–11:00 P.M., weekends 5:00–11:00 P.M. Golden Nugget's newest "in"-spot was voted best new restaurant to open in 2002. Kind of a restaurant of all trades, the menu offers everything from fresh sushi to Bayou Chicken Fingers, Lobster Tostadas, and Mojo steak. $$–$$$

Other Shows and Attractions

Bonanza Gift & Souvenir Shops (all ages)
Corner of Sahara and the Strip.

You can't drive down the Strip and miss this place. It is a hoot to go inside and see the thousands of things that "Las Vegas" can be plastered onto. If you are looking for a kitschy souvenir or gift for Grandma that clearly states where you have spent the last few days, this is the place to shop.

Fremont Street Experience (all ages)
425 Fremont Street; (702) 678–5777. Hourly light shows after dark. Free.

The end of 1995 marked the opening of a $70 million project that transformed a dowdy downtown into a street with palm trees, pedestrian walkways, and a massive, 90-foot semicircular vault spanning four city blocks. A stroll down Fremont Street now provides visitors with an "experience" unlike any other in the world. With more than 2.1 million lights and 540,000 watts of sound, the possibilities are virtually unlimited. Hourly each night, the vault erupts into a brilliant light and sound show.

This show is enhanced by a fiber-optic sound system and computer-controlled lights; kids are in awe, and grown-ups are, too. The constantly changing sound and light shows are seven to nine minutes long and feature themes such as Heartbeat of a Planet, Las Vegas Legends, Dancing in the Street, Odyssey, Country Western Dancing, and the Rescue. Complementing the light show are a variety of street performers including strolling performers, showgirls, and attitude girls.

Stars of the Strip (all ages)
Plaza Hotel, 1 Main Street; (702) 386–2110 or (800) 634–6575. Tuesday through Saturday 1:00 and 3:00 P.M. Free with a two-drink minimum.

Robbie Howard and Kathy Walker produce a high-quality afternoon show that features impressions of famous Las Vegas entertainers—and anyone else they might dream up.

Neon Museum (all ages)
731 South Fourth Street; (702) 229–5366; www.neonmuseum.org. No hours, but lit after dark. Free.

When Las Vegas spruced up its image and decided to toss the old-style neon into the trash, some of us were heartbroken. Those old neon signs may have been a waste of energy, but then, so are Christmas lights. If you are just a sucker for colored lights, don't miss this spot. Nothing beats the nostalgic thrill that comes from looking at these classic signs in action. Unlike most museums, though, the exhibits aren't inside; instead they are doing what they do best, jazzing up our Las Vegas streets.

Still in the development stage at press time, the two-acre Neon Museum Boneyard and Visitor's Center will include the outdoor neon boneyard, the Neon Cafe, a museum with local artifacts (including the original drawing for the Stardust sign and the Sputnik letters that were discarded during a recent "update"), and a retail shop. Plans also call for a separate warehouse/utility building designed around a classroom amphitheater that can be used for educational purposes or for related exhibitions, such as watching a neon artist in action. Supervised tours of the Boneyard will be open to the public at a later date.

Neonopolis (all ages)

450 Fremont Street; (702) 477–0470; www.neonopolis.net. Thursday through Sunday 11:00 A.M.–11:00 P.M., Friday and Saturday until 1:00 A.M.

This mega-entertainment center includes more than 240,000 square feet of nightclubs, shopping, outside entertainment, a fourteen-screen movie theater, restaurants, a food court, and food specialty items like pretzels, ice cream, and cookies.

Neon, Neon Night

As of press time, eleven of the Neon Museum's signs had been relit. Each sign has a dedicated plaque that tells its history.

• The Hacienda's Horse and Rider greet guests on Las Vegas Boulevard at the entrance to the Fremont Street Experience.

• Aladdin's Magic Lamp, Andy Anderson, and the Chief Hotel Court sign are on Fremont Street between Las Vegas Boulevard and Fourth Street.

• The Flame Restaurant sign, the Red Barn, Dot's Flowers, Wedding Information, and Nevada Motel are clustered within the Third Street cul-de-sac.

In addition, be sure to check out these historically significant but commercially working signs:

• **Vegas Vic** (at the Fremont Experience) has been in front of the Pioneer Club for fifty years.

• **Vegas Vickie** sits atop Glitter Gulch at 20 East Fremont Street.

• The **Golden Gate Hotel** sign is on the corner of Main and Fremont.

• The fabulous **Binion Horseshoe** sign, 128 Fremont Street, has 14 miles of neon and seems to encompass the whole building.

Keep abreast of new signs and locations by visiting www.neonmuseum.org.

Jillian's of Las Vegas (all ages)

(702) 759–0450. Thursday through Sunday 11:00 A.M.–11:00 P.M.; Friday and Saturday until 1:00 A.M. $.

Come to Jillian's for dinner, but stay for the games. The 9-Ball lounge has Brunswick pool tables, Ping-Pong, and shuffleboard. Next door the Hi-Life Lanes offer over-the-top bowling with a multimillion-dollar media show and black-light lanes. The electronic games area offers the latest in simulation games in the 12,000-square-foot room.

Lied Discovery Children's Museum (all ages)

833 Las Vegas Boulevard North; (702) 382–3445; www.ldcm.org. Tuesday through Sunday 10:00 A.M.–5:00 P.M. $, members and under age 2 free.

This children's museum has gotten national recognition, and rightfully so. With more than 22,000 square feet of rotating and permanent exhibition space to choose from, including more than one hundred hands-on exhibits exploring the arts, sciences, and humanities, most children will have a hard time deciding what to do next. Two of our favorite stops are the cartoon wheel, where kids use a hand crank to animate their own drawings, and a cool demonstration of the speed of sound: Kids talk into a tube and hear their voices coming out again after an incredibly long delay. Looking up, you see the tube snaking around overhead, but it still seems impossible that sound travels so slowly.

Other spots let kids fly the space shuttle, touch a tornado, and experience wheelchair basketball. The Early Childhood Pavilion is designed especially for little ones under age five to explore at their own pace and includes Boulder Mountain, Cactus Construction, and Desert in the Dark. Baby Oasis! is just for little ones who are not yet walking. The Parent Resource Room, a comfortable place for families to relax and connect with each other, contains parenting books, magazines, and videos, as well as community resource information.

Las Vegas Springs Preserve Volunteers (all ages)

3701 West Alta Drive; (702) 822–8344. Meetings held Tuesday 6:00–8:00 P.M., Saturday 1:00–3:00 P.M. Free.

The Las Vegas Springs were the reason that Las Vegas was born in the first place. A natural artesian spring poured out clear, fresh water that covered the area and made the striking *vegas,* or meadow, that refreshed and encouraged wanderers and made a safe haven for native residents. The 180-acre preserve is home to some of the oldest structures in the valley. It will get a radical face-lift over the next few years, with the environmental and cultural center opening in 2005.

The rare gray fox was recently sighted by a local biologist who spied it resting high in the branches of a native cottonwood tree. The gray fox is the only American canid species that can climb. Lend a hand with this magnificent project and let kids feel as if they are helping to preserve an important part of the American culture.

Inner City **Games**

Someone had his head on straight when he thought of Inner City Games, a free program for ages seven to seventeen that runs from March through August. Actually, this was Arnold Schwarzenegger's baby, begun in Los Angeles with a retired police officer who wanted to give kids positive after-school outlets. Since it was initiated in Las Vegas in 1995, this program has taken off like a shot, providing kids with instruction, encouragement, and more from Henderson to North Las Vegas to Mesquite.

In this cultural/recreational program, kids from across the valley can learn track and field, tennis, soccer, volleyball, hip-hop, dance, basketball, swimming, golf, art, music, drama, chess, computers, bowling, junior broadcasting, and more from professional coaches and teachers. The tennis camps, for instance, are taught by members of the U.S. Tennis Association. Transportation pickup points are at schools throughout the valley.

The program depends heavily on volunteers, with more than 2,000 now helping in various capacities. What better way to spend the summer with your child than to help with this special program that supports all Clark County children? Registration books are available through the schools or may be picked up at the downtown office, 233 South Fourth Street, Suite 205. Call (702) 382–5447.

Desert Demonstration Garden (all ages)
3701 West Alta Drive; (702) 258–3205. Daily, except holidays, 8:00 A.M.–5:00 P.M. Docents available 9:00 A.M.–1:00 P.M. Thursday through Saturday. Free.

The garden was developed to educate the public on xeriscaping—water-efficient landscaping in the desert—but now it is an attraction in its own right. With 2.4 acres of land showcasing more than 180 species of flora in eleven different landscape areas, this garden is a must-see for all those interested in finding out more about our desert environment.

Heritage Park Area (all ages)
Corner of Las Vegas Boulevard and Washington Avenue. Free.

The park includes a desert demonstration garden, a playground, picnic shelter, and more.

Old Las Vegas Mormon Fort State Historic Park (all ages)
500 East Washington Avenue; (702) 486–3511. Daily 8:00 A.M.–4:30 P.M. $, under 6 free.

The pursuit of religious freedom brought some of Las Vegas's first settlers here. Although we still boast a heavy Mormon population, this fort held the first. It is one of the oldest sites in the area. Attend one of the special events scheduled throughout the year.

Las Vegas Natural History Museum (all ages)

900 Las Vegas Boulevard North; (702) 384–3466. Daily 9:00 A.M.–4:00 P.M. $, under 3 free.

Kids like the animated dinosaur exhibit, although it isn't state-of-the-art anymore. The museum also includes a diorama featuring southern Nevada and a shark exhibit with a 3,000-gallon aquarium. We liked the African room, where you can go inside a native hut, and the butterfly display. The museum also includes a children's hands-on room, wildlife room, an icthyosaur exhibit, and a gift shop.

Jana's Junke (all ages)

201 East Colorado; (702) 388–0051. Hours vary.

I don't know who started it, but this corner begins a small cornucopia of antiques and collectible shops. You could easily spend a leisurely afternoon exploring here. With a little of everything collectible, Jana's Junke includes a wide selection of glassware as well as children's books and more vintage hats than even the most partying little girl could desire.

House of Style (all ages)

220 East Charleston Boulevard; (702) 382–5688; www.houseofstylethenandnow.com. Monday through Saturday 11:30 A.M.–4:30 P.M., Sunday by appointment.

Kids love to play dress-up, and who can blame them? Play dress-up together at the place locals go first when they want vintage clothing like the stars wear. I've been a vintage nut for more years than I care to admit, picking up beaded cashmere sweaters, Chinese silk nightgowns, and tailored wool jackets that Katharine Hepburn might have worn. This is the only place in Vegas where you still have a hope of those finds. Owner Mario D'Loe prefers quality over quantity and knows his textiles.

Albion Books (all ages)

2466 East Desert Inn, Suite G (East Desert Inn and Eastern); (702) 792–9554. Daily 10:00 A.M.–6:00 P.M.; buys books until 5:30 P.M.

This bookstore is a local haven on a lazy afternoon. One of my favorite stops is the case of children's vintage books behind the front desk. We love books with cool illustrations. There's room for everyone in the family to span out and find his or her own favorite kinds of book, from modern best-sellers to retro classics. We always look for Edgar Rice Burroughs, especially the *John Carter of Mars* series. There is something for everyone though, and cushy places where you can preview the books before buying. Looking for a first edition or a little educated patter about books? Look no further than the person behind the counter.

Boulevard Kids' Club (ages 2 through 11)

Boulevard Mall, 3528 South Maryland Parkway; (702) 732–8949. Second Saturday of the month, 12:30–1:00 P.M. Free.

Club members meet monthly in back of the food court to do crafts, play games, and enjoy themed events. Sign up for the free newsletter to receive advance notice of upcoming activities.

Sunset Park (all ages)

2601 East Sunset Road; (702) 455–8200; 6:00 A.M.–11:00 P.M. Free.

This 324-acre regional park facility has long been the most recognizable park within the Valley. Sunset Park Nature Area consists of sand dunes and mesquite bosk covering 140 acres. This nature and wildlife habitat area is home to many sensitive species of animals endemic to the area. The park also has one of the widest ranges of recreational activities in the area, including tennis courts, volleyball courts, a fishing pond, grassy open areas, picnic facilities, a large pool with two diving boards, a disc golf course, and lots of play equipment.

Regular fishing derbies are conducted at the Sunset Park Lake in conjunction with the Nevada Fish and Game Department, which usually stocks about 14,000 fish of various sizes so that the kids have something to catch. Adults are welcome to participate, but this really is a great way for kids to catch the fishing bug. Children twelve and younger are not required to have a fishing license; all others must have a current license with a trout tag.

Mystic Falls Park (all ages)

Sam's Town Hotel, 5111 Boulder Highway; (702) 456–7777.

This 25,000-square-foot indoor park, located in the center of the resort, features restaurants, shopping, and the Sunset Stampede, a **free** dancing water, laser, and light show at 2:00, 6:00, 8:00, and 10:00 P.M. daily.

First Friday (all ages)

Las Vegas Arts District, Main and Charleston; (702) 678–6278. First Friday of the month. Free.

Join local artists and arts lovers at this monthly get-together where fine art, entertainment, and a community social combine to create a festive hometown party.

Jam Sessions (all ages)

Lorna J. Kesterson Recreation Center, 500 Harris Avenue; (702) 565–2121. Tuesday 7:00–9:00 P.M. Free.

Bring your guitar to this acoustic bluegrass and old-time music jam session each Tuesday night.

Old-Time Barn Dances (all ages, with adult supervision)

Charleston Heights Arts Center, 800 South Brush Street; (702) 229–6383, 656–9513, or 360–5203. Last Saturday of the month, 6:30 P.M. lessons, 7:10 P.M. dance. $, under 15 free.

Who can keep his or her feet still when a fiddler fiddles his fiddle? We can't. Come early to get your **free** dancing lessons, then grab your child and dance, dance, dance. No partners necessary.

For the **Love** of Poetry

Feel as if you are part of the beat generation who gathered in small cafes and bookstores to chant, cheer, and chortle in iambic pentameter. If your family already loves poetry, you'll fit right in. If you're not too sure, however, ease your way in by just happening to stop by for a cup of hot chocolate during an open-mike session. Like art, these places tend to have their own personalities, however, so just because one doesn't fit, that doesn't mean that your family's poetic bliss isn't just around the next cup of coffee.

If you are developing your children's love of poetry, make sure you let them bring along an unobtrusive toy or book to help them remain quiet during those inevitable breaks in their attention spans. Also, some poets may use mature language or imagery, and just because the content was G-rated the last time doesn't guarantee that it will be G-rated this time. Call to ask the coordinator what to expect.

Young Poets' Corner (ages 8–16). West Las Vegas Arts Center, 947 West Lake Mead Boulevard; (702) 229–4800. Third Saturday of the month, noon–1:00 P.M. Free. Keith Brantley and Pendelita Toney invite young poets to share their words at this monthly event.

Cafe Espresso Roma. 4440 South Maryland Parkway; (702) 369–1540. Monday 8:00 P.M. Free. Enjoy a cup of coffee and open-mike poetry.

Hispanic Poets Society. Clark County Library; 1401 East Flamingo Road; (702) 733–7810. Call for dates. Free. Hear from Hispanic voices in this poetry fest.

Poet's Corner. West Las Vegas Arts Center, 947 West Lake Mead Boulevard; (702) 229–4800. Third Friday of the month, 7:00 or 7:30 P.M. Free. Keith Brantley and Pendelita Toney host established poets in this celebration of their poetry. An open-mike session allows lesser-known authors to share their works.

Wordsmith's Poetry Night. West Charleston Library, 6301 West Charleston Boulevard; (702) 878–3597 or 647–2117. Second Thursday of the month 7:00 P.M. Free. Enjoy free refreshments with your recitations at this monthly event. Some poets may use mature language.

Lights, Camera, **Action!**

Las Vegas is becoming a mecca for entertainment producers. A city with a strong visual personality, it's what lies within that's really important: a fiber optics network. Because Las Vegas's growth has been so recent, the city has one of the highest-tech infrastructures in the world. As the digital age in television, videos, and movies takes over, many producers feel that Las Vegas is not only a great backdrop, it is a fabulous city of entertainment opportunity. Not everyone will become a star, but what a kick to have your family become extras in the next movie filmed here. Television studios are also shooting here more often. Just remember to thank me when you accept that Academy Award.

Casting Entertainment. 4350 South Arville Boulevard, Building D, Suite 27; (702) 252–4442. This company casts locals for union and nonunion work in current and upcoming productions. No experience is necessary. There is a $100 annual registration fee. Registration provides you with access to the weekly hotline of upcoming shoots. During the filming of *Ocean's 11*, for instance, the company had a call for 1,000 extras for one day's shoot. Most of the calls are for adults; when kids are needed, the agency usually makes that announcement on the hotline and asks interested parties to bring along their kids. You may not meet Julia Roberts, but what a hoot anyhow.

Rainbow Company. Charleston Heights Las Vegas Arts Center, 800 Brush Street; (702) 229–6553. This excellent children's theater for ages ten and up stages five productions a year. It's a family favorite for all who love live performances.

Community Youth Theatre Ensemble. West Las Vegas Arts Center, 947 West Lake Mead Boulevard; (702) 229–4800. $$ for eight-week sessions; audition or interview required for admission. Theater-minded kids age ten and up work on writing and improvisational theater to develop youth issue–oriented vignettes.

Children's Theater Classes. Charleston Heights Arts Center and Reed Whipple Center, 800 South Brush Street; (702) 229–6383. $$ for eight weeks. Taught by the staff of Rainbow Company, these classes include basic acting skills that stress the mind, body, and voice and prepare students ages seven to twelve for more advanced theater work.

Ethnic Express Folk Dancers (all ages, with adult supervision)
Charleston Heights Arts Center Ballroom, 800 South Brush Street; (702) 229–6383 or
732–4871. Every Wednesday, 6:30 to 7:15 P.M. class, 7:15 to 8:45 P.M. dancing. $.

This weekly event celebrates the tradition of folk dancing. The early part of the evening is
spent learning or refining a folk dance, with instruction geared toward the level of that
night's participants. Afterward, put the practice to use in the open-dancing session. This
international evening of fun can run the gamut from Russian to Turkish to Macedonian
dance. Children under fourteen must be supervised by parents.

Southern Nevada Zoological-Botanical Park (all ages)
1775 North Rancho Drive; (702) 648–5955 or 647–4685; www.lasvegaszoo.org. Daily 9:00
A.M.–5:00 P.M. $, under 2 free.

"Nevada's Wildest Family Entertainment" is an intimate zoo with more than 300 plant and
animal species displayed throughout the shaded three-acre park. The zoo recently
expanded and upgraded its plant and animal collection.

The zoo boasts a breeding pair of Bali mynah birds, one of the rarest birds on earth.
Only seven of them remain on their native island, with only an estimated 400 to 600 left
on earth. Snow white, with sky blue eye rings and wings trimmed in·black, they are also
one of the most striking bird species, as they rest in their own tropical rain forest exhibit
inside the reptile building.

The zoo also houses representatives from all of the world's venomous lizards (all
three), including a Mexican beaded lizard provided by a zoo in Texas that was the first one
allowed in the state of Nevada. You'll also find an endangered species of small cat from
San Diego, lions Midas and Maniac, and a large underwater alligator exhibit. It may not be
the biggest zoo you'll ever visit, but this clean little zoo has a lot of heart.

Sporting Clubs and Games

Las Vegas Valley Bicycle Club, Inc. (ages 2 and up)
821 Las Vegas Boulevard North; (702) 897–7800.

The Las Vegas Valley Bicycle Club Inc. hosts rides on a weekly basis. Helmets are required
on all rides.

Powerhouse Indoor Climbing Center (all ages)
8201 West Charleston Boulevard; (702) 254–5604. Monday through Thursday 11:00 A.M.–
10:00 P.M., Friday 11:00 A.M.–8:00 P.M., and Saturday and Sunday 10:00 A.M.–8:00 P.M. $.

Powerhouse offers 8,000 square feet of textured climbing terrain that includes roofs, but-
tresses, dihedrals, caves, and gymnastic floor padding. Group and individual classes are
offered. Open to all ages and fitness levels as long as one is heavy enough to get back
down. Not my problem. There is an additional charge for equipment.

Cultural **History**

Currently, there are four properties listed on the City of Las Vegas Historic Property Register:

- **Fifth Street School** at 400 South Fourth Street
- **Moulin Rouge Hotel & Casino** at 900 West Bonanza Road
- **Wait House** at 901 East Ogden Avenue
- **Green Shack Restaurant** at 2500 East Fremont Street

These eight sites are on the National Register of Historic Places:

- **Las Vegas Mormon Fort** at 500 East Washington Avenue
- **Railroad Cottages** at Second to Fourth Street, Garces Avenue to Clark Avenue
- **Post Office/Federal Building** at 301 East Stewart Avenue
- **Westside School** at 300 West Washington Avenue
- **Big Springs** at Las Vegas Water District property (east of Meadows Mall, near the expressway and Valley View Boulevard); not open to the public
- **Old Las Vegas High School/LAS VEGAS Academy** at 315 South Seventh Street
- **Smith House** at 624 South Sixth Street
- **Huntridge Theater** at Charleston Boulevard and Maryland Parkway

For more information call the city's Historic Preservation Officer at (702) 229–2087.

The 51s (all ages)
Cashman Field; (702) 386–7200 or 474–4000. $.

We love watching the Stars—whoops! I meant the 51s—play baseball at Cashman Field. For one thing you can actually see the ball. Every game is something like a party; kids are free to get up and move or drop their cotton candy on the ground. Frankly, we love the slightly wild atmosphere. Everyone knows everyone, and we like it that way. We buy the cheap seats because we're only in them about half the time and they're close to the restrooms.

Lorenzi Adaptive Recreation Center and Programs

333 West Washington; (702) 229–6358 or 229–4905. The city runs the only adaptive recreation program in the state to ensure that kids with special needs also have opportunities for special fun.

Programs include everything from Project D.I.R.T. (Developing Interest in Risk Taking) to F.L.O.A.T. (Forming Leisure Opportunities using Aquatic Techniques). R.E.A.L. provides year-round opportunities for people with disabilities to participate in organized sports, including aquatics, soccer, skiing, basketball, and track and field. Leisure Buddies/P.A.L. is a program for ages seven to twenty-one that helps kids find friends. The Teen Club and Youth Council extend regular programming to encourage a healthy, independent, and well-balanced leisure lifestyle.

To find out more about these and other programs, call (702) 229–4900 or TDD 386–9108 (for the hearing impaired), or write to Adaptive Recreation Program, 749 Veterans Memorial Drive, Las Vegas, Nevada 89101.

Flyaway Indoor Sky Diving (40 pounds and up)
200 Convention Center Drive; (702) 731–4768. Monday through Saturday 10:00 A.M.–7:00 P.M. Cost per flight includes training, gear, and flight instruction. Under age 18 must be with parent or guardian, minimum weight, forty pounds. $$$.

Flyaway offers indoor skydiving in a vertical wind tunnel. High-flying families can experience the thrill of skydiving, then be captured for eternity on video. The last instruction is offered one hour before closing.

Where to Eat

Coffee Pub. 2800 West Sahara Avenue; (702) 367–1913. Monday through Friday 7:00 A.M.–3:00 P.M. Who knows how long this place has been around? Come here for breakfast, served until 2:00 P.M., or for the great selection of pastas and sandwiches. You almost feel as if you are in New York—it's crowded and friendly. At least that's my story. $–$$

Ellis Island Restaurant. 4178 Koval Lane; (702) 733–8901. Open twenty-four hours. This is another of those local secrets for bargain hunters. The steak dinner comes with soup or salad, baked potatoes, garlic bread, and dinner rolls. The rest of the food isn't bad either, so go ahead and splurge. $–$$

Huntridge Drug Store Restaurant. 1122 East Charleston Boulevard; (702) 384–3737. Monday through Saturday 8:00 A.M.–6:00 P.M., Sunday 9:00 A.M.–11:00 P.M. This place serves Chinese food the way your mom made it with Chop Suey and Chow Mein the top sellers. The old-fashioned hamburgers are also a hit.

But the real draw is that this place hasn't changed in more than thirty years, giving families a taste of old Vegas. $

In-N-Out Burger. Numerous locations. Just burgers, fresh-cut fries, and real milk shakes here, but everything tastes so fresh that fast food takes on a new meaning. With numerous locations throughout the valley, stop in here for a cheap meal that is wholly satisfying. Don't expect toys, though, if that's why you stop at a burger place. $

Iowa Cafe. 300 East Charleston; (702) 366–1882. Daily 8:00 A.M.–4:00 P.M., Thursday night until 9:00 P.M. This homey little cafe offers great handmade sandwiches, a wide variety of drinks, and the chance to get to know the locals. A favorite hangout of businesspeople and local artists, the Thursday evening poetry readings are fun for everyone. The Cafe is also open for First Friday and other special occasions. $

Mediterranean Cafe. 4147 South Maryland Parkway; (702) 731–6030. Sunday through Thursday 10:00 A.M.–9:00 P.M., Friday and Saturday until 10:00 P.M. My kids are willing to try new foods and discovered, to their surprise, that they like almost anything that they can dip into. This restaurant offers dips aplenty and a festive atmosphere that seems more exotic than it is. For the vegetarian in your crew, this is the place to go. The cafe also offers an amazing array of tasty teas. $–$$

Salvadoreno. 720 Main Street; (702) 385–3600. Tuesday through Sunday 10:00 A.M.–9:00 P.M. Come for lunch with the kids. The location is a little rough at night, but that often means that the food is authentic and cheap. That is the case here, where Central American food is dished up in generous portions. The stuffed *papusas* are a real hit with my kids, as are the fried plantains with cream. If your family is feeling adventurous, this is the place to feed that adventure. $–$$

Off the Beaten Strip

The area right around the Strip offers a variety of family-friendly hotels, amusements, and restaurants. Many of the hotels offer **free** shuttles to the Strip, so that you can see the sights without having to deal with the megacrowds. Because they are out of the way, they often do a little more to bring people in. The Hard Rock and the Rio are two hotels that have found their own niches: the first with the beautiful people, the latter with discerning clients.

But as you move away from Las Vegas Boulevard, other interesting sights and sounds appear. As we speak, more and more entertainment and educational opportunities are being created for families and kids, not by the megaresorts, but by individual businesses, government services, and nonprofit arts and service organizations that understand and value the rich infrastructure that makes a great city. It is exciting to live and visit here, and nowhere else is it more accurate to say, "The best is yet to come." In fact, it is coming right now.

The Rio

3700 West Flamingo Road; (702) 252–7777; www.playrio.com. $–$$$$

The Rio has one of the best views of the Strip, although it isn't part of it. Located 1 block west, its twin towers are distinctive and easy to locate. The first all-suite hotel/casino in Vegas, each of its 2,563 suites contain in-room coffeemakers, refrigerators, safes, and ironing boards. *Travel and Leisure* magazine readers named it the "Best Value in the World." The suites overlooking the Strip offer some of the best views in Vegas; the ones looking to the western mountains offer a contrasting view that is equally stunning when the sun sets. One things families don't like, though, is that it seems to take forever to get from one place to the next. Ask for the new tower and a bellboy to take your luggage up. That way, the entrance to Masquerade Village will be close, even though the check-in desk is not.

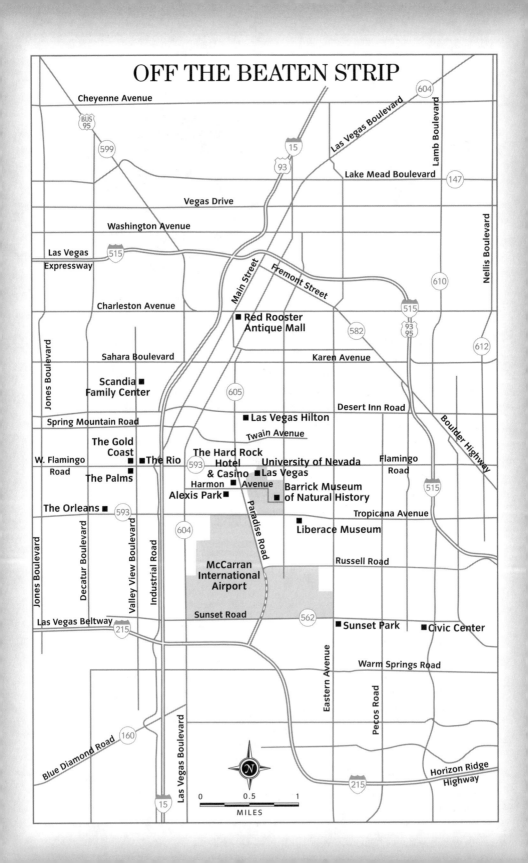

OFF THE BEATEN STRIP

Cheyenne Avenue

BUS 95

599

I15

93

Las Vegas Boulevard

604

Lamb Boulevard

Lake Mead Boulevard

147

Nellis Boulevard

Vegas Drive

Washington Avenue

Las Vegas Expressway

515

Main Street

Fremont Street

610

Charleston Avenue

■ Red Rooster Antique Mall

582

515 93 95

Sahara Boulevard

Karen Avenue

612

Jones Boulevard

■ Scandia Family Center

605

Desert Inn Road

Boulder Highway

Spring Mountain Road

■ Las Vegas Hilton

Twain Avenue

W. Flamingo Road

The Gold Coast

■ The Rio

593

The Hard Rock Hotel & Casino

University of Nevada Las Vegas

Flamingo Road

■ The Palms

Harmon ■ Avenue

■

Barrick Museum of Natural History

515

■ The Orleans

593

Alexis Park ■

Paradise Road

Tropicana Avenue

604

■ Liberace Museum

Jones Boulevard

Decatur Boulevard

Valley View Boulevard

Industrial Road

McCarran International Airport

Russell Road

Sunset Road

562

■ Sunset Park

■ Civic Center

Las Vegas Beltway

215

Eastern Avenue

Warm Springs Road

Pecos Road

Blue Diamond Road

160

Las Vegas Boulevard

Horizon Ridge Highway

I15

215

N

0   0.5   1
MILES

The Pool (all ages)

A sand beach lies at the edge of a tropical lagoon, complete with waterfalls, four nautical-shaped swimming pools, and five Jacuzzi-style spas. Although the area is not huge, kids will enjoy going from pool to pool while little ones dig in the sand.

Butch Harmon School of Golf at the Rio Secco Golf Club (all ages)

Okay, we admit this isn't for everyone, but if you are willing, you and your kid can get trained by the same guy who keeps Tiger Woods at the top of his game—not his training minions, but the man, himself. Golf packages are available from $1,250 to $4,600 per person. A one-day package with Butch Harmon includes a two-night stay at the Rio, a complete day of instruction with Harmon, computerized video analysis of your game, on-course playing lesson at the Rio Secco Golf Course, lunch, and transportation to and fro. Harmon trains kids or grown-ups and ensures that each student is fit with the right equipment. He also has a training school where, for the lower fee, you can receive training by his instructors. Just make sure you book ahead of time, because Tiger doesn't have to wait.

The Rio Secco Golf Course nests amid the rolling foothills of the Black Mountains. An eighteen-hole championship course, it was designed primarily for the guests of the Rio by Rees Jones, *Golf World* magazine's 1995 "Golf Architect of the Year" and mastermind behind more than one hundred of the world's top courses.

The Goyas' TopPicks for fun off the Strip

1. Have a picture taken while floating above the crowd as part of the Rio's Masquerade Show in the Sky
2. See the Smothers Brothers at the Orleans
3. Bowl with the family at the Gold Coast
4. Attend an "all ages" concert at the Joint
5. Rest in the shade of a desert willow at UNLV
6. Try an exotic taste at Chinatown Plaza
7. Catch your reflection in a rhinestone piano at the Liberace Museum
8. Have dinner with a Klingon at the Star Trek Experience
9. Find a Las Vegas hidden treasure at the Red Rooster Antique Mall
10. See a world-class performer at the UNLV Performing Arts Center

Climb **Aboard**

You can become a part of the $25 million masquerade show in the sky. Show up an hour before the performance to get all gussied up to ride in one of the floats. That way you can wave and watch at the same time. The cost is $9.95 (must be 48 inches or taller). Those under age sixteen must be accompanied by parent or guardian. Reservations required.

With six featured shows, you won't mind seeing it more than once. Shows include Ipanema Beach Party, Street Party, Venice Masquerade, and Disco Swing Parade.

Masquerade Show in the Sky (all ages)

(702) 252–7776. Every two hours daily from 2:00 P.M.–midnight except Wednesday. Free.

The Rio hosts a twelve-minute THEA award–winning parade in the sky. Loud music and floats that really float combine to make this spectacle spectacular. For families, the best view is from the balcony overlooking Masquerade Village, where kids can get an ice cream or hot dog while waiting. If you want one of those shiny plastic beaded necklaces that performers throw into the audience, however, you'd better move fast, because so does everyone else.

Buffets According to the **Buffet King**

You can't write a guide book about Las Vegas without recommending where to buffet it. My personal opinion is that buffet food is rarely excellent, no matter how hard they try. Even the most upscale casinos offer buffets, but at such high prices that I don't really see the advantage, since there is only so much food you can down at one time. The best reason to go to a buffet is to satisfy a group who can't seem to agree on a common food theme. Modern buffets often have multiethnic food stations where dishes are prepared on the spot and offer a variety of culinary options.

For the best value in buffets, consider a late lunch; prices are often half of what you pay for dinner, and the selection is nearly the same. Places like the Bellagio and Bally's offer delicacies and prices that most of us can't afford to miss. Paris Las Vegas has also gotten good reviews from those who like French food.

When dining with kids, one of the advantages of buffets is the fact that you don't have to wait for the food once you are seated. Lines to get in, however, can be exceptionally long. Tipping at the 15 percent range is appropriate; these servers often work harder for you than standard restaurant servers.

I consulted the Buffet King, a high school teacher and the father of a three-year-old known for his buffet passion. He has been sampling local buffets for years, first with his parents, and now with his own child. Here are his recommendations.

- **Golden Nugget.** 129 East Fremont Street; (702) 385–7111. Daily 7:00 A.M.–10:00 P.M., Sunday brunch 8:00 A.M. "If you do the Fremont Street Experience, try this buffet. The restaurant is pretty and serene. The selection is small, but the food is terrific." $$

- **Palace Station The Feast Gourmet Buffet.** 2411 West Sahara Avenue; (702) 367–2411. Daily 7:00 A.M.–10:00 P.M., weekends until 3:30 P.M. "The pasta bar and the ice-cream bar are very good." $$

- **Texas Station Feast Around the World Buffet.** 2101 Texas Star Lane; (702) 631–1000. Daily 8:00 A.M.–10:00 P.M. "The food is good." $$

- **Sunset Station Feast Around the World Buffet.** 1301 West Sunset Road; (702) 547–7777. Daily 8:00 A.M.–10:00 P.M. "The biggest and best buffet of all of the Stations has a wide selection of food, including Italian, Chinese, Mexican, and American." $$

- **Sam's Town Firelight Buffet.** 5111 Boulder Highway; (702) 456–7777. Daily 11:00 A.M.–9:00 P.M., weekends 10:00 A.M.–3:00 P.M. "They have some unusual foods that you don't usually see at buffets, like Jamaican duck, and Coca-Cola Chicken. There is a good ice-cream and dessert bar. The hotel is beautiful and they boast a spectacular free laser show in the middle of the hotel." $$

- **Rio Carnival World Buffet.** 3700 West Flamingo Road; (702) 252–7777. Daily 8:00 A.M.–11:00 P.M. "In my opinion, overrated." $$

Other Popular Buffets

- **Aladdin Spice Market Buffet.** 3667 Las Vegas Boulevard South; (702) 785–9005. Daily 7:00 A.M.–10:00 P.M. $$

- **Main Street Station Garden Court Buffet.** 200 North Main Street; (702) 387–1896. Daily 7:00 A.M.–10:00 P.M., weekend brunch until 3:00 P.M. $$

Ronn Lucas (ages 5 and up)
Masquerade Showroom; (888) 746–7784. Daily 3:00 P.M., dark Friday. $.

Using a variety of puppets and props, this talented ventriloquist mixes stand-up comedy and improvisation into a family-friendly mix that leaves everyone laughing.

Tony 'n' Tina's Wedding (ages 5 and up)
Calypso Room; (888) 746–7784. Daily 7:00 P.M. $$$$.

This dinner show lets you come to the nuptials of Anthony Nunzio Jr. and Valentina Lynne Vitale, a comical mock ceremony that became an off-Broadway wedding-day non-bliss sensation. The dinner-reception includes an Italian buffet and champagne toast and the chance to dance with your own little girl.

Where to Eat

It is hard to beat the Rio for choices in tasty eating. It boasts the largest private wine cellar in the world, but it also takes food preparation seriously, making its own fresh pasta, baking its own breads in a state-of-the-art bakery, and hand cutting each piece of beef, chicken, and seafood. The Rio even makes its own ice cream. So whichever of the fifteen restaurants you choose, the Rio has a reputation for overall food excellence that extends throughout the hotel.

Buzio's Seafood Restaurant. (702) 247–7923. Daily 11:00 A.M.–11:00 P.M. Reservations suggested. Chef Kolanchai Ngimsangaim flies the seafood in daily to ensure its ultimate freshness. The open kitchen adds to the entertainment as guests watch the preparation of lobsters, oysters, mussels, clams, and more. The chef personally plucks the room's daily selection of delicate seafood from the Rio's own live aquarium habitat. Locals consistently rate this one of the best seafood experiences in the city, as well as one of the most romantic dining places. Come for lunch with the kids and watch the beautiful people at the pool, or get a sitter and enjoy more romantic evening fare. $$–$$$

Carnival World Buffet. (702) 252–7777. Daily 8:00 A.M.–10:00 P.M. Voted by locals as the "Best Buffet in Las Vegas" year after year, this all-you-can-eat buffet has twelve distinct dining experiences from around the world, including Asian, Italian, American, and Brazilian food. At each station, on-site chefs prepare fresh food so junior can have lasagna while dad has prime rib. The pastry roundtable has more desserts than you can shake a spoon at. Kids will love the variety, but not the long line that can extend enough to make a two-hour wait. Come at off times if you don't like lines. $–$$

Fiore Rotisserie. (702) 247–7923. Nightly 6:00–11:00 P.M. Reservations suggested. Awarded the prestigious Five Star Diamond Award by the American Academy of Hospitality Science and under the direction of Chef Jean-Louis Palladin and Chef Gervais Henric, this restaurant celebrates culinary delights from the south of France to the northern coast of Italy. $$$–$$$$

Gaylord India Restaurant. (702) 252–7777. Daily 11:00 A.M.–2:30 P.M. and 5:00 to 11:00 P.M., weekends to 1:00 A.M. My kids love Indian food, although one has to make sure that there are plenty of nonspicy choices. Served family-style (or should we say Chinese-style?), dishes are usually shared by the entire table. $$

Rosemary's. (702) 777–2300. Daily 5:00–11:00 P.M. Or 8125 West Sahara; (702) 596–2251. Monday through Friday 11:30 A.M.–2:30 P.M. and Monday through Sunday 5:30–10:30 P.M. (I had the best mandarin martini I have ever had in my life here, but that is another book.) This local restaurant has taken on legendary proportions in the Vegas Valley with innovative, fresh, and startlingly deli-cious fare. Elegant, but not pretentious; take kids who love good food. $$–$$$

Toscano's Deli. (702) 252–7777. Daily 7:00 A.M.–1:00 A.M. This New York–style deli features sandwiches, salads, soups, and pizza as well as fresh-baked breads and desserts. $

VooDoo Cafe. (702) 247–7923. Daily noon–3:00 P.M. and 5:00–11:00 P.M. Reservations suggested. This restaurant boasts one of the best views of the Strip; be sure to ask for a window table. Choose shrimp Creole or sweet curry spiced Chilean sea bass with grilled prawns from the Cajun-inspired menu. Once the kids are safely in bed, this is one of the hottest dance spots in town, regularly attracting Hollywood stars and other celebrities to its lounge. $$–$$$

The Orleans

4500 West Tropicana Avenue; (702) 365–7111 or (800) 675–3267; www.orleanscasino .com. $–$$$$

With more than 800 rooms, the Orleans appears to be intimate when compared to some of the megaresorts in the area. It has some of the best family-friendly performers, including the fabulous Smothers Brothers. Although not flashy, it is one of the best values you will find, with top-notch friendliness and quality dining. Visitors can enjoy the full-size swimming pool and the health club before heading off to the Strip or to the open space just outside of Vegas. A **free** shuttle gets you to and from the Strip. The Century Orleans 12 is a twelve-screen movie theater with state-of-the-art digital and THX sound. The Time Out Arcade features the latest and greatest in video and interactive games for every member of the family and is open seven days a week.

Bowling Center (all ages)
Open bowling hours vary. $.

With seventy lanes and a full-service pro shop where you can get everything from coaching instruction to a new ball, drilled to order, this place has everything a bowling family would need, including shoe rentals.

Kid's Tyme (ages 3 months to 12 years)
Open daily 9:00 A.M.–midnight, until 1:00 A.M. Friday and Saturday. Cost is per hour (three-and-a-half-hour maximum). $.

Let the kids be wild at this play area, which includes a jungle gym, movie room, arts and crafts area, Sega Dreamcast, Lego station, and more. A licensed day care, all providers are CPR trained. The center stops accepting children younger than two and a half at 10:00 P.M. and all other children at 10:30 P.M.

Taking a Break

One of the pitfalls of a family vacation is that the parents are usually occupied with keeping the kids happy. Wouldn't it be nice to have a few hours' break so you'd get to miss the little buggers?

Sitters aren't cheap, but they will give you a chance to experience the adult Las Vegas. Usually there is a fee, a minimum, and an hourly rate. At these prices, however, you can—and should—expect a lot. Minimally, the sitter should have had a background check and be bonded, licensed, and insured. Ask if the sitters are CPR trained and if the agency has minimum age requirements for its sitters. Find out what the sitters do after they arrive. Do they bring age-appropriate toys and games? Will they get the children ready for bed? Do you want the sitter to bathe the children, read them a story, take them to the arcade, or just sit in the corner while the kids watch a video? Is there an additional fee for more than two children? Will they put children to bed at a certain time?

Around the Clock Childcare. (702) 365–1040. Price varies. In business for more than sixteen years, this agency requires a background check and is bonded, licensed, and insured.

Four Seasons Babysitting Service. (702) 384–5848. Around for more than twenty-five years, owner Opal Holton claims not to have hired anyone new for "years." She employs women ages thirty-eight to sixty who are licensed, bonded, and insured and who have health cards and background checks. "I only hire new people if they are someone I know very well," she says, "And I haven't needed to do that for years." The sitters cannot drive the children anywhere, but they are willing to walk with them to a nearby arcade, amusement, or show, at parental request. The cost is $35.00 for the first four hours (one or two children), $7.00 each additional hour; $45.00 for the first four hours (three or four children), $10.00 each additional hour.

The Orleans Showroom (age appropriateness varies)

The 827-seat Orleans-style showroom features theater-style design and a technically superior sound and lighting system, which ensure a sensational entertainment experience for guests of all ages. Expect to see such legendary acts as Jerry Lewis, Willy Nelson, Pat Benatar, Bo Diddley, Tanya Tucker, and the Smothers Brothers, with tickets usually in the $30 to $45 range.

Ba Da Bing (all ages)

(702) 992–7970. Thursday through Monday 7:30 P.M. VIP package $$$$, dinner and show $$$, children under 13 $$.

Join the birthday bash for a mythical Las Vegas Don and his gang of Italian "friends."

Where to Eat

Don Miguel's. (702) 365–7550. Daily 11:00 A.M.–11:00 P.M. They try hard to please here, with traditional Mexican dishes as well as creative menu items, like the chicken Baldastano or the filet Colorado. But we can't resist the beans, guacamole, and salsa served with chips and the **free** margarita that makes waiting for your food a genuine pleasure. The kids always enjoy watching the fresh tortillas being made. Don't go home without trying the tequila flan or my daughter's favorite, fried ice cream. $–$$

French Market Buffet. (702) 365–7111. Monday through Saturday 7:00–10:00 A.M., 11:00 A.M.–3:00 P.M., 4:00–10:00 P.M.; Sunday 8:00 A.M.–3:00 P.M., 4:00–10:00 P.M. The French Market Buffet is the Orleans's action buffet featuring Italian, Mongolian, barbecue, American, seafood, Mexican, and Chinese cooking, as well as an oversize dessert bar. From eggs prepared before your eyes just the way you like them to house-smoked ribs, families are sure to find something to satisfy every palate. $–$$

The Rib Joint. (702) 365–7111. Daily 5:00–11:00 P.M. This is our kind of place; my kids have always called ribs "barbecued bones." The family feast is perfect for us who love to "just taste" each other's food, and, quite frankly usually order too much for one meal anyway. If kids like pizza, there's that too. $–$$

Sazio's. (702) 365–7111. Daily 11:00 A.M.–10:00 P.M. Thin-crust pizzas, fried ravioli, a fabulous spinach salad with walnuts, veal, chicken, and seafood make this another welcome addition to chef Gustav Mauler's local repertoire. $–$$

The Gold Coast

4000 West Flamingo Road; (702) 367–7111 or (888) 402–6278. $–$$

The Gold Coast Hotel and Casino is a 711-room resort destination located 1 mile west of the Strip and a half mile from Chinatown. Surrounded by acres of **free** parking and two easy-access parking garages, the Gold Coast also has a **free** shuttle bus that carries guests to and from its sister properties, the Barbary Coast on the Las Vegas Strip and the Orleans. The hotel features a swimming pool and a fitness area.

Pool (all ages)

The small heated pool is open year-round.

Bowling Center (all ages)
Open twenty-four hours (no open lanes from 5:00 to 9:00 P.M.). $.

A seventy-two-lane bowling center, one of the largest in the country, occupies the entire second floor of the Gold Coast's 1988 casino addition. Amenities include a pro shop with instructor, 1,400 equipment lockers, a video arcade, and a snack bar specializing in pizza. The center features Brunswick 2000 bowling equipment and automatic scoring that is

"Taxi!!"

Actually, you have a snowball's chance in summer of hailing a cab from the streets of Las Vegas. Instead, taxis regularly pick up passengers at hotels' entrances for those patrons patiently waiting in queues. Charges are regulated, so there is no need to call around for the best rates. You will pay $2.20 for the first eighth mile. Each additional eighth mile is 20 cents; waiting time per minute is 35 cents; and McCarran charges a fee of $1.20 per trip, collected by the cab company. Expect to pay $15.00 to $20.00 from downtown to the airport, $8.00 to $12.00 from the Strip to the airport; traffic may make these fees vary.

- Ace Cab, 736–8383
- Blue Cab, 384–6111
- Deluxe Cab, 568–7700
- Henderson Taxi, 384–2322
- Nellis Cab, 248–1111
- Western Cab, 382–7100
- Yellow Checker Star Transportation, 873–2000

state of the art. The Gold Coast offers a league program for everyone: competitive scratch leagues, mixed adult programs, and one of the city's largest junior leagues, plus bumper bowling for the little ones. Show up Sunday morning at 8:45 or 10:15 for the pro sessions ($8.00 per session, $36.00 per hour private lessons) to learn or improve your technique.

Child Care (ages 2 through 8)
(702) 367–7111. 9:00 A.M.–midnight. Free.

Let your children have a little playtime during vacation at this **free** child care center. The kids must be potty trained and out of pull-ups, and may not stay at the center for more than three hours per day. Parents must leave a photo ID and stay at the casino.

Honky Tonk Angels (all ages)
Gold Coast Showroom; (702) 251–3574. Wednesday through Monday 8:00 P.M. $$; additional charge for dinner.

If you like Southern country women, you'll like this show that features three local angels who pay tribute to Patsy Cline, Dolly Parton, Reba McEntire, Brenda Lee, Tammy Wynette, the Judds, and Faith Hill. One of the best show values in town, the place really rocks when the three are on stage together.

Where to Eat

Arriva. (702) 367–7111. Daily 5:00–11:00 P.M. Reservations suggested. Fresh seafood and Italian specialty dishes are served in a warm atmosphere. House favorites include a wide range of appetizers, seafood, milkfed veal, chicken dishes, and pasta. $–$$$

Cortez Room. (702) 367–7111. Daily 5:00–11:00 P.M. Generous portions of prime rib, steak, and seafood make this dining room an exceptional value. An informal, yet warm and comfortable atmosphere contributes to this dining experience. $–$$$

Hot Dog. Daily 10:00 A.M.–6:45 P.M. This is one of those Vegas secrets. The best hot dog in town is from the vendor cart in the sports book area. You can load on the usual fixings or add sauerkraut or onions, just like on the streets of New York. My favorite? Mustard and kraut. $

The Hard Rock Hotel & Casino

4455 Paradise Road; (702) 693–5000 or (800) HRD–ROCK; www.hardrockhotel.com. $–$$$$

If you wanna be a rock star, this is the place to hang out. Young, hip, and trendy, the Hard Rock's nightclub, the Joint, is one of the hottest places in town to see real stars in action; most of the bands that play here, stay here. So does everyone else who is, wants to be, or wants to see the beautiful people in action. The Hard Rock is relatively small compared to some of the newer hotels, with only 668 rooms and suites. The $100 million expansion includes a tower where oversize guest rooms sport sleek lines, lush materials, and a subtle color palette. In each of the rooms guests can throw open their French windows for a view of the Beach Club or the Strip, or for some fresh air. Entertainment centers, sitting areas, and deluxe bathrooms with marble and stainless steel sinks add to the sophisticated feel. A **free** shuttle service gets guests to and from the Strip.

Beach and Cabanas (all ages)

For my money, this is the coolest pool in town. With two acres of sandy beaches, ocean-like pools, underwater music, spectacular landscaping, and gorgeous private cabanas, who wouldn't want to hang out here? The thirty-five Tahitian-style cabanas that line the pool's edge and amble through its center offer cable TV, a telephone and refrigerator, and overflowing bowls of fresh fruit. Best of all, cooling mists of spray emanate from the cabana's ceilings throughout the day. While mom swims with the kids, dad can go work out in the nearby Rockspa, the Hard Rock's athletic club and wellness center. It sports top-of-the-line workout equipment. Then while dad supervises, mom can get in touch with her inner soul at the wellness center or get a longed-for pedicure. The center has everything from aromatherapy and salt scrubs to glycolic peels and reflexology pedicures, or just enjoy the Vichy showers, steam rooms, and Jacuzzi spas.

Watching the hordes of skimpily clad singles search for mates may be the biggest entertainment of all as they saunter between the swim-up gaming area and the poolside bar and grill.

World's Largest Neon Guitar (all ages)

Another Vegas world's largest: The largest neon guitar sign in the world (is there stiff competition among neon guitars?) can be seen beckoning from the Hard Rock Hotel and Casino. Lit nightly.

Rock Tour (all ages)

Not really a tour, but a massive collection of rock 'n' roll memorabilia. Stop at the front desk to ask for a tour map before hunting for the treasures displayed throughout the hotel. Look for the Women of Rock display, the Beatles collection, and clothes worn onstage by the Red Hot Chili Peppers.

The Joint (age appropriateness varies)
(702) 226–4650. Hours and prices vary.

Rolling Stone magazine calls the Joint "the rock and roll equivalent of the Grand Ole Opry." Not all acts would be appropriate to bring the kids to, but call to find out who's playing. During "all ages" nights, the price drops and the chairs disappear, but the bands live on.

Where to Eat

Mr. Lucky's 24/7. (702) 693–5592. Open twenty-four hours. This is one of the best cafes in town, with lots to choose from. The secret steal here is the steak and shrimp special that isn't on the menu. You have to ask for it. Shhh! Don't tell anyone. $–$$

The Pink Taco. (702) 693–5525. Daily 11:00 A.M.–10:00 P.M., Friday and Saturday noon until midnight. Kids will love the black beans served here, if you can get them to try them. Otherwise, well-prepared tacos, burritos, and more will satisfy everyone. $–$$

Las Vegas Hilton

3000 Paradise Road; (702) 697–8700 or (888) 462–6535; www.lvhilton.com. $$

As other resorts have turned away from families, the Hilton appears to be more inclusive. Its entertainment venues include shows that are often appropriate for the whole family and often priced so that families can afford to go. The tram connects the Hilton to the Strip, so you can avoid driving. Much of the hotel has also been recently renovated, so you don't have to sacrifice luxury to take advantage of this bargain.

Star Trek: The Experience (all ages)
North Tower of Las Vegas Hilton, 3000 Paradise Road; (702) 697–8700 or (888) 462–6535. Daily 11:00 A.M.–11:00 P.M. $$ for anyone 42 inches or taller.

You could spend a morning here, first checking out the space-age shops and exhibits—including a complete re-creation of the promenade from *Star Trek: Deep Space Nine*—shopping at Zek's Grand Emporium and Moogie's Trading Post, then going through The History of the Future, a self-guided museum tour. The museum includes props from original productions and a time line of space exploration up through Star Trek expeditions. Finally, beam aboard the bridge of the USS *Enterprise* in Voyage Through Space, a twenty-two-minute interactive ride that lets you battle Klingons on your way back to Earth. After all that, you will need a bite to eat at Quark's Bar & Restaurant, where you never know who—or what—you will be sitting next to. Star Trek fans will love the place; others may think the restaurant and the ride rather pricey for what you get.

Summer Pool Parties (all ages)
(702) 732–5755 or (800) 222–5361. Various dates throughout the summer, 6:00–10:00 P.M. $$ for adults, $ for children 12 and under.

This all-ages pool party features an unlimited buffet with burgers, hot dogs, chicken sandwiches, beer, soft drinks, and a roasted pig on a spit. As the evening wears on, it may become a little wild as sexy legs contests and limbo competitions heat up. If you go early and leave early, you should have a fun time.

Where to Stay

Alexis Park. 375 East Harmon Avenue; (800) 582–2228. Entering Alexis Park is like stepping back to a romantic '40s movie set. Stroll among lush landscaping and soothing fountains. Winding pathways lead you past the two-story white stucco buildings that house the 500 guest suites. There is no gaming here, so parents can breathe a sigh of relief. There also aren't a lot of entertainment options for kids other than the pools and the all-suites hotel room, but the quiet of this resort is a welcome contrast to the jangle of the megaresorts. Alexis Park offers three sparkling pools and a series of wandering paths for kids to explore. Despite the relative peace, however, you are right across the street from the Hard Rock and only a couple of blocks from the heart of the Strip itself. $$–$$$

Other Shows and Attractions

Senator Howard Cannon Aviation Museum (all ages)
McCarran Airport, open twenty-four hours. Free.

The most visited museum in the state, the main exhibition area of this tribute to aviation lies in the heart of McCarran Airport on the second floor above the north end of baggage claim. Artifacts, pictures, memorabilia, and more pay tribute to Howard Hughes, George Crockett, Howard Cannon, Pat McCarran, and others who have contributed to the history of aviation in southern Nevada.

Kids love the large items, like the Cessna 172 that set the world endurance record by staying aloft for 64 days and 22½ hours without touching ground. A 1956 Thunderbird that sits outside the museum was the car of choice to lead small planes back on the runway for Alamo Airways. Thirty-eight other exhibits include information on the impact of aviation on Las Vegas tourism, commercial aviation, and children and women in aviation.

The southeast corner of the museum includes a new store with books and airplane models related to the history of aviation. Plans are under way to construct a child-friendly exhibit in the airport's D section that looks like an airplane engine and will include lots of interactive buttons.

Dirk Arthur's "The New Art of Magic" (ages 5 and up)
Plaza Hotel and Casino, 1 Main Street; (702) 386–2110. Wednesday through Saturday 7:00 P.M. with a Sunday matinee at 3:00 and 7:00 P.M. $$.

If you don't want to spend big bucks, try Master Magician Dirk Arthur who performed for seven years with "Jubilee." His larger-than-life magic tricks feature exotic tigers, leopards, and a rare snow-white tiger; an "appearing helicopter" illusion; a levitating Lamborghini; and an escape trick called the "Giant Drill." He also performs traditional illusions and sleight-of-hand tricks. Like Siegfried and Roy, Arthur has also established his own captive breeding program.

Riding in Style

It isn't just celebrities who ride in limos. A variety of limousines is available for hourly rental around town. The average price for a town car is $40 per hour for up to four people, a basic limo runs about $55 per hour and holds up to six people, and a super stretch averages $80 per hour and holds up to ten people. Most services prefer forty-eight hours' notice. There's a two-hour minimum on Friday and Saturday after 4:00 P.M.

Many of the limousine companies also provide shuttle service from McCarran International Airport. Take a limo to your Strip hotel for an average of $4.00 per person ($7.50 per person round-trip). Just walk out door #4 and purchase your ticket at the booth, then catch a ride in style.

- Ambassador Limousine, 362–6200
- Bell Trans, 385–5466
- CLS Transportation, Las Vegas, 740–4545
- On Demand Sedan, 876–2222
- Presidential Limo, 731–5577

Red Rooster Antique Mall (all ages)
1109 Western Avenue; (702) 382–0067. Weekdays 10:00 A.M.–6:00 P.M.

This is our favorite place to find old books, linens, pictures, glassware, toys, and other odds and ends that people who love to find a bargain love to find. My kids love antiques shops for the same reason that grown-ups do: hidden treasures at a bargain. While antiques are not particularly cheap here, it is always a kind of cultural excursion to see what kind of stuff people treasured.

Going west on Charleston, pass I–15, turn left on Martin Luther King Boulevard, then make the first left on Wall Street that allows you back under the freeway. Make the first left again on Western Avenue, continue to the end of the street, and park at the big red barn. It is the only way I know to get there.

Las Vegas Sports Park (all ages)
1400 North Rampart; (702) 233–3600. Weekdays 9:00 A.M.–9:00 P.M. Hours vary with activity.

This facility offers a wide variety of classes and clubs including fencing, karate, ballet, lacrosse, and hockey. Drop-in activities include batting cages, ice-skating, and an arcade.

The **Big M**

McCarran International Airport is the twelfth busiest airport in the United States, with an average of 84,000 passengers daily. In 1997, thirty million passengers passed through the airport, including two million international travelers. While there, take the time to see the little touches that make this airport unique: the large panels of children's art tiling the walls on either side of the D concourse tram, the landscape scenes by internationally recognized local artist Robert Beckmann, and the **free** whimsical children's area where kids can fly over the observation deck. The **free** Howard Cannon Aviation Museum has interactive exhibits that will interest most kids. Additional exhibits are located in ticketing at the A and B gates, in Terminal 2, at the North Las Vegas Air Terminal, and in the general and corporate aviation terminal operated by Signature Flight Support.

If you still haven't gotten your plane fix, park in the area south of the airport on Sunset Road where **free** transceivers let you listen to the tower's communications with the aircraft landing and take-off crews. Tune your AM radio to 810.

Scandia Family Center (all ages)
2900 Sirius Avenue; (702) 364–0070. Daily 10:00 A.M.–10:00 P.M., until midnight Friday and Saturday. Pay per activity; $, ages 5 and under free with partner.

This fun center offers three eighteen-hole miniature golf courses, the Lil' Indy raceway, bumper boats, eighteen automated hardball and softball pitching machines, a snack bar, and an arcade. A group or all-day pass costs $17.50; a supersaver pass costs $12.95.

Chinatown Plaza (all ages)
4255 Spring Mountain Road; (702) 221–8448. Daily 10:00 A.M.–9:00 P.M.

Although small, this tiny treasure of a shopping center is a real cultural excursion. We love wandering through the Asian grocery store to see the exotic foods and the dried plums. Then we head to the incense and herb shop where we buy loose teas. Packed full of Asian wares, from furniture and clothing to pottery and fine hand-carved jade, this plaza has it all. Kids will love the hot dogs baked in pastry at the Diamond Bakery or dim sum, noodles, or a spicy hand-tossed concoction from any of the nine Asian eateries.

National Vitamin Company Factory Tour (all ages)
7440 South Industrial Road; (702) 269–9600. Monday through Saturday, 10:00 A.M.–4:00 P.M. "Dino" greets kids daily at 2:00 P.M. Free.

A twenty-minute tour takes you behind the scenes of this state-of-the-art vitamin and cosmetic factory, where visitors can view educational displays and then receive complimentary samples of vitamins or skin care products. The smoothie bar is a great way to end the tour before heading to the gift shop to purchase botanicals, hair and skin care products, vitamins, herbals, and lotions.

Elvis-A-Rama Museum (all ages)

3401 Industrial Road; (702) 309–7200. Daily 10:00 A.M.–8:00 P.M. $, ages 12 and under free.

This museum dedicated to Elvis contains more than $5 million worth of cars, gems, and other personal memorabilia, including a love letter written while he was in the Army and his only pair of blue suede shoes. A **free** Elvis tribute show is performed every hour on the hour.

Liberace Museum and Center for the Arts (all ages)

1775 East Tropicana Avenue; (702) 798–5595. Monday through Saturday 10:00 A.M.–5:00 P.M., Sunday noon–4:00 P.M. $, free for museum members and children 5 and under.

Liberace's estate, through his Foundation for the Performing Arts, has awarded talented students with millions of dollars in scholarships in music, dance, drama, film, and the visual arts. Liberace's museum is a must-see and a great pair with Elvis-a-Rama. Elvis must have taken some of his later flamboyance from this master of excess who owned the largest rhinestone in the world and a series of rhinestone-encrusted cars and pianos. Unfortunately, many people have forgotten that Liberace's glitzy costumes dimmed in

Pool. The other kind.

Knocking a ball around is always fun. Alexander is tall enough to play pool, but even older elementary school kids love to see their ball slide into the side pocket. For a couple of hours of air-conditioned fun, check out these pool palaces. All are open twenty-four/seven, but will enforce curfew.

Crystal Palace Billiards. 2411 East Bonanza; (702) 384–6734. $ per hour per person. For ages 11 and up. Multiple tables are available.

Las Vegas Cue Club. 953 East Sahara; (702) 735–2884. $ per hour. The club offers thirty-five tables, ½ quarter tables, video games, and a full kitchen.

Mickey's Cues and Brews. 7380 South Eastern; (702) 361–2060. $ per hour. While the only thing served here is wine, beer, and soda, Mickey's offers menus from other restaurants that you can order from and have delivered. Play at the regulation tables or bar tables, or try your hand at foosball, pinball, golf, or Pac Man while you eat.

comparison with his talent. As you wander through the museum looking at his outra-geously outré costumes, his music filters through the air and one has to fall in love again with a talent and a man who knew no bounds.

Local **RV** Parks

With the abundance of RVs on the freeways, it makes sense that local facili-ties are plentiful both in town and out. There are more than 200 licensed RV parks, state parks, and recreation areas throughout the state. More than twenty-five RV parks lie within and around Vegas itself. Just outside Nevada's borders, yet within an easy half day's drive from Las Vegas, lie natural won-ders like the Grand Canyon, Grand Staircase Escalante, Havasu Falls, Death Valley, Zion National Monument, and much, much more. Before you head off into the wild blue yonder, take a couple of days to relax Vegas-style. Here are our favorite in-town stops:

Destiny's Oasis. 2711 West Windmill Lane; (702) 260–2020; www.destinyrv .com. Rates vary seasonally. This is one of the most luxurious RV resorts you will find, with a restaurant, an adults-only pool, and a children's pool. Each grassy site has a private patio, picnic table, cable programming, security, and phone service. The pool area has waterfalls, white sand beaches, a lagoon, and poolside cabanas. Families can practice their golf strokes at the eighteen-hole putting course or relax at the clubhouse. Kids enjoy the video arcade, playground, tennis and volleyball courts, and horseshoe pits. A free daily shuttle service from 9:00 A.M. to 11:00 P.M. takes guests to Beltz Outlet Mall, Fashion Show Mall, and the Strip.

Sam's Town. 5225 Boulder Highway; (702) 454–8055 or (800) 634–6371. Rates vary seasonally. This resort features a midsize pool, showers, a dog run, and a laundry.

Silverton. 3333 Blue Diamond Road; (702) 263–7777 or (800) 588–7711. Rates vary seasonally. This RV park is located near the south end of the Strip and includes a charming little water park for children.

Circusland RV Park. 500 Circus Circus Drive; (702) 794–3757 or (800) 634–3450. Rates vary seasonally. Although there are 369 spaces, this Circus Circus RV park, which offers laundry, showers, a store, a fenced pet run, and a monorail to the main casino, fills up quickly. The park has its own pool; guests are allowed to use the casino pool as well.

Las Vegas Villa (all ages)

4982 Shirley Street; (702) 795–8119. Price varies (groups only).

Families in small groups can now tour the home of the late Liberace. For an additional fee you may enjoy either morning tea, lunch, or afternoon high tea (groups of twenty-five or more people). Tour guide is extra.

University of Nevada Las Vegas (UNLV) (all ages)

4505 South Maryland Parkway; (702) 895–ARTS; www.unlv.edu.

Las Vegas isn't exactly a college town, but UNLV does a surprisingly good job of upping the cultural ante. From showcasing internationally recognized local fine artists to importing exciting Broadway performers, the Performing Arts division is a real cultural boon. The Performing Arts center tries to bring in children's programming as well. Check out the Web site www.unlv.edu/Colleges/Fine_Arts/Theatre or call the box office at (702) 895–ARTS to see what family events are scheduled.

Ask to be put on the mailing list for the *Best of Broadway Series,* which has brought in stars like the late Gregory Hines, a regular on *Sesame Street;* Rockapella, the group that sings for the Carmen San Diego shows; and Disney's Belle from *Beauty and the Beast.*

The World Stage Series brings in performing arts groups from all over the world, with emphasis on cultural programming. Two groups in recent years were Ladysmith Black Mambazo, the Zulu group that inspired Paul Simon's *Graceland* album, and Fiesta Navidad, a joyous Mexican Christmas pageant.

The **Masters Series** brings in internationally acclaimed classical dance and music groups such as Yo-Yo Ma, now familiar to older kids for his haunting cello in *Crouching Tiger, Hidden Dragon;* the Bolshoi Ballet Ensemble; and the St. Paul Chamber Orchestra with Bobby McFerrin. Dress the kids up in real shoes and velvet and take advantage of these wonderful cultural opportunities.

Marjorie Barrick Museum of Natural History (all ages)

4505 South Maryland Parkway; (702) 895–3381. Monday through Friday 8:00 A.M.–4:45 P.M., Saturday 10:00 A.M.–2:00 P.M.; closed holidays. Free.

The UNLV Marjorie Barrick Museum, founded in 1969, is dedicated to collecting and preserving the natural and human history of the southwest United States and its surrounding regions. Museum staff scientists in the fields of ornithology, entomology, herpetology, and archaeology conduct essential research and documentation emphasizing the Mojave Desert. The Harry Reid Center for Environmental Studies (HRC), housed in the museum, includes divisions in biological studies, analytical chemistry, microbiology, sensor chemistry, DNA studies, and indoor pollutant studies.

The main exhibit hall not only holds the museum's permanent collection (check out the 9-foot-tall stuffed polar bear) but also features a 3,000-square-foot gallery that is host to international, national, and regional exhibitions. The museum features exhibits on Mojave Desert wildlife, Native American artistry, and early Las Vegas history, as well as Mexican dance masks, Guatemalan huipils, and pre-Columbian pottery. Artists and art groups recognize the exhibition space as one of the best in the state of Nevada.

Donna Beam Fine Art Gallery (UNLV) (all ages)

(702) 895–3893. Monday through Friday 9:00 A.M.–5:00 P.M., by appointment Saturday 9:00 A.M.–5:00 P.M., closed holidays. Free.

This has to be one of the most fun places in town to view art. From the wild to the contemporary to the mystic, the Donna Beam features an outstanding and diverse schedule of changing exhibitions throughout the year. Whether one-person shows, group shows, theme shows, or competitions, exhibitions feature work by regionally and nationally recognized contemporary artists as well as UNLV faculty and students. So you never know what you are going to get. The gallery also has been host to exhibitions organized by such groups as Crayola Crayon, Inc., American College Theater Festival, and the National Council on Education for the Ceramic Arts. The variety and verve of these exhibitions make it a perfect starting place to turn your little one into a fine-arts lover.

UNLV Arboretum (all ages)

4505 South Maryland Parkway; (702) 895–3392. Free.

Less formal than the Desert Demonstrations Garden, the entire UNLV campus is designated as an arboretum. However, the Xeric Garden, located near the Museum of Natural History, is the place most people refer to when they think of the UNLV Arboretum. The garden functions as an exhibit of the Museum of Natural History, with many species of drought-tolerant desert plants from the Mojave and from all over the world. The garden is most colorful from February through May when spring flowers bloom, although other plants bloom sporadically throughout the rest of the year. For a self-guided tour, pick up a brochure inside the museum gift shop. Plan to spend less than an hour touring the garden, then look for trees with labels throughout the campus. End up by the concert hall, where a cluster of weeping specimens in a grassy area provides cool shade in which to picnic and play. Guided tours are offered monthly.

UNLV Runnin Rebels (all ages)

Thomas & Mack Stadium, 4505 South Maryland Parkway; (702) 739–3267. $.

Live sports are always a blast, and we are loyal Rebels fans. Catch some top-notch basketball played by these college giants.

UNLV Lady Rebels (all ages)

Thomas & Mack Stadium, 4505 South Maryland Parkway; (702) 739–3267. $.

Women's basketball just might be the hottest sport going, with fans from all over the country rootin' and tootin' them on. Catch our local team in action.

Superheroes Galore

Comics are back with a vengeance. Become a kid again with your kid at any of these top shops.

Woody's World. 2704 Sunset Road; (702) 898–7717. Monday through Saturday 10:00 A.M.–7:00 P.M., Sunday 11:00 A.M.–6:00 P.M. Browse among the classic and new comics and trading cards, or just chat up the new Marvel Comic–based movies.

Silver Cactus Comics. 480 North Nellis Boulevard; (702) 438–4408. Monday through Saturday 11:00 A.M.–8:00 P.M., Sunday 11:00 A.M.–6:00 P.M. Classics from the gold and silver age of comics can be found here, as well as a variety of collectibles, action figures, and even cookie jars. The large collection of statues is the specialty, however, so make sure to check them out.

Cosmic Comics. 3330 East Tropicana; (702) 451–6611. Daily 11:00 A.M.–7:00 P.M., Sunday until 5:00 P.M. If you're looking for comic books, animated movies, cartoons, collectibles, action figures, or statues of your favorite comic character, come here. The selection is sure to please your kids.

Where to Eat

Big Mama's Soul Food Cooking. 2230 West Bonanza Road; (702) 597–1616. Daily 10:00 A.M.–10:00 P.M. Another Southern-style favorite; get your hush puppies here. $–$$

Bootlegger Ristorante. 7700 South Las Vegas Boulevard; (702) 736–4939. Open twenty-four hours. The new location hasn't changed the basic charm of this classic family-style restaurant. Although service is superb, the southern Italian-style food is the real draw. Don't miss the ravioli or the eggplant parmigiana. All meals are served with salad, soup, and garlic-soaked bread with marinara dipping sauce. Go between 4:00 and 6:00 P.M. for the early bird specials. Reservations are required on weekends, when the parking lot fills with expensive cars

and their romancing inhabitants. Although the atmosphere is warm and inviting, it is usually fairly quiet as well, so don't expect a loud family party to go unnoticed. $$

Cafe Heidelberg. 610 East Sahara Avenue; (702) 731–5310. Daily 11:00 A.M.–10:00 P.M. This was the first place we ate at when we visited Las Vegas to decide whether to move here. The festive German atmosphere has since proven itself to be unique. Most evenings have live entertainment, the German beer keeps coming, and the food is always substantial, with enough of a selection for everyone to find something to enjoy. $$

Fong's Garden. 2021 East Charleston Boulevard; (702) 382–1644. Daily 11:00 A.M.–11:00 P.M. Fong's opened in 1933 as the Silver Cafe and has been going strong ever since. You can't miss the giant neon pagoda outside. Pat Buddha's belly inside for good fortune. Then dig into the savory Philippine and Chinese cuisine. Or try the almond duck. A classic restaurant that serves classic dishes, just like in the good old days. $–$$

The Hush Puppy. 1820 North Nellis Boulevard; (702) 438–0005. Daily 5:00–10:00 P.M. This local legend features catfish and alligator. The food can be uneven at times, but if you're looking for a down-home experience from the bayous of southern Louisiana, this is the place to go. $–$$

India Oven Restaurant. 226 West Sahara (½ block west of the Strip); (702) 366–0222. Daily 11:00 A.M.–2:00 P.M. and 5:30–10:00 P.M. Tandoori chicken and fresh hot naan (bread) out of the oven could make up a meal for Seiji. The rest of us like to include some of the wonderful spicy vegetarian fare as well as the creamy *raita,* a cucumber and carrot yogurt dip that cools our mouths. $

La Scala. 1020 East Desert Inn Road; (702) 699–9980. Weekdays 11:30 A.M.–2:30 P.M. and 5:00–10:00 P.M., weekends 5:00–10:00 P.M. Expect a great dining experience, complete with fresh homemade breads and pastas and the freshest hand-picked ingredients. $$

Memphis Championship Barbecue. 4379 North Las Vegas Boulevard; (702) 644–0000. Monday through Saturday 11:00 A.M.–10:00 P.M., Sunday noon–9:00 P.M. A second restaurant is located at 2250 East Warm Springs; (702) 260–6909. Sunday through Thursday 11:00 A.M.–10:00 P.M., Friday and Saturday until 10:30 P.M. I guess when you eat smoked food, it just feels as if you are sitting around an open fire digging in with your cave buddies. Whatever the primal appeal, smoke and barbecue are favorites in our house. Try the deep-fried pickles (Seiji's favorite food) as an alternative to overeating

the cornbread and baked beans. Mama Faye's Down Home Super Dinner serves the five of us easily, with take-home portions, while we all get to pick and choose our favorite combinations of foods. $–$$

P. F. Chang's. 4165 South Paradise Road (Flamingo and Paradise), (702) 792–2207; 1095 Rampart Boulevard (Charleston and Rampart), (702) 968–8885; 3667 Las Vegas Boulevard (Aladdin Resort), (702) 836–0955; www.pfchang.com. Daily 11:00 A.M.–11:00 P.M., Friday and Saturday until midnight. The wide variety of Asian pastas, rice dishes, and vegetarian fare draws families and trendsetters alike. Kids love the Peking dumplings and Harvest Spring Rolls. Adults adore the messy but luscious lettuce wraps. $

Pho Vietnam Restaurant. Chinatown Plaza, 4215 West Spring Mountain Road, Suite B-201. Daily 10:00 A.M.–10:00 P.M. Exotic dishes may be too exotic for most kids, but no one will turn down the fried egg rolls served with lettuce. Chloe and Alexander sneak each other's iced French coffee with condensed milk. Other exotic drinks we mean to try include fresh young coconut milk; the pickle lemonade; and Che Ba Mau, mung bean and red bean with gelatin in light syrup. We feel so culturally rich here. $

Speedway Café or Ricky's Bar & Grill. 3227 Civic Center Drive; (702) 399–3297. Open twenty-four hours. Take your pit stop at this race-themed restaurant near the Speedway adjacent to the Speedway Casino and Ramada Inn. Check out the two restored gas pumps, the mural of a surfing "woody," and the mag wheels as backrests. The cafe features breakfast, lunch, and dinner items like pork chops, meat loaf, sandwiches, pastas, prime rib, fresh fish, and omelettes. $

Togoshi Ramen. 855 East Twain Avenue; (702) 737–7003. Daily 11:30 A.M.–9:30 P.M. Ramen has become a staple in our house, and when we go out for noodles, this is one of our favorites. I don't know whether it is the tasty food or the added attraction—Japanese comics and magazines—that make this a kid's haven. $–$$

Tokyo. 953 East Sahara Avenue; (702) 735–7070. Dinner only. Get a taste of Japanese cooking at two large hibachi tables, a fourteen-seat tatami room, or the sushi bar. With dozens of adventurous and not-so-adventurous entrees, there should be something for everyone here. The tabletop hibachi cooks beef, chicken, seafood, and vegetables on skewers. Dinners come with miso soup, pickles, rice, dessert, and green tea. $$

Where to Stay

Artisan Hotel. 1501 West Sahara Avenue; (702) 214–4000 or (800) 554–4092; www .artisanhotel.com. This small art-themed hotel is a quiet getaway without being too far from the action. $–$$

Carriage House Deluxe Suites. 9105 East Harmon Avenue; (702) 798–1020 or (800) 221–2301; www.carriagehouselasvegas.com. This small suite hotel has a pool, tennis courts, and a top-notch restaurant that features a fabulous view. Across the street from the back entrance to the Desert Passage, families can still enjoy being in the heart of things without being overwhelmed by crowds. $–$$

Beyond the Neon

Like many big cities, sometimes it is hard to tell where Las Vegas begins and where it ends. The Strip is actually not in Las Vegas at all; it is part of Clark County. Henderson and North Las Vegas are separate townships within Clark County, but the physical boundaries that distinguish one township from the next have long since blurred. The Clark County School District, which includes the public schools of Summerlin, Las Vegas, North Las Vegas, and Henderson, also includes small towns as far away as Laughlin, Boulder City, and beyond. In addition, large swatches of Bureau of Land Management land also lie within Clark County, snaking throughout the area to provide our own kind of open space.

What everyone *can* see is that all these areas are merging visually. The explosion in new casino growth has led to a concurrent explosion in home building, making this the fastest-growing area in the country. With nearly 8,000 new residents setting up house here each month, the greater Las Vegas metropolitan region jumped to more than 1.3 million residents by the beginning of the new millennium. People who project those things expect the area to support two million residents by 2005.

In addition, Las Vegas attracts about thirty-four million visitors annually. Tourism generates more than $29 billion in local revenue, $22.5 billion of which is spent on nongaming goods and services. Those are the numbers that fuel the claim that Las Vegas is the number one tourist destination in the world, generating more tourist dollars than New York City and San Francisco combined. And the city is still on a roll, annually increasing the number of tourists it attracts by more than 10 percent, with an increasing number of those visitors bringing their children.

That still may not make Las Vegas a kids' town, but clearly, family-friendly entertainment, attractions, and services are expanding and doing well here, as are cultural activities appropriate for the whole family. As residents support local arts and artists, the rich infrastructure enjoyed by older cities will also become more available here, but always with the Vegas touch. Take a day to saunter out beyond the bright lights of the Strip. You may be surprised what you will discover.

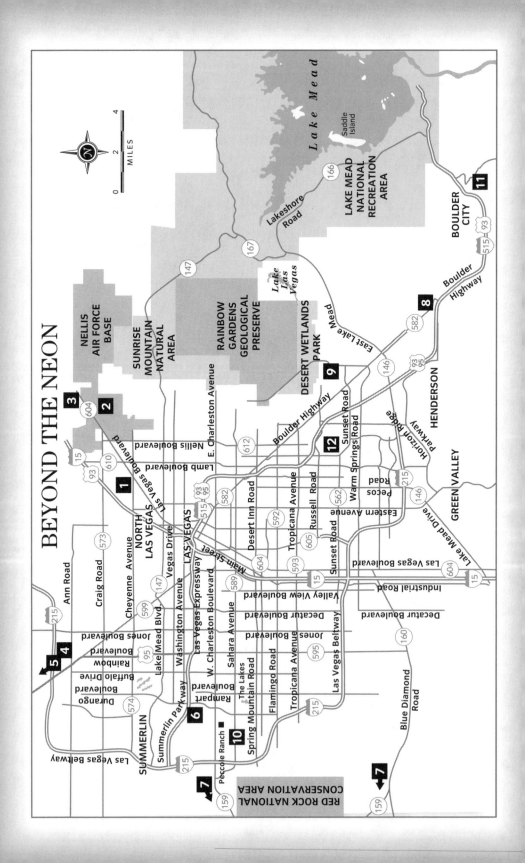

BEYOND THE NEON

Map Destinations

1. Planetarium—3200 East Cheyenne Avenue (SE Entrance of Community College of Southern Nevada)

2. U.S. Air Force Base Thunderbirds Tour—Nellis Air Force Base, Craig and Las Vegas Boulevard North

3. Las Vegas Motor Speedway—7000 Las Vegas Boulevard North

4. Gilcrease Orchard—7800 North Tenaya

5. Floyd Lamb State Park—U.S. 93/95 west from Las Vegas to Tule Springs Road

6. The J. W. Marriott Las Vegas—221 North Rampart Boulevard

7. Spring Mountain Ranch State Park—State Route 159 between Blue Diamond and Red Rock Canyon

8. Clark County Museum—1830 South Boulder Highway

9. Henderson Bird Preserve—2400 Moser

10. Las Vegas Art Museum—West Sahara Library, 9600 West Sahara Avenue

11. Elephants are Forever—Boulder Dam Hotel

12. Ethel M. Chocolate Factory—2 Cactus Garden Drive

Henderson/Green Valley

Henderson has the distinction of being the fastest-growing city in the country, so much so that visitors flying into Vegas will have a hard time distinguishing it as a separate city at all. With all of its growth, however, it just may be the most family-friendly area in the entire Las Vegas valley. In fact, it has garnered national awards that honor it as one of the most family-friendly cities in the nation.

The extensive trail system within Green Valley, the public artwork scattered around town—often depicting children in a Norman Rockwell–type situation—and the impressive array of public recreational opportunities have won the Henderson Parks and Recreation Department the honor of being named the top agency of its kind in the nation. It is also one of the safest places to live and one of the top places to start a home-based business (a mom thing, I suspect).

For a small town, Henderson has made a big commitment to the families within the area. City officials cajoled and coerced developers into interlacing Green Valley with leafy trail systems, parks, and outdoor rest areas. Old Henderson is being regenerated with public funds to revitalize the downtown and to bring in additional public facilities and

The Goyas'
TopPicks for fun beyond the neon

1. Writing like an astronaut with a pen from Fisher Space Pens in Boulder City

2. Drinking an iced coffee while the kids play in the water feature at Green Valley Center

3. Eating a chocolate at Ethel M. Chocolate Factory

4. Seeing the sunrise while birding at the Clark County Wetlands Preserve

5. Picking ripe apricots at Gilcrease Orchard

6. Hiking to a petroglyph in Red Rock Canyon

7. Listening to a concert under the stars at Spring Mountain State Park

8. Riding horses at Floyd Lamb State Park

9. Practicing disc golf at Peccole Ranch Trails

10. Putting on white gloves and a hat and having an elegant all-girl's lunch at Ceres J. W. Marriott Las Vegas

green spaces. Henderson Parks and Recreation is the local leader for innovative athletic, cultural, arts, and human services programs, as well as the state-of-the-art public facilities that include water-play areas and luscious public pools. Green Valley competes with Summerlin for upscale residential development. In this "master planned community" set against the backdrop of Black Mountain, Henderson city fathers and mothers have made sure that outdoor space is within reach of every child.

Sky's the Limit Climbing Center (40 pounds and up) ⬤
3065 East Patrick Lane, Suite 4; (702) 363–4533; www.skysthelimit.com. Monday through Friday 9:00 A.M.–9:00 P.M., Saturday 10:00 A.M.–8:00 P.M., Sunday 10:00 A.M.–6:00 P.M. $, equipment rental extra.

Rock climbing seems like one of the more extreme sports, but our family has been climbing indoors for a few years now (Seiji started when he was three). I must confess that it sure is fun. It is also a great workout for the arms, legs, gluteus maximus, and more. The best climbers use their brains as well as their brawn, and because all climbers climb in pairs, it also builds family connections. Getting back down safely is just as important as scaling that wall; with Sky's the Limit, we always feel safe. This center features 6,400 square feet of fully contoured structures with walls 30 feet high and expert climbing instruction.

Ethel M. Chocolate Factory (all ages)

2 Cactus Garden Drive; (702) 458–8864. Daily 8:30 A.M.–7:00 P.M. Free.

This is the kind of place where one would expect to find Lucy and Ethel, either behind the scenes or trying to sneak another free chocolate. They say Mr. Mars, of Mars candy bar fame, still lives above the factory, but Ethel M. is his high-end confection, with truffles and liquor candies a house specialty. Self-guided tours end with a **free** chocolate sample and the chance to fill a personal Valentine's heart with your own sweet treats. Make mine raspberry cream. Take the conservation tour to see how the factory reprocesses its water. It shows how unusable water can become clean enough for fish to live in, and it makes one happy to see a corporation that cares about the community.

Ron Lee's World of Clowns (all ages)

330 Carousel Parkway; (702) 434–1700; Monday through Friday 8:30 A.M.–4:30 P.M. Free.

The hand-carved carousel is the draw for many, but inside the museum clown memorabilia, statues, figurines, cartoons, and a small restaurant fill out the excursion. Small viewing windows let kids see how those expensive little character statues are created. My kids loved the stacks of Warner Brothers cartoon figures that were halfway completed. Interesting for adults, as well, to witness the process that takes you from the mould to seeing the final brushwork applied. The collection of clown costumes from some of the most famous circuses is also a treat.

Coffee and a Dip (all ages)

Green Valley Town Center (Sunset Road and Green Valley Parkway). Free.

Grab a cup of coffee and park your seat next to the local fountains. If you haven't seen one of these fountains before, they are a blast! Literally. Water shoots out of hundreds of little holes in the ground, varying the rhythm, height, and combination of jets into a percussive water dance that kids can't resist. Kids should wear water-friendly clothes that can dry in the sun. Water shoes keep little ones from slipping. This is not a place to come if you want your kids to stay dry.

Liberty Pointe Park (all ages)

Green Valley Parkway and Paseo Verde Parkway (south of I–215).

Forty acres of grass, recreation, culture, and community come together at this multifaceted center.

Henderson Pavilion

Liberty Pointe, 200 South Green Valley Parkway; (702) 384–TICS (8427). Prices vary with venue.

This state-of-the-art performing arts venue supports a world-

class stage that can host anything from a solo artist to a full-scale Broadway production. With 2,500 seats and an overflow lawn that can seat another 5,000, this new venue should be a boon to the whole valley.

The open-air Promenade in front of the Pavilion has already hosted numerous arts programs including the Vegas Valley Book Festival.

Multigenerational Center and Aquatic Complex
Liberty Pointe, 250 South Green Valley Parkway; (702) 492–4622. Seasonal hours.

With 84,000 square feet to play with, it isn't surprising that this community center offers something for everyone. It includes a 12,000-square-foot gym, an elevated jogging track, a fitness room, a climbing wall, a game room, dance and aerobics rooms, an adult lounge, a computer lab, a demonstration kitchen, an arts and crafts room, and a set of pools that include everything from a 50-meter lap pool to a zero-depth splash pool with water slides and other play features.

Paseo Verde Public Library
Liberty Pointe, 280 South Green Valley Parkway; (702) 492–7252. Daily 9:00 A.M.–9:00 P.M., until 5:00 P.M. on Saturday, Sunday noon–4:00 P.M.

One of the newest libraries in the valley, this 42,000-square-foot facility includes a children's library, round adult area, reading room, and the Heritage Genealogical Research Center.

Clark County Archery Range (ages 4 and up)
6800 East Russell Road. Open during daylight hours. Free.

Robin Hood never had it this good. With an outdoor range, practice range, and yardage from 10 to 100 yards, there is something for archers of all ages and abilities.

Pacific Archery Sales (ages 6 and up)
4084 Schiff Drive; (702) 367–1505. During summer open to families, hours vary seasonally. $ entry fee for unlimited time; equipment rental, $.

This archery range has an indoor range of 20 yards. There are various programs and free-shooting times. Kids (ages five to eighteen) may train for the junior Olympic program. The center also works with the Boy Scouts and supervises the Clark County Archery Range.

Dog Fancier's Park (all breeds) 🐾
5800 East Flamingo Road (adjacent to Horseman's Park). Free.

A special park just for dogs and their pet owners, this is a great place to get out and run the kids. With numerous canine trials, training, and club meetings for dog lovers, it is also a place to come watch man's best friend strut his stuff. For upcoming events, clubs, and training opportunities, many of which are **free**, call the Dog Fancier's Hotline at (702) 564–3647. The fenced, open area allows for training your favorite pup off leash (as long as you have control of your animal).

Horseman's Park (all ages)

5800 East Flamingo Road; (702) 455–8281. Free.

This equestrian park provides 320 stalls and pens, two lighted arenas, and a cutting area for day use on thirty-eight acres of parkland. The park hosts jumping, rodeo, and other equestrian events. Call for a schedule or just show up and see what is happening.

Athletic Arts Academy (ages 3 and up)

6150 Annie Oakley Drive; (702) 450–2787. Call for open skating times, usually noon–3:00 P.M. on weekdays, Saturday 1:00–7:00 P.M., Sunday noon–5:00 P.M. Open skating $.

Built by the designer of theatrical flying apparatus (think Peter Pan and Wendy), this facility teaches children to ice-skate, but there's a whole lot more, including weeklong summer camps. Included in the 14,000-square-foot facility are a theater dance room, a climbing wall, and a 60-by-120-foot ice rink. The large warming room has card tables and places to sit and chat while watching the kids skate. Specializing in instructing kids ages three to six, instructors skate with the children to help with tricky moves. Skate rental available for a nominal fee. Children who are taking classes are considered "members" and are offered special free monthly membership appreciation classes, including hip-hop, children's theater, rock climbing, Irish dancing, and more. Free family skates are offered on Wednesday nights from 7:00 to 8:00 P.M. for members active in the ice-skating classes. On Friday nights, all families can attend the D.J. skating party from 6:00 to 9:00 P.M.

Empire of Chivalry and Steel (all ages)

2601 East Sunset Road; (702) 455–8200. Sunset Park; (702) 877–9254. Wednesday 7:00 P.M. Free.

Anyone interested in Middle Ages arts and crafts, historical research, and swordplay (hmm. . . . I wonder which one of my boys would be interested in that) can get together to practice fighting (swords not provided) and relive a little history.

Alexander's Favorite **Henderson Parks**

My eldest son likes to *do* stuff, and Henderson parks offer a lot of choices in outdoor activities. Henderson does do a great job, with its programs and with the park facilities themselves. Here is a list of my son's favorite Henderson parks. For more information, call (702) 565–2063 or log on to www.cityof henderson.com/parks.

O'Callaghan Park. 601 Skyline Road. O'Callaghan Park area includes thirty acres of expansive green that just makes kids want to run and play. In addition, there are softball and baseball fields, a basketball court with six backboards, two handball courts, two horseshoe pits, two Frisbee golf target baskets, four lighted tennis courts, two playground areas, two covered picnic

(continued on following page)

tables, and barbecue grills. The park also includes a half-mile fitness and jogging course and a restroom. Of course, we have to play Three Billy Goats Gruff under the bridge—great fun. We also love the old playground equipment, a relief from the ubiquitous play gym at every other park in the city. We hope they never "upgrade."

Mission Hills Park. 551 East Mission Drive. This twenty-five-acre park consists of two lighted baseball fields, three lighted tennis courts, two lighted basketball courts, a lighted trail system, tot-lot play amenities, custom slides on a hill, a picnic complex, a lighted arts and crafts plaza with central shade sculpture, restrooms, and a huge in-ground water play area with cushy, non-slippery flooring. Extensive cement walkways are perfect for learning or perfecting tricycling, biking, skateboarding, or in-line skating techniques.

More is planned for the park; future phases could include a group ramada complex, two lighted volleyball courts, and four horseshoe courts.

Arroyo Grand Sports Complex. 298 Arroyo Grande. This sixty-acre park is designed for league sports and lots of viewers, not all of whom will pay attention to the game. A large play structure has slides built into the hills, expansive cement walkways for any kind of rolling apparatus, and picnic facilities large enough for a family, a neighborhood, or a company party.

Hayley Hendricks Park. 811 Ithaca Avenue. With ten acres, this park includes a water play area similar to the one at Mission Hills but smaller, a playground, sand volleyball courts, a skateboard park, a soccer field, barbecues, picnic tables, a covered picnic shelter, horseshoe courts, a walking course, and restrooms.

Civic Center Plaza. 200 Water Street. Not exactly a park, this is a great place to bring the kids for quiet time: reading, drawing, watching the water sparkle in the sun. This open-air plaza has bench seating, water fountains, and beautiful views.

Vivaldi Park. 1249 Seven Hills Drive. This ten-acre park has a covered picnic shelter, a basketball court, tennis courts, and sand volleyball courts. We like the bike trails that lead to other parks.

Table Tennis Tournaments (ages 8 and up)

Silver Springs Recreation Center, 1951 Silver Springs Parkway; (702) 566–2710. Third Sunday of the month, 2:00–4:00 P.M.

Bring your buddy to compete in these low-key, high-fun, fast-paced games.

Borders Books (all ages)

1445 West Sunset Road; (702) 433–6222. Monday through Friday 9:00 A.M.–10:00 P.M., Saturday until 11:00 P.M., Sunday 9:00 A.M.–9:00 P.M.

Borders is our favorite new-book store, not just for the great selection of books and the large selection of books on tape, classic radio shows, and an impressive children's area, but for the other offerings as well. For one thing, the lunchtime wraps are a family favorite—one of the best lunch values around. We also love the array of **free** community events, everything from music (Irish, blues, jazz, Native American flute, bluegrass) that is appropriate for the entire family to the poetry discussions and bedtime stories. I read once that bookstores are becoming the new community centers, and for us, at least, there is a lot of truth in that assessment.

Young Chautauqua (ages 8 to 17)

(702) 564–4128; www.hdpl.org/chaut2000.html. Thursday 6:30–8:00 P.M., June through August. **Free.**

For ten weeks during the summer, kids can become a part of history. During this program, kids research a favorite character, create costumes, write a twenty-minute monologue, and practice performing. Although the program is free, each child is required to provide a

East Side **Recreation** Centers

Rec centers offer families a great way to spend time together shooting baskets, playing pool, lifting weights, or taking classes together. These are our favorites.

- **Black Mountain Recreation Center.** 599 Greenway Road (Horizon Drive and Greenway Road); (702) 565–2367. **Free.**
- **Valley View Recreation Center.** 500 Harris Street; (702) 565–2367. **Free.**
- **Whitney Ranch Recreation Center.** 1575 Galleria Drive; (702) 450–5885. **Free.**
- **Clark County Parks and Recreation.** 2601 East Sunset Road; (702) 455–8200. **Free.**

notebook and appropriate costume (expenses average $40 to $50 per character). Other family members can help with the costumes, listen to the monologues, and provide additional support. The kids take turns performing within the Las Vegas area. Previously they have been invited to the Boulder City Chautauqua, Las Vegas Chautauqua, assisted living homes, and other special events within the area. Call for further information.

Henderson Bird Preserve (all ages)

2400 Moser Drive; (702) 566–2940. Daily 6:00 A.M.–3:00 P.M. (gates are locked at 3:00 P.M.).
Free.

Since 1998, bird lovers and other naturalists have been trekking to this 147-acre preserve to cool down and relax amid nine settling ponds, lagoons, basins, and luxuriant foliage. The Henderson Bird Preserve is a collaborative effort among the city, the Audubon Society, and the wastewater treatment facility. They hope the preserve will increase the haven for nearly 200 species of migrating and native birds that alight here, from bald eagles to hummingbirds.

The increasingly lush oasis is a welcome resting place. Families can walk the trails themselves or arrange for a **free** guided tour with resident experts who have access to a wide variety of resource material that can help kids understand this habitat. Tours must be set up at least two weeks prior to the tour date. The best tour size is ten people or fewer, especially if small children are involved, so that everyone will get a chance to see birds in action.

The trails and picnic areas are for foot traffic only. Although strollers and wheelchairs are permitted, no other "vehicle" is, including bicycles, skateboards, in-line skates, or anything else that rolls. Friends are welcome, but not pets.

Clark County Wetlands Park (all ages)

Temporary Information Center, 6800 East Russell Road; Permanent Information Center,
7050 East Tropicana Avenue; (702) 455–7503. Daily 10:00 A.M.–4:00 P.M. Free.

Thirty years ago the Las Vegas wash supported more than 2,000 acres of wetlands; by the new millennium there were fewer than 400 acres left. Ironically, the increased population in Las Vegas has disturbed the natural balance of this desert wash by increasing the amount of water that flows through the wash, resulting in erosion and up to 1,000 tons of sediment being deposited into the Las Vegas Bay each day. This critical habitat is home to plants, animals, and migratory birds that count on open water and patches of lush vegetation to survive. Efforts are underway to stabilize the wash and revitalize and expand the existing wetlands. Still in the process, the master plan calls for a variety of trails throughout the nearly 2,700 acres of the park, including horse trails, walking trails, and biking trails.

The **Nature Preserve** includes 5 miles of trails that are now in place, and will eventually become part of the **River Mountain Loop Trail,** which will be more than 60 miles long. With multiple trailheads, the River Mountain Trail loops around much of the eastern portion of the valley, including Lake Mead. The Nature Preserve will house a visitor center, a small amphitheater, footpaths, and more than 2,000 trees and shrubs, and will provide educational opportunities for the community. Paved trails are for hiking only and are wheelchair accessible. Construction began in July 2000 and is scheduled to be completed in 2015.

If your family is interested in volunteering, ask about Friends of the Desert Wetlands Park.

Duck Creek Trail and Coyote Loop Trail
(all ages) 🚶 🚴

Take Tropicana Avenue to the east end, turn right on Broadbent Boulevard. Coyote Loop begins about 100 yards into the Duck Creek Trail.

These two popular trails are some of the first completed at the Wetlands Park. Open daily, both trails start from the Duck Creek Trailhead. Check in with the visitor center to get a map of new and existing trails. Duck Creek is a ¾-mile dirt trail for hikers and bikers, with a shade shelter along the trail overlooking the wetlands.

Las Vegas Fencing Club (ages 5 and up)

Southern Nevada Fencing Center, 100 South Maryland Parkway, second floor; (702) 366–7005 or 242–0765; www.lasvegasfencing.com. Weekdays 5:30–9:00 P.M., Saturday 9:00 A.M.–2:00 P.M. Times may vary during tournament weekends. Free introductory lesson.

I took fencing in college and found it absolutely fun, as well as an excellent workout. If you have boys, it would be difficult to find a sport that they would consider more exotic and enjoyable than swordplay. The great thing about fencing is that size and weight aren't as important as in other sports, so kids can quickly give their parents a real contest, and girls are not at a disadvantage. If your family enjoys swashbuckling movies, then try fencing. (Just don't allow them to swing from the chandeliers.) The annual Duel in the Desert competition usually takes place in January and can inspire would-be fencers. The Las Vegas Fencing Club is a member of the United States Fencing Association.

Fencing Junior Olympics Training Program (ages 5 and up) 🤺

American Foundation for Ballet and Fencing, 2949 East Desert Inn; (702) 866–2323 or 866–2325.

A fencing professional for more than forty years, Maître Mel North has worked with some of the greatest fencers of the world, first as a student, then as a teacher and innovator. The former head coach for fencing at UCLA, his coaching has led to fencing championships for his teams and for individuals. The foundation now claims to have the largest junior Olympic program in the state. Adults are finding fencing increasingly attractive as well. Train together at this facility.

Chloe's Favorite Bookstores

We love going to Borders or Barnes and Noble with their chichi coffee shops, stacks of best-sellers, and huge banks of periodicals. However, when you enter a used-book store, it is somehow more adventurous, almost as if one were Indiana Jones searching for a lost treasure. You just never know what you will find, a first edition of *John Carter of Mars*, a Japanese picture book, a two-inch hardcover set of Beatrix Potter, or an unknown author in a gilded binding. My kids love going to used bookstores to just see what is out there. The best part, however, may be talking with the shopkeepers, usually bibliophiles who love to discuss books, illustrators, and favorite authors.

Book Magician. 2202 West Charleston #2; (702) 384–5838. Daily 9:00 A.M.–7:00 P.M., Sunday noon–5:00 P.M. This isn't your typical used-book store. Instead, books are treated as prized artifacts, displayed in the style to which they should be accustomed. First editions, collectibles, signed editions, and works by individual authors the owner has met along the way (Irving Stone, Ray Bradbury, Gail Heath) are lovingly laid out. Stop by for a chat or to get help finding your favorite book.

Dead Poet Books. 3874 West Sahara; (702) 227–4070. Daily 10:00 A.M.–6:00 P.M., closed Sunday. Ask the helpful staff about your can't-live-without-it first edition and they'll search for it for free. Most likely, it is the enthusiasm of the staff that makes this place such a hit with locals, or the extensive children's section, or the military section, or the art section . . . need we go on?

Plaza Books. 7380 South Eastern Avenue; (702) 263–2692. Monday through Friday 10:00 A.M.–6:00 P.M., Saturday and Sunday noon–6:00 P.M. We've been going to this bookstore for years to exchange books and look for new treasures. This is a great place to shop for paperbacks; there's an extensive selection of science fiction, romance, and all of those other trashy novels into which we love to escape. Tell them whom you've read and you will get a free recommendation of other authors you may enjoy. We've found our first editions of *John Carter* here, along with newer copies of Jane Austen, Willa Cather, Agatha Christie, and more.

Clark County Museum (all ages)

1830 South Boulder Highway; (702) 455–7955; www.co.clark.nv.us. Daily 9:00 A.M.–4:30 P.M.; closed Thanksgiving and Christmas. $, under 3 free.

Kids get a real dose of the past at this meandering museum that features historic homes, railroads, and a time line from 12,000 years ago to the present. The railroad exhibits have been steadily increasing, although not all are available for public inspection. The museum now owns an engine, a passenger car, an express car, and a caboose; the caboose is open to the public. The Boulder City Train Depot has also been acquired recently and houses railroad memorabilia. Look for the peacocks that hide in the brush nearby.

The Heritage Street area is a unique collection of various buildings, mostly homes, from the 1900s to the 1950s, complete with appropriate furnishings. The outdoor mining exhibits, ghost town, and nature trail provide plenty of opportunities for kids to let off a little steam.

Inside, our kids' favorite stop is the old-fashioned scale where pocket change provides your weight and fortune. Changing exhibits expand upon local historical themes, from frontier photographs to traveling exhibitions from the Smithsonian. Annual events, like the Native American Festival, further explore our relationship with the past.

D & R Balloons (all ages)

(702) 248–7609. Sunrise and sunset rides. One-hour flight $$$$$ per person; half-hour flight $$$$, with a two-person minimum.

Private rides, groups, and children are invited to float over the city. With D & R's thirty years of experience, hotel pickup and return, and FAA inspection, the only thing on your mind should be the glittering lights of the Strip. D & R flies some of the newest equipment in the valley. Ask about coupons.

Las Vegas Soaring Center (ages 4 and up)

23500 Las Vegas Boulevard South; (702) 874–1010. Daily 9:00 A.M.–dusk. $$ and up.

Have you ever wanted to ride in a high-performance sailplane or the open cockpit of a biplane? Take one- and two-passenger rides with this company. When conditions are good, it may extend the flight.

Air Vegas Airlines (all ages)

500 Highway 146, Sky Harbor Airport; (702) 736–3599 or (800) 255–7474. $$$$$.

This company conducts air tours to the Grand Canyon, Bryce Canyon, Monument Valley, Zion National Park, Glen Canyon Dam, and Lake Powell. Tours vary from three hours to overnight and include lunch and hotel pickup and return.

Lake Las Vegas (all ages)

1600 Lake Las Vegas Parkway; (702) 564–1600 or (800) 564–1603; www.lakelasvegas.com.

This private 320-acre lake on the edge of Lake Mead National Recreation area seemed to be a massive undertaking, but I have to admit that they pulled it off. The most beautiful planned community in the area is surrounded by the best of southern Nevada landscapes. Striking mountains and a clear blue lake complemented by a crystalline sky create a stunning environment for acres of green golf courses and old-world Mediterranean-style architecture. That Celine Dion chose to build her home here just cements the notion that the area will take off as a celebrity retreat and a luxury home market. The rest of us can visit.

Guests and residents can stargaze with a local astronomer, rent mountain bikes for guided or nonguided tours, learn to sail at the Yacht Club, or learn archery or rock climbing. Book through the local hotels' concierge desks or ask for a local trails map.

The new MonteLago Village is designed to resemble a fabled European waterfront village with a beautifully designed shopping area, winding cobblestone streets, numerous water features, and charming cafes and shops. The Ponte Vecchio–style bridge spans the waterway with classic arches and bridge-top shops.

Gondola Adventures, Inc.
220 Grand Mediterra; (877) 4–GONDOLA; www.gondola.com. $$$$$.

Ride a silent-motored gondola at sunset for one of the most original views of Las Vegas. Various cruises include iced champagne or cider, dinner, or a basket lunch. Prices quoted are for two, with an additional "couple" (of kids) for $20 for the one-hour champagne ride. Prices go up from there.

Where to Eat

Baja Fresh Mexican Grill. Sunset Galleria, 675 Mall Ring Circle; (702) 450–6551; www.bajafresh.com. Daily 11:00 A.M.–9:00 P.M. "No microwaves, no can openers, no freezers, no lard, no msg," it claims. I have to admit that one son doesn't like the food. However, the rest of us think the marinated, charbroiled meats, the fresh vegetables, the homemade guacamole, and the handmade tortillas are absolutely wonderful. The kid-size meals are a great deal. Fresh salsas and herbs are there for the taking, and the drinks include refills. What a deal! $

Bull Shrimp. Green Valley Ranch, 2300 Paseo Verde, I–215 and Green Valley Park-

way; (702) 942–4110. Weekdays 11:30 A.M.–2:00 P.M., daily 5:00–10:00 P.M., until 11:00 P.M. Friday and Saturday. Fabulous chopped avocado salad, tender grilled lobster, and melt-in-your-mouth steak are presented at Chef Gustav Mauler's signature restaurant. For the adventurous, try the ahi tuna. Everyone loves the coconut shrimp. Seiji couldn't stop eating the irresistible fresh bread. For the truly indulgent, the lobster is the best I've ever had. Don't be surprised to be sitting next to local or visiting celebrities such as Tony Curtis or Brad Pitt. $$–$$$

Carrabba's Italian Grill. 10160 South Eastern Avenue; (702) 990–0650. Dinner only. Monday through Thursday 4:00–10:00 P.M., Friday and Saturday until 11:00 P.M. Sit at the pasta bar to watch the chefs toss pasta, pizza, and more. The fresh bread that you can dip in an herbed olive oil is the kind of hands-on eating our kids adore. My daughter asks for the spaghetti al dente, and we all share the Dessert Rosa, a butter cake with fruit and real whipped cream, or the Chocolate Dream, a fudge brownie drenched in chocolate mousse. $$

Chevy's Fresh Mex. Galleria Mall; (702) 434–8323. Monday through Thursday 11:00 A.M.–10:00 P.M., Friday and Saturday until 11:00 P.M., Sunday 11:00 A.M.–9:30 P.M. Kids love the ball of tortilla dough they get to play with. The large kids' menu and the ice cream for dessert are also hits. $–$$

Chicago Tasty Dog. Silverado Ranch Plaza, 9711 South Eastern Avenue; (702) 914–3451. Sunday and Monday noon–6:00 P.M., Tuesday through Saturday 11:00 A.M.–8:00 P.M. We looked all over town for great cheese fries and finally found them here. Sit out in the spring sun to eat richly authentic Italian beef and sausage sandwiches, pizza puffs, whole deli pickles, breaded mushrooms, and Vienna Beef hot dogs. $

Chuck E. Cheese. 1521 West Sunset Road; (702) 547–0059; www.chuckecheese.com. I get the hot Italian sandwich here, which is really pretty good. Both parent and kids get their hands stamped on entering, so kids can go wild with little chance of disappearing for more than a few minutes. The pizza keeps the kids fed, but the real attraction is the games. Look for coupons in the paper, or go online for **free** tokens. $

Fatburgers. Sunset Station and other locations; (702) 898–7200. Daily 10:00 A.M.–10:00 P.M. The best cheap burgers in town, these hand-packed patties are thrown onto a grill in the classic manner. The onion rings are just the way you remember them, and the kid-sized portion means that you won't be tossing half of this hefty sandwich in the trash. $$

5 & Diner. 375 North Stephanie Street; (702) 940–2050. Monday through Thursday 6:00 A.M.–10:00 P.M., Friday and Saturday until midnight. They call this comfort food now: hamburgers, chicken-fried steak, ham sandwiches, meat loaf, and spaghetti. The malts are thick and satisfying, the atmosphere inviting for kids, and the classic '50s attitude a real family pleaser. Check out any of the seven locations scattered throughout the valley. $–$$

Japengo. Hyatt Regency Lake Las Vegas, 101 Montelago Boulevard; (702) 567–1234 or (800) 554–9288. This La Jolla restaurant was a big hit when it opened, with innovative cuisine that wasn't like any other restaurant. The open kitchen here makes for an entertaining evening while you wait for creative dishes influenced by the Pacific Rim. Many consider the sushi the best in the valley. Adventurous families will love to eat here. $$–$$$

Joe's Crab Shack. 1991 North Rainbow Boulevard; (702) 646–3996. Daily 11:00 A.M.–10:00 P.M., until 11:00 P.M. on weekends. Try the barbecue crab, eaten in a messy manner that won't make kids feel intimidated. The large outdoor play area and sandbox can be viewed from the patio dining area, so have a glass of wine while little Johnny plays. $$

Johnny Mac. 842 Boulder Highway; (702) 564–2121. Daily 10:30 A.M.–11:00 P.M., or whenever they feel like opening and closing. Pizza, pasta, and the best chicken wings you are likely to find. Johnny Mac's wings converted Alexander into a chicken wing fanatic, sending us on a cross-town quest to see if anyone else could compete. So far, they can't. Pizzas are handmade and the place is loud enough to muffle any cranky kid you happen to have in tow. $

Lotus of Siam. 953 East Sahara Avenue, Suite A-5; (702) 735–3033. Lunch buffet weekdays 11:30 A.M.–2:30 P.M., dinner 5:30–9:30 P.M. *Gourmet* magazine calls this "the best Thai restaurant in the United States." Make sure you order dishes that the kids can eat, as many of them are very spicy. Pad thai is usually a good bet. $$

Mimi's Cafe. 596 North Stephanie, (702) 458–0726; 1121 Fort Apache, (702) 341–0365. Daily 7:00 A.M.–11:00 P.M. Meaty chicken pot pie, barbecue meat loaf, quiche, and endless strawberry lemonade make this California chain a local hit. Come early, though, because there is almost always a wait. $–$$

Minnie's Frozen Custard. 565 College Drive (College and Horizon); (702) 566–8338; Monday through Thursday 2:00–9:00 P.M., Friday and Saturday 3:00–10:00 P.M., Sunday 2:00–8:00 P.M. Frozen custard is a rich, creamy ice cream and is all the rage, now. This is the latest entry into the market and a welcome treat after a spray day in Mission Hills Park. $

Old Spaghetti Factory. 721 Mall Ring Circle (behind the Galleria); (702) 458–0845. Daily 11:30 A.M.–9:30 P.M. The food is inexpensive and the kid's meal, which comes on cute little dinosaur plates, includes plenty of food, dessert, and a bag of goodies. There is even a separate dining room for families. $$

Panera. Galleria Pavilion, 605 Mall Ring Circle; (702) 434–4002. Daily 5:00 A.M.–9:00 P.M. Fabulous breads make fabulous sandwiches. Alexander fell in love with the turkey and artichoke sandwich on focaccia. Of course, the fresh desserts and pastries are Seiji and Chloe's downfall. $

Wild Oats Market & Cafe. 517 North Stephanie Street; (702) 458–9427. Daily 7:00 A.M.–11:00 P.M. Using organic produce, the cafe makes tasty salads, pizza, pasta, and other yummies for lunch or a great quick take-home meal. Kids love the organic soups and the smoothies. $

Willy and Jose's Cantina. Sam's Town, 5111 Boulder Highway; (702) 456–7777. Wednesday through Saturday 5:00–11:00 p.m. Voted a "Best of Las Vegas" honor by the *Review-Journal* (which can seem ubiquitous), this spicy Mexican restaurant serves up a variety of kid- and adult-friendly entrees. Grown-ups may want to try the Six-Shooter steak and chicken; my kids almost always order a bean burrito. It is hard to resist the fried ice cream or the chocolate tacos to cool your mouth after a sizzling main course. $–$$

Where to Stay

Green Valley Ranch. 2300 Paseo Verde, I–215 and Green Valley Parkway; (702) 617–7777. This Vegas hot spot is reputed to be one of Brad Pitt's favorite hangouts when he's in town. Locals are equally impressed.

Day or night, the **Backyard** has plenty to offer—live music, a relaxing getaway, or a place to hang out with friends. The Backyard is the most- happening spot for parties, special events, and concerts. It also features one of the nicest pools in Vegas with a walk-in sand beach, disappearing-edge waterfall, and a bridge that spans the entire length of the pool.

The 10,000-square-foot **Grand Dolphin Court Spa** at Green Valley Ranch is a European day spa that offers a multitude of therapies, a full-service salon, and workout facilities. The glass bottom of the reflecting pool in front of the spa forms the ceiling of many of the treatment rooms. $$–$$$

Hyatt Regency Lake Las Vegas. 101 MonteLago Boulevard; (702) 567–1234 or (800) 554–9288; www.lakelasvegas .hyatt.com. Built around a 320-acre lake with more than 10 miles of shoreline, this 500-

room Mediterranean-style resort is just 17 miles from the Strip. Kids aren't just shuttled off into a corner here, they are pampered, scampered, and unhampered to their heart's content. With two spacious swimming pools (including a water slide), sandy beaches, kayaking, fishing, windsurfing, boating, swimming, hiking, croquet, golf, volleyball, and spacious areas waiting to be explored, kids will have more than enough to keep them busy for as long as you want to stay. As an added attraction, the casino is set off from the rest of the resort, making the experience more elegant for players while keeping kids well away from the adults-only area.

Camp Hyatt is typical of the Hyatt's family-friendly attitude. The renowned children's program features a variety of activities for kids ages three to twelve. The program offers half off a second room (if available), children's menus, and supervised daytime and evening camp activities. Parents with kids in diapers are offered outside baby-sitting services on request. **Camp Hyatt Mud Castle** is a kids' club room that looks like a Moroccan mud palace. Age-appropriate activities are supervised by CPR- and first-aid-trained attendants who specialize in working with children. Finger painting, arts and crafts, field games, sand castle and mud castle building, playtime, and swimming are all part of the program. At night ask for a **free** "planisphere" from the Concierge Desk to help identify distant stars and galaxies, visible with desert-sky clarity. Fly-fishing lessons and fishing guides can be booked for the whole family. Use the hotel's birding backpack for **free** (deposit required), complete with binoculars, a map, and a bird identification book, or ask for the **free** hiking map. The **Reflection Bay Golf Club,** designed by Jack Nicklaus, was listed in *Golf* magazine's 1999 top ten courses. Set up some private or family lessons with the Nicklaus/Flick Golf School.

The **upper pool,** heated in winter months, features shaded tables, chaise longues, and a hot tub; the **lower activity pool** has a playground, a wading pool, and a water slide. The **swimming lagoon and beach,** below the activity pool, lets families have access to lakeside water play. Cabanas and raft rentals are available.

Spa Moulay offers everything from Swedish massage to a Moroccan Rhassoul clay wrap. I say, let the boys fish while the girls get their toes polished. $$$–$$$$

The Ritz Carlton, Lake Las Vegas. 1610 Lake Las Vegas Parkway; (702) 568–6858 or (800) 241–3333; www.ritzcarlton.com. The Mediterranean-style resort offers 349 rooms and suites that overlook Lake Las Vegas, complete with an arched bridge that floats over the warm waters. As of press time, there were no special children's programs available. However, with the swimming pool, white sandy beaches, and the numerous Lake

Las Vegas amenities including boating, mountain biking, kayaking, hiking, golfing, stargazing, nature seminars, sailing lessons, fishing and more offered throughout the resort, kids should be able to find plenty to do.

The only U.S. location for Italy's La Culla treatment, the spa retreat and fitness center, **Spa Vita di Lago** (702–567–4700), offers a variety of treatments as well as wholesome health food at its cafe. It's open every day from 6:30 A.M. to 7:00 P.M.

Sam's Town. 5111 Boulder Highway; (702) 456–7777 or (800) 634–6371. The recent renovation of Sam's Town, including the **free** water/laser light show that occurs four times daily at the **Mystic Falls Indoor Park,** has made this one of the best places for families to stay. **Sam's Town Live!** often has concerts that are very appropriate for children, such as its opening with Kenny Loggins. **Century 18 Sam's Town** contains a six-theater movie complex on one floor, with twelve smaller screens on the first level. The **child care center** includes an outdoor play area and more than seventy nongaming amusement games. The **Firelight Buffet** has been a great success and is frequently cited as one of the best buffet bargains in town.

A **free** shuttle takes guests from the Stardust on the Strip and the Fremont and California Hotels downtown. $–$$$

Sunset Station Hotel and Casino. 1301 West Sunset Road; (702) 547–7777 or (888) SUNSET9; www.sunsetstation.com. Station Casinos consistently cater to locals and bargain travelers who don't want to spend a fortune but still want a quality experience. Sunset is one of the best properties in the bunch, with magnificent stained glass throughout the building. The hotel includes a pool, movie theaters, an arcade, and a variety of high-quality fast food including Krispy Kreme, Fatburger, Ben and Jerry's Scoop Shop, and pizza by the slice. The live concerts often are very appropriate for kids, and prices can start as low as $19. Specializing in country and jazz music, the venue has recently expanded to comedians and rock bands; think the Charlie Daniels Band, B. J. Thomas, and Dave Koz. Comedians tend to be family-friendly, but ask anyway. $

Guests and other patrons can use the secure, fun-filled **Kids Quest** child care services while they are on the property.

For everyone from the gourmet to the buffet buff, Sunset Station's food is consistent, high quality, and reasonably priced. **Sunset Cafe** is perfect for a late-night feast or a hearty breakfast; the **Feast Around the World buffet** has five cooking stations and special pricing for kids; the new **Sonoma Cellar** steak house offers an extensive wine list and top-notch food. $–$$$

For More Information

www.cityofhenderson.com.

North Las Vegas Chamber of Commerce. 1023 East Lake Mead Boulevard, North Las Vegas, Nevada 89030; (702) 642–9595. The bureau's Web site is http://nlvchamber.com/.

Henderson Chamber of Commerce. 590 South Boulder Highway, Henderson, Nevada 89015-7512; (702) 565–8951. Or visit the Web site at www.hendersonchamber.com/.

Henderson Convention Center and Visitors Bureau. 200 Water Street, Henderson, Nevada 89015; (702) 565–2171.

Boulder City

Take I–15 north to U.S. 93/95 east until you see the green trees and grass that signify Boulder City, a Nevada exception for a number of reasons. The first ever planned community, it was commissioned in the early 1930s by the federal government to house the workers needed to build Hoover Dam. Today it remains a charming small town that stands apart. You won't see slot machines here. Boulder City is the only town in Nevada that has chosen to remain gaming free. Instead it boasts small arts and antiques shops, quaint restaurants, and unique low-key entertainment. The increasingly popular and numerous festivals can attract thousands, sometimes tens of thousands.

Boulder City has thirty-four acres of landscaped parks, including year-round swimming, racquetball, shuffleboard, tennis, and basketball, but these are the least of the area's outdoor charms. It is also fast becoming internationally recognized for its wide variety of extreme—and less extreme—world-class sports. From its onset, this small desert town has attracted outdoor adventurers from gold prospectors to big-game hunters. Since then the area has engaged hang gliders, land sailors, hikers, anglers, birders, bicyclists, hot springs enthusiasts, naturalists, boaters, and more. With Lake Mead National Recreation Area right next door, it may be the most versatile little town you will ever visit.

Hunters come to hunt bighorn sheep and anglers compete for sixty-five-pound striper. Bird-watchers enjoy seeing everything from osprey to bald eagles, while mountain bike enthusiasts barrel down some of the best tracks in the world. With the new world-class municipal golf course, it may seem as if the only outdoor sport not available is dogsledding. Knowing Boulder City, however, all it may take is one local enthusiast and that, too, may come.

Boulder City is a small town. At most of the businesses here, when you talk to the person behind the counter, you're talking to the owner. Frankly, I love that, and have always supported local stores, even when prices are slightly higher. I have been repaid with personal service and interesting products. One caution: Although most businesses try to maintain regular hours, the smallest and most intimate shops sometimes close despite their posted hours. Be forgiving and come again. The wait is almost always worth it.

Bootleg Canyon Mountain Bike Trail (all ages)
Yucca Street and Industrial; (702) 293–2453 or (702) 896–6882; www.bootlegcanyon.com. Free.

This hand-built trail is strictly for mountain bikes. "It isn't necessarily a walking or horseback riding trail," advises local trail builder Brent Thomson. "It is all about momentum and flow. Imagine how snow skis deal with gravity. There is a flow and a rhythm to the descent."

Remember **Bowling?**

I was told recently that bowling is one of the most watched sporting events on TV. Go figure. I had forgotten all about bowling until new owners took over Boulder Bowl in Boulder City and starting having after-school leagues. Now it isn't unusual to see second graders toting their bowling bags up to the alley after school any day of the week. Some of the casinos have also rediscovered bowling, and the alleys are filling up. Not only are youth leagues hot, a growing number of leagues feature parents and kids bowling as partners. Open bowling sessions are a great way to spend a couple of hours with the kids. While you are not bowling, you may be surprised at what revelations appear during casual conversation between those waiting their turn. Most bowling alleys charge around $2.50 per game, with a $2.00 shoe rental.

- Boulder Bowl, 504 California Street, (702) 293–2368
- Gold Coast Hotel & Casino, 4000 West Flamingo Road, (702) 367–4700
- Mahoney's Silver Nugget Bowling Center, 2140 North Las Vegas Boulevard, (702) 320–2695
- Orleans Bowling Center, 4500 West Tropicana Avenue, (702) 365–7111
- Primm Valley Resort, 31700 Las Vegas Boulevard South, (702) 382–1212
- Sam's Town Bowling Center, 5111 Boulder Highway, (702) 454–8022
- Santa Fe Lanes, 4949 North Rancho Drive, (702) 658–4995
- Silver Nugget, 2041 Las Vegas Boulevard, (702) 399–1111
- Suncoast, 9090 Alta Drive, (702) 636–7111
- Sunset Lanes & Casino, 4451 East Sunset Road, (702) 736–2695
- Terrible's Casino & Lanes, 642 Boulder Highway, (702) 564–7118
- Texas Station, 2101 Texas Star Lane, (800) 654–8888

Most of the trail was built within the last few years, but already it has garnered international admiration. The International Mountain Biking Association designated it as an Epic Destination, one of only twenty-four "must-do" trails in the nation. With a variety of special events, bikers and their admirers may find this new set of trails a must-do event.

Boulder Creek Golf Club (all ages)

1501 Veteran's Memorial Drive; (702) 294–6534. Daily, dawn to dusk. Prices vary, ranging from $ to $$$$$ depending on age, residency, time of day, day of the week, and season.

Boulder Creek, which opened to the public January 3, 2003, makes Boulder City the only town in the valley to be home to two municipal golf courses. This course sports twenty-seven holes of championship golf with three distinct themes: oasis, arroyo, and desert. Boulder Creek will also have a night-lighted double-ended practice facility, or driving range, and a night-lighted par-3 state-of-the-art training center on 430 acres of land. It also has an extensive junior golf program.

Boulder City Golf Course (all ages)

1 Clubhouse Drive; (702) 293–9236. Daily, sunrise to sunset. Prices vary, ranging from $ for junior golfers to $$$ for out-of-town adults.

Boulder City residents and guests have experienced the pleasure of this 6,600-yard championship eighteen-hole, par-72, golf course since 1973. Designed by Billy Casper and David Rainville, the rolling fairways overlooking Eldorado Valley are lined with trees, while several integrated water features add to the lush feeling. Guests may also take advantage of the 5,000-square-foot clubhouse and full-service golf shop. The bar and grill are open for breakfast and lunch.

Boulder City BMX, Inc. (all ages)

Veteran's Memorial Park, Buchanan Boulevard and Airport Road; (702) 293–6787; www.bouldercitybmx.com.

This family sport attracts individuals of all ages who compete within their age and class, from beginning to expert. The Boulder City BMX track in Veteran's Memorial Park features weekly practices and races. The track is sanctioned and governed by the rules of the National Bicycle League, which promotes bicycle racing as a fun sport with emphasis on safety and sportsmanship. Riders can compete at the local, regional, and national levels. Local BMX enthusiasts are organizing National Bike League pro series and national series events.

Skateboard Park (all ages)

Veteran's Memorial Park, Buchanan Boulevard and Airport Road. Free.

Skateboard enthusiasts consider this wooden skateboard park one of the best in the Vegas area. "This skate park has two levels," says Winston MacDonald, "perfect for beginners and advanced skaters." The facility includes ramps and quarter pipes.

Art Center at ABC Park (all ages)

Adams Avenue and Georgia Street; (702) 294–0335 or (702) 293–9256. Prices and hours vary with projects.

This 2,800-square-foot facility includes a kiln room, ceramics and pottery classes, quilting, and sewing and needle art projects. The center's first major project includes a tile art project called "Tile Our Town." Staff, students, visitors, and community members may come to the facility to hand-paint 800 ceramic tiles that will be placed along the baseboard area of the Art Center.

Southern Nevada Paddling Club (all ages)

Location rotates to accommodate members from all parts of the valley; (702) 255–5926; www.kayaknevada.org. First Wednesday of the month at 7:00 P.M. $$ annual dues.

This relatively new organization was formed to gather people who have an interest in paddle sports, particularly, although not exclusively, kayaking. The group organizes paddling trips, arranges water safety training and other clinics to improve paddling techniques, and hosts monthly membership meetings, often with educational speakers. Outings can be geared toward the ability of interested participants. Although the initial members were primarily adults and their dogs, families are welcome.

Labyrinth (all ages)

St. Andrew's Catholic Church, 1399 San Felipe Drive; (702) 293–7500. Free.

Labyrinths were traditionally a tool for meditation and spiritual healing. Walking the intricate pattern calms, collects, and refreshes kids and adults alike. Afterward, the serene setting is conducive to intimate conversations, spiritual discussions, or self-reflection.

Fisher Space Pen Company and Factory (all ages)

711 Yucca Street; (702) 293–3011; www.spacepen.com. Weekdays 8:00 A.M.–3:00 P.M.

The complete line of what many consider to be the world's best writing utensil is available to the public in the reception area of the factory (no public tours though). These pens have accompanied every manned space flight since 1968. Paul C. Fisher invented and sold the rights to erasable ink, but the ink that can write in zero gravity, upside down, in water, over grease, and in extreme temperatures still remains his secret. Fisher's newest pen is guaranteed not to run out of ink for the rest of your life. The Fisher Bullet pen is displayed in the New York Museum of Modern Art and has been the topic of many art books; a Fisher pen has been to the top of Mount Everest, and Jacques Cousteau has used one on his undersea adventures.

With luck, you might see the stately, white-haired Fisher himself, who lives in a small apartment above the factory. In his late seventies, he still goes to work every day.

Boulder Gem Club (all ages)

1204 Sixth Street; (702) 293–7853. Second Wednesday of the month, 7:30 P.M.; no meetings in July and August. Family membership $ per year.

Meet with fellow rock hounds who can find something good to say about almost any rock found during their seasonal excursions. Attend a free monthly meeting (about some aspect of nature) to see how your family fits in. Although the group is mostly adults, they welcome fellow ooohers and aahers of any age.

Six Company Visitors Bureau (all ages)

441 Nevada Highway; (702) 293–1823. Daily 9:00 A.M.–4:00 P.M. Free.

Stop here to see Hoover Dam videos and to purchase Southwest gifts, film, Indian jewelry, and pottery. You can also pick up information on the surrounding area.

Reynolds' Dolls Gifts & Collectibles (all ages)

552 Nevada Highway; (702) 294–2448. Daily 10:00 A.M.–5:00 P.M.

Enjoy this large selection of porcelain dolls, collectibles, and Southwestern jewelry. People who are in the know tell me this shop has some of the best prices around.

St. Jude's Ranch for Children (all ages)

100 St. Jude's Street; (702) 294–7100 or (800) 492–3562; info@stjudesranch.org.

"We pray for children who put chocolate fingers everywhere, who like to be tickled, who stomp in puddles and ruin new pants, who sneak Popsicles before supper, who erase holes in math workbooks, who can never find their shoes.

. . . And we pray for those who never get dessert, who have no safe blanket to drag behind them, who watch their parents watch them die, who can't find any bread to steal, who don't have any rooms to clean up, whose pictures aren't on anybody's dresser, whose monsters are real." (from the St. Jude's Web site)

St. Jude's has become known around the world as a sanctuary for abused, neglected, and abandoned children. The beautiful campus overlooks Lake Mead and might provide the perfect counterpoint to any visit to Las Vegas. The **gift shop** offers a wide selection of recycled greeting cards made by the children who live here to raise money for themselves and the shelter. Souvenir and religious items, handmade crafts, and donated articles from supporters across the United States are also available. Guests may purchase a rosary or St. Jude medal and have it blessed in the nearby chapel.

The **Chapel of the Holy Family** is also worth a visit to see the dramatic murals, antiques, handmade tapestries, and other treasures, including an original Salvador Dali cross.

A segment of the **River Mountain Loop Trail** runs by St. Jude's. Instead of bicycling by, take a rest on one of the benches nesting under a shaded tree and breathe in the healing atmosphere. Then stop by the **Thrift Shop** to see whether you can discover another man's treasure. The shelter, now expanded to three locations, including two in Texas, is always in need of donations and volunteers of all ages. Consider chipping in to discover how lucky you are.

A **Baby** in a **China Shop**

My kids love to go to old bookstores, antiques shops, and other places where unique items may be picked up for a song. They also love to look at lovely things in art shops or other places. Since the time my eldest shopped with me from her stroller, we have had three categories of behavior that all three kids have always thought fair and have always respected. Not only does it make shopping with them relaxing and fun, whether we are in a china shop or a toy store, it relieves the shopkeeper who may not otherwise be too happy with your little one's patronage. Before we enter a store, I let the kids know which kind of place we are entering.

Look but don't touch! That means they keep their hands inside the stroller or, when older, in their pockets. If they really want to see something, I pick it up and hold it. They still don't touch anything.

Ask permission to touch carefully. I let the child ask the owner or clerk whether they may look at an item more closely. This allows the shopkeepers to politely set parameters to protect their merchandise.

Go ahead and touch all you like. At a bookstore, toy store, or a place with kid-friendly merchandise, I let well-behaved children go as they please, within reason. It helps if you actually buy something.

Before we go anywhere, I always tell them exactly what I expect from them and what they can expect. When the kids were very little, I let them know that they could buy one item anytime throughout the day. (When they got older, they had a budget.) My littlest would usually pick out something at the beginning of the day and play with it while we shopped. My oldest usually kept her options open until the day was nearly over (sometimes that meant that we returned to a store to quickly pick up her choice). My middle child often didn't feel that anything at all merited that final commitment. In any case, merchants have repeatedly told me that the children behave beautifully and are welcome to return whenever they like. And that's something you can't purchase for any price.

Back in Thyme (all ages)
524 Nevada Highway; (702) 294–1983. Daily 10:00 A.M.–5:00 P.M. Closed Wednesday.

This charming antiques and collectibles store has new antique-looking items, crafts, and genuine antique furniture, glassware, jewelry, toys, and more.

Central Market (all ages)

1101 Arizona Street; (702) 293–4213. Monday through Saturday 8:00 A.M.–9:00 P.M., Sunday until 8:00 P.M.

Step into the past at this classic market known for its fresh meat. If you're picking up supplies for a barbecue on the lake, make sure you stop here. Locals and old-timers prefer this friendly, cozy, and fairly well-stocked market to any of the big chains. It's a Boulder City institution.

Fiddlesticks Quilts (all ages)

1229 Arizona Street; (702) 293–2979; www.fiddlesticksquilts.com. Tuesday through Saturday 10:00 A.M.–5:30 P.M.

Full of quilters and quilting supplies, as well as other crafts, the lessons and sewing projects draw quilters and crafters of all ages. Make a holiday hanging or a handmade bear that can be cherished for generations.

Boulder City Museum and Historical Association and Gift Shop
(all ages)

Boulder Dam Hotel, 1305 Arizona Street; (702) 294–1988. Daily 10:00 A.M.–5:00 P.M., from noon on Sunday. $, ages 6 and under free.

Plan to spend at least an hour exploring the creation of Hoover Dam through the eyes of the men who built it and their families. Kids enjoy the interactive displays, including listening to tape-recorded stories from the children who lived in Boulder City during the dam's construction.

Nevada State Railroad Museum, Boulder City (all ages)

600 Yucca Street; (702) 486–5933.

Although the museum isn't technically open to the public, if the gate is open and anyone is there, and you are interested in trains, you can probably get a private tour of the restorations and plans to build a local facility. The cars are enclosed within a chain-link fence and are visible from outside the fence. There has been talk of developing a train track between Henderson and Boulder City, strictly for tourist excursions.

Cristina's Treasures (all ages)

1400 Wyoming Street; (702) 293–3440; www.christmastreasures.com. Monday through Saturday 10:00 A.M.–6:00 P.M., Sunday 11:00 A.M.–3:00 P.M.

Girls will love this store with lots of white painted furniture, lacy linens, and whimsical candleholders.

Ace Shopper Stopper (all ages)

541 Nevada Highway; (702) 293–3373. Monday through Saturday 7:00 A.M.–6:00 P.M., Sunday 8:00 A.M.–5:00 P.M.

While the girls are at Christina's, send the boys to Ace, an old-fashioned hardware store with everything from paints and balsa wood for model planes to bouncing balls to hand tools. If Ace doesn't have it, you don't need it—at least that's what my husband tells me.

Lake Mead National Recreation Area (all ages)

601 Nevada Highway; (702) 293–8907 or 293–8990; www.nps.gov/lame.

The juxtaposition of the bright blue lake against the stark desert hills is a study in con-trasts, and the cool water is the perfect complement for the searing desert heat. There are a variety of ways to take advantage of the water: Look at it, swim in it, fish in it, or ride on top of it. But whichever you choose, Lake Mead sure feels good on a sizzling summer day.

Founded in 1935, when the Hoover Dam was completed, Lake Mead is the largest man-made lake in the United States. It offers a world of recreational opportunities. Anglers come from all over to fish for the legendary striped bass, the wind offers great sailing opportunities, and a beach is available for waders and swimmers. A number of businesses specialize in renting everything from canoes and ski boats to paddleboats and luxurious houseboats. Many visitors simply enjoy the contrast between the crystal blue waters and the stark desert terrain. At the end of the day, the hills pick up the magnificent colors of the sun to glow against the darkening sky.

Stop by the **Alan Bible Visitor Center** to explore "Discovering the Desert." These interactive, hands-on exhibits invite visitors to discover the Mojave Desert of Lake Mead National Recreation Area. The visitor center is located about 4 miles east of Boulder City, at the junction of U.S. Highway 93 and Lakeshore Scenic Drive. Members of park staff are available to provide information, books and maps, and other materials for sale. The visitor center is open from 8:30 A.M. to 4:30 P.M. every day except Thanksgiving, Christmas, and New Year's Day.

Lake Mead Cruises (all ages)

480 Lakeshore Road; (702) 293–6180; www.lakemeadcruises.com. Prices begin at $.

Explore the lake on a beautiful paddle-wheel boat. The cruise line offers day cruises and a romantic nighttime dinner-dance cruise. The captain invites kids to steer the boat and get a special patch.

Lake Mead Resort & Marina (all ages)

322 Lakeshore Road; (702) 293–3484; www.sevencrown.com. Hours vary seasonally.

Come down here to feed the gigantic fish or rent a boat. Or just look at the lovely lake.

Hoover Dam Museum (all ages)

1305 Arizona Street; (702) 294–1988. Monday through Saturday 10:00 A.M.–5:00 P.M., Sunday opens at noon. Closed Easter Sunday, Mother's Day, Thanksgiving, and Christmas. $, members free.

View historic artifacts from the time that Hoover Dam was built.

Craft Cottage (all ages)
1326 Wyoming; (702) 294–4465. Weekdays 9:00 A.M.–5:00 P.M., Saturday opens at 10:00 A.M.

This tiny little shop should be part of some fairy tale—stuffed with beads, clay, ribbon, buttons, thread, yarn, and other crafty items as it is. Not only is the owner one of the nicest women in the world, she is a local fixture. She is happy to sit with you and teach you knitting or just shoot the breeze. She has also been known to offer two hot and thirsty kids a welcomed glass of water on their way home from school. Thanks, Mrs. Frazier.

Elephants Are Forever (all ages)
1305 Arizona Street, Suite 100; (702) 294–7717. Daily 10:00 A.M.–4:00 P.M., until 6:00 P.M. on weekends.

Elephant-related gifts, jewelry, art, cards, and clothing as well as other gift items such as candles, cats, and dolphins.

Bike Stuff (all ages)
1647 Nevada Highway; (702) 293–2453. Daily 10:00 A.M.–4:00 P.M., until 6:00 P.M. on weekends.

Stop in to pick up a free map of the Bootleg Canyon Trails. Rent road, juvenile, tandem, and various kinds of mountain bikes at this small shop, or join the owner for a free weekly ride geared to the levels of experience of those who show up.

Veteran's Memorial Park (all ages)
Buchanan Boulevard and Airport Road.

The small town is outdoing itself with this multi-use park. Along with the regular soccer fields and baseball diamonds, the park includes a **Desert Demonstration Garden** with Joshua trees and other southern Nevada native plants; a **children's spray park** with a variety of **free** water-play equipment; a **wetlands park** that is home to local waterbirds including a blue heron; a **fishing pond;** a small **radio-controlled sailboat pond;** a **dog park;** and more. The wind and wide-open spaces are perfect for local kite flying, as well. The **BMX park** and **skateboard park** are considered two of the best facilities in the region.

Boulder City Radio Controlled Speedway (all ages)
Veteran's Park; (702) 293–3758. Call for events.

A full-service facility at the speedway includes a prepared track, stadium seating, and a covered pavilion for ⅒-scale racing.

B.C. Cinemas (all ages)
Hacienda Hotel and Casino, Highway 93; (702) 293–7221. Daily hours vary with the movies.

Local movie man J. J. Brennan shows first-run movies in this independently owned double-screen cinema complex. Check out the concession prices if you want to see a family-friendly operation in action.

Seiji's Favorite Places to **Splash**

We love those outdoor splishy-splashy **spray parks** that are the newest rage (yeah!) with local park planners. Kids can run in and out of the water all day, and they don't even have to ruin your lawn. Most spray parks are open 9:00 A.M.–8:00 P.M. during the summer. If we aren't at **Veteran's** spray park sipping an iced tea with our girlfriends, you might find us at one of these.

Acacia Park. 50 Casa Del Fuego (southwest of U.S. Highway 95 and Lake Mead Drive). This park hopes to promote desert-conscious landscaping and offers a water-play feature, a backyard garden demonstration area, an edible garden, an allergy-free garden, an animal habitat garden, a wetlands demonstration area, and a Mojave Desert demonstration area, as well as play areas and a dog park.

Hayley Hendricks Park. 811 Ithaca Avenue (next to Brown Jr. High School); (702) 565–4264. This spacious multi-use park offers Henderson's first skate park, a tot-lot playground, lighted horseshoe courts, an equestrian trail, lighted tennis courts, covered and trellised picnic areas, and a spray park.

Mission Hills Park. 551 East Mission Hills Drive. Enjoy the tube slides, fabulous concrete pathways to learn how to ride a bike or to in-line skate, and acres of green grass.

Sunny Springs Park. Elk Horn and Buffalo. They packed this nine-acre park with four basketball courts, two tennis courts, a water-play feature, a beginners' skate park, an area to play horseshoes, and a large playground as well as a picnic area. Sunny Springs has squirt guns, spray fountains, and a rubber deck.

W. Wayne Bunker Family Park. Alexander Road and Teneya Way. A skate park, horseshoe pits, a jogging track, and barbecue grills make this a local favorite.

Winchester Park. 3130 South McLeod. This park has things to do for kids of all ages. The spray pool is there for the little ones, and there is a skate park for the older kids. There is also a community center, fitness course, picnic area, playground, tennis court, and walking course.

Periwinkle Cottage (all ages)
503 Hotel Plaza; (702) 293–5767. Monday through Friday 10:00 A.M.–5:30 P.M., Saturday 10:00 A.M.–5:00 P.M, Sunday noon–4:00 P.M.

Come to the quaint Coffee and Tea Room to enjoy a little local flavor with your morning coffee. The adjacent shop carries Ty products, jewelry, antique furniture, European bath soaps, greeting cards, bath and body products, candles, potpourri, jams, coffee beans, and scone mixes. I'll take home the antique china.

Grandma Daisy's Candy & Ice Cream Parlor (all ages)
501A Hotel Plaza; (702) 294–6639. Daily 11:00 A.M.–5:00 P.M.; www.grandmadaisys.com.

Homemade fudge, chocolates, bulk candy, ice cream, and coffee. You can find Seiji here most days after school.

Dance Works (all ages)
410 Nevada Way, #160; (702) 294–1180. Monday through Saturday 11:00 A.M.–5:00 P.M.

One of the area's newest shops, this small store offers great deals on dance wear, active wear, and gifts related to dance.

Dam Helicopter Company, Inc. (all ages)
(702) 294–2200. $$–$$$$.

Enjoy inexpensive helicopter tour rides over Lake Mead and Hoover Dam.

Black Canyon/Willow Beach River Adventures (all ages)
(800) 455–3490; www.blackcanyonadventures.com. $$$ per person, including lunch; $$ ages 5–12, under 5 free.

Enjoy breathtaking scenery on a floating trip that all ages can enjoy through the steep cliffs and smooth waters of Black Canyon, just below Hoover Dam. Canoe and rafting is restricted to this single concessionaire, so you won't be bumping into lots of other folk. Depending upon the season, you may be treated to a hiking excursion to a hot springs waterfall.

Where to Eat

Bob's—Best Food by a Dam-site! 761 Nevada Highway; (702) 294–BOBS. Daily 7:00 A.M.–9:00 P.M., closes at 4:00 P.M. on Wednesday. Dam-site jokes aside, Bob's used to be a place to avoid. Under new ownership and with a terrific local chef, it has become another Boulder City staple. The fried chicken is excellent. Traditional cafe fare like salads and biscuits and gravy are interspersed with a pretty good range of choices for the never-ending multitude of Atkins dieters. $–$$

Carlos' Mexican Cafe. 561 Hotel Plaza Street; (702) 294–6640. Daily 11:00 A.M.–8:30 P.M., Saturday 4:00 –8:30 P.M. Crowds from all over Vegas patiently wait their turn to eat at Carlos'. Vegetarians will find plenty to choose from here (our favorite is the broccoli and pine nut burrito). My daughter loves the seafood burrito. $$

Casa Flores Restaurant. 93 Nevada Highway; (702) 294–1937. Daily 11:00 A.M.–9:00 P.M. Traditional Mexican food served in a friendly atmosphere. Great soup. $–$$

Chiarelli's Deli & Market. 1224 Arizona Street; (702) 293–6600. Daily 10:00 A.M.–6:00 P.M. Stop by here to satisfy your balsamic vinegar needs and your cravings for a good Italian sub. $

The Coffee Cup. 512 Nevada Highway; (702) 294–0517. Daily 6:00 A.M.–8:00 P.M. That crowd you see on the sidewalk on Sunday morning is the one waiting to get into this classic breakfast cafe. Portions are large, homemade, and filling. Plan on sharing with a little one. $

Evan's Old Town Grille. 1129 Arizona Street; (702) 294–0100. Tuesday through Friday 11:00 A.M.–3:00 P.M. and 4:00–10:00 P.M., Saturday 4:00–10:00 P.M. Pastas, soups, and salads are served here. Sit outside on a hot summer night with the misters creating a cooling breeze. Don't forget to say hi to the local politicians who hang out here on Friday nights. $$

Golden City Chinese Restaurant. 1420 Nevada Highway; (702) 294–1818. Daily 11:00 A.M.–9:00 P.M. The buffet lunch is always packed due to the fresh and varied all-you-can-eat menu. Make sure that you order orange chicken in the evenings. $–$$

Le Bistro Cafe. 1312 Nevada Highway; (702) 293–7070. Monday through Saturday 5:00–9:00 P.M., closed Sunday. Not a typical kids' place, the friendly staff and owner make it family friendly nonetheless. There's no children's menu, but homemade soups, tasty breads, and pastas made to order fill adult and kid bellies alike. Intimate, yet with a touch of class, this is a great place to celebrate an illustrious occasion or carve out a space where family conversation gets priority. Everyone will feel special here. $$

Milo's Best Cellars. 538 Nevada Highway; (702) 293–9540. Daily 11:00 A.M.–9:00 P.M., until midnight on Friday and Saturday. Sophisticated ladies and their charges may enjoy open-air dining at this Boulder City hotspot. With a fine selection of wines by the glass, this little bistro offers an inexpensive way to feel upscale. Stop by for some baked brie covered in nuts and served with green apples, red grapes, and a sliced baguette, or the wonderful soup du jour. Ask the waitperson to simplify the sandwiches for the kids, then relax and enjoy an afternoon along the Boulder City parkway. If your kids are a little older, they may enjoy their own outdoor dining (within view) at either Tony's Pizza or the Fifties Diner next door. $

Montana's at Boulder Creek Golf Course. 1501 Veteran's Memorial Drive; (702) 294–6538. Daily 7:00 A.M.–9:00 P.M. or so, until 6:00 P.M. on Tuesday and Wednesday. Enjoy gourmet pizzas, burgers, and steaks along this beautiful golf course. $–$$

The Pit Stop. 802 Buchanan Boulevard; (702) 293–7080. Daily 10:00 A.M.–9:00 P.M. Connoisseurs of burgers love The Pit Stop, which also serves corn dogs (my little one's choice) and excellent fish baskets. $

Roberto's Taco Shop. 1645 Nevada Highway; (702) 294–3893. Daily 7:00 A.M.–10:30 P.M. If you crave or have never had real Mexican food, don't miss Roberto's. The success of a group of San Diego food stands has led to a flurry of small shops throughout Vegas. Thick, chewy chips, chunks of chicken, pickled carrots and onions, *hot* sauce, and freshly made beans all taste as if you were dining in a Mexican home. Kids almost unanimously adore the bean burritos, cheese quesadillas, and rolled tacos. When they get adventurous, let them add the homemade guacamole. My kids love the shrimp burritos and the fish tacos. $

Southwest Frosty Freeze Diner. 825 Nevada Highway; (702) 293–1537. Daily 6:00 A.M.–8:00 P.M., open until 9:00 P.M. in summer. A local tradition for shakes and malts, this place has been around for years and years. The sandwiches are fresh and generous, and the cucumber salad that often accompanies them is fresh, crisp, and tangy. Salads are made with iceberg lettuce. $

Tony's Pizza. 546 Nevada Highway; (702) 294–0023. Daily 11:00 A.M.–8:30 P.M., weekends noon–8:30 P.M. Tossed pizzas with gourmet or standard toppings keep this place hopping. Tony's also does stuffed shells and tasty hot subs. The dine-in special is a large one-topping pizza with a pitcher of soda. An old Pac Man keeps everyone entertained while waiting. $

Toto's Mexican Restaurant. 806 Buchanan Boulevard #10; (702) 293–1744. Daily 11:00 A.M.–9:30 P.M., Friday and Saturday until 10:30 P.M. Okay, I'll tell you a story: One night Alexander asked if they had Tapatio sauce for his bean burritos. The waitress said she'd look, then didn't come back. The busboy couldn't understand what we were saying. So, finally, a little miffed, I told Alexander to eat his burrito before everything got too cold. Just as he was finishing the last bite, the waitress, who seemed to have disappeared for at least fifteen minutes, arrived breathlessly at our table. "Here," she said, as she handed my son a small bottle of sauce. "I had to run over to the grocery store for it." Portions are generous and freshly made, and the chips are thin, crisp, and hot. The two-person dinner special feeds our whole family—twice—and is cheaper than feeding the family at a typical fast-food restaurant. $–$$

Where to Stay

Hacienda Hotel & Casino. U.S. Highway 93; (702) 294–2200. The only full-service hotel in the Lake Mead National Recreation Area, but don't expect a lot of frills. Still, with the lake on one side, Hoover Dam on the other, and Boulder City five minutes up the hill, you may not need much more than a place to lay your head and a little nightlife. $–$$

Historic Boulder Dam Hotel Bed & Breakfast. 1305 Arizona Street; (702) 293–3510; www.boulderdamhotel.com. Clark Gable and Carole Lombard stayed here, as did other Hollywood types like Jimmy Durante. During Hollywood's golden age, when celebrities came to Las Vegas to party, play hearty, and get out of the limelight, nowhere provided a retreat like the classy Boulder Dam Hotel. Stars came here to hunt big game, take advantage of the newly

More **Lodging** Options

- Sands Motel of Boulder, 809 Nevada Highway; (702) 293–2589. $
- Starview Motel of Boulder City, 1017 Nevada Highway; (702) 293–1658. $
- Lighthouse Inn and Resort, 110 Ville Drive; (702) 293–6547 or (800) 934–8282. $
- El Rancho Boulder Motel, 725 Nevada Highway; (702) 293–1085. $
- Flamingo Inn Boulder City, 804 Nevada Highway; (702) 293–3565. $
- Nevada Inn, 1009 Nevada Highway; (702) 293–2044 or (800) 638–8890. $
- Super 8 Motel, 704 Nevada Highway; (702) 294–8888. $
- Western Inn, 921 Nevada Highway; (702) 294–0393. $

formed lake, and get away from crowds. Celebrities still come here for those things. The rooms are relatively small, with individual collections from closed local casinos contributing to the classic atmosphere. $$$

Within the hotel are also a series of small shops and studios, with crafts and paintings from local artists. Prices are very reasonable.

The BDH Cafe (702–293–0098) is in the hotel. This lovely dining room has changed hands several times in recent years. The latest incarnation serves hearty breakfasts and a great lunchtime chicken salad, as well as an assortment of sandwiches and pasta dishes. $–$$

For More Information

Boulder City Chamber of Commerce. 1305 Arizona Street, Boulder City, Nevada 89005; (702) 293–2034. Accessible on the Web at www.bouldercitychamber.com.

Boulder City Visitors Center. 100 Nevada Highway, Boulder City, Nevada 89005; (702) 294–1220. Or visit www.bouldercity.com/visitors.html.

North Las Vegas

Before you head out of town, experience the charms of North Las Vegas, a township with its own character. It was traditionally considered home to the horsey set, with extensive equestrian trails into the desert and up into the Spring Mountains. Now, horse property, pig farms, and other agricultural interests have been largely replaced by new home developments and shopping malls.

Nevada's love affair with horses goes way back. Until a few years ago, herds of wild horses still roamed over public lands west of Vegas. Throughout the state, Nevada could

Sports Parks

Spend a lovely afternoon in these active arcades where video games are replaced by the real thing.

Dansey's Indoor Race Track. 741 North Nellis; (702) 453–7223. Daily 10:00 A.M.–9:00 P.M. Races held 6:30 P.M. on Tuesday and Friday, 5:00 P.M. on Sunday. A day at the races can be a fun treat. Come and watch the races or take part in the fun and rent a car. Car rental is $15.00 per hour; $6.00 for the day if you bring your own.

Event Center Las Vegas. 121 East Sunset Road; (702) 317–7777. Winter and summer hours vary, but generally open daily from 11:00 A.M.–11:00 P.M. Some afternoons closed to the public. Call for specific times. Cost varies by height for unlimited attraction passes. $–$$, under 36 inches free. The park has it all, from indoor rock climbing to batting cages to a NASCAR speed park. Nevada residents save $5.00 with ID.

boast one of the largest wild horse populations in the country. During the last few years, though, most of this area's wild horses have been removed. Yet the horsey set holds on, with acre-size parcels that remain one of the last reserves for the urban cowboy.

Kyle Ranch (all ages)
Corner of Losee Road and Carey Avenue; (702) 633–1020. Currently no facilities are available to the public.

Debate continues on whether this adobe building is the oldest or the third-oldest structure in the area. Established in 1875, this was one of only two major ranches in the Valley throughout the nineteenth century. The old ranch house burned down in the late 1990s; a lower water table has since turned the artesian spring that supplied the ranch into a marsh. Nestled in the heart of an industrial area, it stands, guarded only by a slim fence. As one state historian put it, "One good rain could wash it away." Those who decry that fate hope to move the adobe structure, brick by brick, to the site of the Las Vegas Springs Preserve, where measures can be taken to maintain it.

Las Vegas Mini Grand Prix (ages 4 and up)
1401 North Rainbow Boulevard; (702) 259–7000. Daily 10:00 A.M.–10:00 P.M., Friday and Saturday until midnight. $–$$.

Not ready to test your racing skills on the Speedway? Check out this seven-acre family fun center with four minitracks, a banked oval Super Stock Car track, a dragon roller coaster, and a slide. Go-carts can be driven by those 54 inches and taller; littler ones may be passengers. The two adult tracks (sixteen or older) are the real challenge: Grand Prix is a

Kids on Ice

Consider cooling off during the hottest summer days on a giant ice cube—well, not a cube, but icy cool just the same. Take lessons, just flounder around, or consider watching young skaters train. For a more exciting viewer's sport, attend the adult hockey league games for **free** during tournament time. Although these players aren't part of the NHL leagues, tournaments like Global Sports or Canadian Hockey Enterprises can create a lot of excitement. Ask for a schedule of upcoming games at the counter.

Santa Fe Ice Arena. Santa Fe Station, 4949 North Rancho Drive; (702) 658–4991. Tuesday through Thursday 3:00–5:00 P.M. and 7:45–10:00 P.M., Friday 8:00–11:00 P.M., Saturday 2:30–4:30 P.M., Sunday 1:00–4:00 P.M. No skating Monday. The only year-round rink in Vegas, this stadium-size arena offers public skating as well as private and group lessons for figure skating and hockey. This is a fun place for an adventurous kid's birthday party; birthday packages make the party a piece of cake. $5.00, $4.00 for children 12 and under, skate rental $2.00. Sunday family special: $4.00 includes skate rental. Tuesday 3:00–5:00 P.M., two for the price of one.

timed lap racecourse; Superstock is a mini-stock-car racetrack. Take a break or get refreshed inside at the arcade and snack bar. The cost is $5.50 per ride or 5 rides for $25.00; kiddie rides are half price or less.

Gilcrease Nature Sanctuary (all ages)
8103 Racel Street; (702) 645–4224. Wednesday through Sunday; 10:00 A.M.–3:00 P.M. $.

Spend the day at this nature sanctuary and enjoy the walking trails, petting zoo, picnic area, and exhibits. You might see everything but cats and dogs here, including upland birds, indigenous game birds, exotic birds, llamas, specially bred chickens, lizards, and more. Individual and group tours are available.

Gilcrease Orchard (all ages)
7800 North Tenaya Way; (702) 645–1126. Saturday 7:00 A.M.–noon. Free.

Kids and parents love coming to one of the oldest ranches in the Valley to pick seasonal fruit, wander through shady orchards, or purchase fresh produce from the stand. From local pears to apricots, apples, plums, and pumpkins, there is almost always something fresh and juicy to eat here. Call to see what luscious delectable is in season.

Las Vegas Drive-In Theatre (all ages)

4150 West Carey Avenue (across from the Fiesta); (702) 646–3565. Weekdays 8:00–11:30 P.M., weekends until midnight; opens at 7:00 P.M. in winter. $, children under 12 free.

When we were kids, the only movies we saw were at drive-ins, where a children's play area, a grassy knoll, and a snack bar kept us entertained even when the movie did not. One of the last drive-ins in the country, and the last in the Valley, this family-friendly outdoor movie house is a welcome relic from the past and a great treat for parents of very little ones who are looking for a place the whole family can enjoy. Tuesday is family night; adults pay $4.00, children are still free, and hot dogs are only a buck twenty-five.

Floyd Lamb State Park (all ages)

U.S. 93/95 west from Las Vegas to Tule Springs Road; (702) 486–5413. Open sunrise to sunset; $ per car. Trail rides for ages 4 and up; (702) 604–0689. Special horses for small children, $$ per hour, $ per half hour.

Everything seemed fun in the old days—even divorce. In the '40s and '50s, instead of battling it out in the courts, Eastern socialites would hightail it to Nevada to exchange bridal bonds for saddle sores. Clare Boothe's wickedly witty movie *The Women,* in which Norma Shearer trades verbal barbs with supposed friend Rosalind Russell and husband stealer Joan Crawford, takes place in a six-week-residency dude ranch similar to the former Tule Springs Ranch just outside of Las Vegas. The ranch offered soon-to-be divorcees a chance to wrangle, ride, swim, shoot, or just get a desert tan.

Now it's called Floyd Lamb State Park, and visitors can still imagine the ghosts of these upper-crust women in and around the ranch. This lovely little oasis has peacocks, four small stocked fishing ponds, and sixty-year-old trees.

A relatively new park, rangers are working with the recently formed Tule Springs Historic Preservation Committee to renovate the main house, guest cottages, and riding stables. The park has reinstated horseback and surrey rides.

Where to Eat

Anthony and Mario's Broadway Pizzeria. 850 South Rancho Drive; (702) 259–9002. Daily 11:00 A.M.–11:00 P.M. "Tomato pies" served the New York way: thin, crispy, without too much topping so that you can fold it in half to keep it off your shirt. The pastas here are also an excellent choice, for those with a kid who doesn't like pizza, like our eldest. She prefers the ravioli. Try the Italian ices and gelatos for dessert. $

Gallo's Pizza Company. 3250 North Tenaya Way; (702) 656–9191; www.famous pizzacompany.com. Daily 10:00 A.M.–10:00 P.M. Get a wide selection of gourmet pizzas, pastas, heroes, calzones, and strombolis here. $

Joey's Only. 3455 South Durango Boulevard; (702) 242–2888. 7450 West Cheyenne Avenue; (702) 395–4313. Daily 11:00 A.M.–9:00 P.M., until 10:00 P.M. Tuesday and Friday. Opens at noon on Sunday. Come for the fish and chips or the battered shrimp dinner, then expand from there. Joey's also offers salmon, mahimahi, catfish, crab, scallops, mussels, rib eye steak, and chicken, all at prices families will appreciate. $

Tenaya Creek Restaurant and Brewery.
3101 North Tenaya Way; (702) 362–7335.
11:00 A.M.–9:00 P.M., until 10:00 P.M. on Friday and Saturday nights. The versatile menu includes gourmet pizzas, pastas, barbecued honey beer ribs, pan-roasted salmon, dinner-size salads, and a selection of sandwiches. The homebrew is also tasty. Kids will love the house-made root beer. Try it in a float for an extra-special treat. $$

Summerlin, Peccole Ranch, and The Lakes Area

These upscale neighborhoods have always been family oriented, at least in the ten or so years they've been around. They are so family-friendly, in fact, that they actually use *"children and families"* in their marketing materials. Not only that, they emphasize the proximity to Red Rock Canyon to encourage outdoor enthusiasm among their residents. Biking and hiking paths are often shaded by a canopy of maturing trees. Public spaces include lots of recreational activities. Youth-oriented public facilities encourage peer and family play. Residents are extremely loyal to this area and proud to show it off to visiting South-siders or out-of-towners. If you don't live here, make sure you spend a day exploring these lovely neighborhoods.

Children's Memorial Park (all ages)
Rainbow Boulevard and Gowan Road. Free.

This beautiful park will make you grateful for the gift of your children. Enjoy two playgrounds and a large picnic area. Full of shady trees, the park also has walking trails, a roller hockey field, and Little League fields. The large kiosk in the center of the park lists each tree in the park, when it was planted, and the name of the child in whose memory it was dedicated.

Pueblo Park (all ages)
Lake Mead Boulevard and Buffalo Drive. Free.

A park that works hard to combine natural landscaping with more people-friendly areas, Pueblo Park follows a natural arroyo as it meanders alongside Lake Mead. The natural slope and concrete pathways make it great for teaching little ones how to ride rolling apparatus such as skateboards, in-line skates, bikes, or scooters. Natural flora and fauna are intermingled with low-water landscaping, small grassy areas, and quiet retreats that become intoxicatingly fragrant after a desert rain.

Movies in the Park (all ages)
Cimarron Rose Track Break Center, 5591 Cimarron Road; (702) 638–8036. Third Friday of the month, 6:30 P.M. Free.

Bring your lawn chairs or a blanket to this movie displayed on a huge projection screen in a park. The center concentrates on G-rated Disney fare, although an occasional PG-13 film

Winston's Favorite Skate Parks

Athletic and energetic, Winston and his mom have explored parks all over town. Here is his critical assessment of the best and worst. Rumor has it that the city is planning to add more skate parks.

Veteran's Memorial Park in Boulder City. "This skate park has two levels, perfect for beginning and advanced skaters. The top level has all the huge ramps for the skaters and bikers who like to get tons of air. The bottom level is better for skaters like me, who like the smaller ramps and rails. The ramps and quarter pipes are really smooth and solid; they're made of wood with some kind of outer coating that makes them smooth and hard. Just the ground is concrete. If you go on the weekend during the day, it's pretty packed, but if you come early or late or on the weekdays, it's not that bad."

Henderson Boys and Girls Club. One of the first skate parks in town, the Boys and Girls Club is open to everyone, although children must be registered by their parent or guardian. "It's a parking lot with all kinds of ramps set out. Some things can be moved around. The ramps are big—it's hard to get enough speed. It's not for skateboards; with in-line skates, you'd be able to do some things."

Desert Breeze. An all-concrete park; make sure kids wear their protective gear. "This park for the average skater is second to Boulder's Veteran Memorial Park. It's got a few metal capped curbs and one really good rail. It's crowded with younger, not-so-good skaters on the weekend days and fairly empty during the week when you'll find the older kids, who are really good."

Skate City. 4915 Steptoe Street; (702) 433–5544. Saturday–Monday noon–8:00 P.M., Tuesday–Friday 2:00–8:00 P.M. Miniramps, ¼-pipes, box jumps, and other ramps can keep active boarders happy all day. "One of the most fun new skate parks in the city." Members pay $8.00/two hours, $12.00/all day.

will play if nothing else is available. Picnickers are welcome, but there are usually concessions sold as well. If rain threatens, the whole thing moves indoors. Although most appropriate for families with younger children, everyone is welcome.

Peccole Ranch Trails (all ages)
Peccole Ranch. Free.

You'll feel as if you are in another part of the world while within this meandering, shaded path system. With miles of landscaped play area, there is something for everyone to do here. Walking, in-line skating, biking, scootering, jogging, or just plain lounging under the trees is okay in this shaded bower. Extensive grassy areas studded with drinking fountains, benches, and tables are lit at night so that a moonlight stroll is also a possibility. Disposable scooper stands make it easy to pick up after dogs, keeping the grassy areas clean for the rest of us.

Move along to the path off Grand Canyon Drive to take advantage of the Healthline Workout Stations. My kids love to see if they are getting bigger and stronger at these exercise areas. All in all, this is a great place to picnic, spend the day, or just bring a blanket and read a book in the shade while the little one sleeps. The disc golf course is off Red Hills Road and Apple Drive.

Las Vegas Flyfishing (all ages)
7520 Washington Avenue, Suite 140; (702) 838–6669. Weekdays 10:00 A.M.–6:00 P.M., Saturday 9:00 A.M.–5:00 P.M.

A complete shop of fly-fishing fun including apparel, tying supplies, rods and reels, waders, and the men who stand behind them. Ask about guided trips and classes.

Las Vegas Royals Extreme Hockey (all ages)
Venue varies; (702) 278–2711. $.

Families can catch hard-hitting, rugged hockey (part of the USA Hockey Elite Division) on Friday and Saturday nights from November through March. Facilities in transition: keep checking in to get updates on a November 2005 reopening.

Las Vegas Art Museum (all ages)
9600 West Sahara Avenue; (702) 360–8000. Tuesday through Saturday 10:00 A.M.–5:00 P.M., Sunday 1:00–5:00 P.M.; closed Monday. $, under age 12 free.

This small but worthy museum concentrates on fostering the great artists of the twentieth and twenty-first centuries. The museum has featured Marc Chagall, Salvador Dali, and more recently Dale Chihuly, with his collection of spectacular colored-glass works. Chihuly's work can always be seen in the lobby of the Bellagio, in a garden of luminous flowers that grows from the ceiling. Permanent pieces include some of Las Vegas's internationally recognized local artists. Regular showings also include up-and-coming artists whose work is exhibited by juried selection.

Farmers' **Markets**

Arts and crafts mix with homemade jams, popcorn, chewy breads, handmade crafts, and fresh produce from California, Utah, Arizona, and Colorado at these weekly markets.

Expect more booths during prime harvesting seasons, although you're always sure to find something of interest.

- Peccole Ranch, Village Square Shopping Center. Sunday 9:00 A.M.– 1:00 P.M.
- Bruce Trent Park, Rampart Boulevard and Vegas Drive; (702) 869–2877; www.lasvegasfarmersmarket.com. Wednesday 4:00–8:00 P.M. (no market in January).
- Colonnade Shopping Plaza, 8878 South Eastern at Pebble. Saturday 9:00 A.M.–1:00 P.M.
- Boulder City Bicentennial Park. Thursday 9:00 A.M.–1:00 P.M.
- Water Street, downtown Henderson; (702) 565–2181. Thursday 3:00–7:00 P.M. November through March, 4:00–8:00 P.M. April through October.

Clark County Adventurers (age appropriateness varies)
2601 East Sunset Road; (702) 455–8121. Some excursions have fees.

This group just likes to get out. Join fellow adventurers for day hikes and weekend outings throughout the year. Call the information line for upcoming events.

Where to Eat

Danielle's Chocolates and Ice Cream.
Sahara Town Plaza, 6394 West Sahara Avenue; (702) 259–7616. Seagull Park Plaza, 4840 East Bonanza Road, #1; (702) 362–3983. Daily 10:00 A.M.–9:00 P.M., until 11:00 P.M. Friday and Saturday. The family that owns Danielle's has been making hand-dipped chocolates since before their ancestors moved from England. The homemade ice creams, added as a hot-weather refresher, come in a variety of unique flavors, including brownie chip and strawberry rhubarb. Old-fashioned jet stream sodas bring back grandma's youth when both she and the sodas were sweet and tangy. The cup of sparkling water on the side lets you fizz the drink up to your personal liking. If you prefer, try the raspberry cremo, a shake made of fresh raspberry and vanilla ice creams blended together and topped with another scoop of raspberry ice cream.

The glass display case is filled with mouth-watering chocolates and candies. In addition to the normal varieties, you will also find unusual candies like hoarhound drops, a hard, toffeelike frontier candy dusted with white powder; and white-chocolate popcorn, a sweet and salty treat laced with colored syrup. $

Diamond China Restaurant. 3909 West Sahara Avenue; (702) 873–6977. Daily 11:00 A.M.–5:00 A.M., until 4:00 A.M. on Sunday. After a late-night movie fest or on your way home late from an adventure, this is the place to fill the tummy before heading off to bed. It is also good enough for a quick school-night dinner. $–$$

Gandhi. 4080 Paradise Road at Flamingo; (702) 734–0094 or 734–3444. Daily 11:30 A.M.–10:00 P.M. If you have vegetarians in the crew, it is often difficult to find a place where you can all eat. This is such a place, serving Indian cuisine like deep-fried vegetable fritters, *matter paneer,* spicy cottage cheese and peas, and vegetable curries. Nonvegetarians also find an assortment of goodies, including tandoori, chicken, and shrimp. The buffet-style servings make it easy to encourage kids to try something new without breaking the budget or going home hungry because of an unlucky choice. $$

Jamms. 1029 South Rainbow Boulevard; (702) 877–0749. Daily 7:00 A.M.–3:30 P.M. Repeatedly voted among the best breakfasts and coffee shops in town; locals come to enjoy each other as much as the food. $

King & I II. 2904 Lake East Drive, The Lakes; (702) 256–1568. Daily 11:00 A.M.–9:30 P.M., Friday and Saturday, 11:00 A.M.–10:00 P.M., Sunday 3:00–9:00 P.M. A local favorite for Thai food, this reasonably priced restaurant has a steadfast and loyal clientele. Thai food can be hot, however, so make sure that you ask, and order at least some dishes that are not highly spiced so that the kids can eat, too. $–$$

Lindo Michoacan. 2655 East Desert Inn Road; (702) 735–6828. Daily 11:00 A.M.–11:00 P.M., Saturday and Sunday open at 9:00 A.M. Ever since my husband took my son to Baja, they have been on a quest for the perfect

flan. Go to this place for soup, flan, and a cheap eat that is wholly satisfying. $–$$

Metro Pizza. 4001 South Decatur Boulevard; (702) 362–7896; 1395 East Tropicana Avenue; (702) 736–1955; www.metropizza.com. Daily 11:00 A.M.–10:00 P.M. Not the cheapest pizza around, but regularly cited as one of the best, Metro is the pizza child of two cousins who have created a slew of pizzerias. Kids love the big ball of pizza dough that keeps them entertained while waiting for the food. Parents love the salads, particularly the Tuscan salad with pears, glazed walnuts, and blue cheese. The garlic may be a little heavy, but if it's all in the family, who cares? Bring your own parsley, however, if you are meeting friends, to ensure that you keep them. We can't recommend everything on the menu, because we haven't tried everything. But we're working on it and will let you know if we find something sub par. They're friendly here, too. Take advantage of the Calendar of Savings with daily specials, including free bread days, free fries, free kid's pizza with adult purchase, or, our favorite, free cannoli with any dine-in meal. Download the calendar from the Web site or pick it up at the store. $–$$

Photos & Flowers Garden Cafe. 3818 Meadows Lane; (702) 258–1554. Weekdays 7:30 a.m.–3:00 p.m., until 4:00 p.m. on Friday, Saturday 8:00 a.m.–3:00 p.m. Okay, we admit it, for lunch this is kind of a "girl" place. The sandwiches, like the curried egg salad I love, are a little too froufrou for my boys. They're happy with the smoothies and soups, but really prefer coming for breakfast (served all day on weekends) when there are more macho choices like the tortilla omelette. $

Yolie's Brazilian Steakhouse. 3900 Paradise Road; (702) 794–0700. Daily 5:00–11:00 P.M., weekdays for lunch 10:00 A.M.–2:30 P.M.

At a certain point in a child's life, the appetite begins to seem insatiable, and meat is the order of the day to ensure that growing bones and muscle have enough to grow *on*. If your kids are at that stage and enjoy food that is a little different, try this steak house that specializes in spicy Brazilian-herbed barbecue carved tableside. Best of all for those insatiable appetites, it's an all-you-can eat kind of place. $$

Where to Stay

Suncoast Hotel and Casino. 9090 Alta Drive; (702) 636–7111 or (877) 677–7111; www.suncoastcasino.com. Many families swear by this Mediterranean-themed resort with 400 oversized rooms and suites in the heart of Summerlin surrounded by a golf course. Families will enjoy the sixty-four-lane bowling center, 160-seat movie theater, and the state-of-the-art fitness center that overlooks the swimming pool. Then don't forget to take in Red Rock Canyon. $$

J. W. Marriott Las Vegas Resort, Spa, and Golf

221 North Rampart Boulevard; (702) 869–7725 or (877) 869–8777. $$$–$$$$

This beautiful, high-end resort offers a family the chance to be twenty minutes from either the Strip or the spectacular Red Rock Canyon. Surrounded by golf courses and trickling streams, one feels safe and relaxed here. The large pool area doesn't have the fancy slides, but it is surrounded by large grassy lawns instead of crowded cement "lounge areas." The small streams and water features beg exploring by curious kids and the casino is completely separate from the rest of this quiet jewel, so families can feel free to move around without the usual clanging, banging, and crowds.

Carmel Room (all ages)
(702) 507–5955. Sunday through Thursday, 5:00–10:00 P.M., Friday and Saturday, 5:00–10:30 P.M. $$–$$$.

Enjoy continental cuisine in a luxurious setting. This resort makes it easy to find time for a romantic dinner for two.

Ceres (all ages)
(702) 869–7381. Daily 6:00 A.M.–10:00 P.M. $.

On the Strip, this would be a very high-end setting, with the large room's glass walls overlooking spectacular water features. The food is wonderful and the prices are a boon to a traveling family's pocketbook. Or a local's, for that matter.

J. C. Wooloughan's Irish Pub (all ages)

221 North Rampart Boulevard; (702) 869–7725. Daily 11:00 A.M.–1:00 A.M., Friday and Saturday until 2:00 A.M., Saturday and Sunday opens at 10:00 A.M. $–$$.

Authentic Irish food that is good for your soul includes an all-day Irish breakfast as well as hearty meat pies and stews that will warm you all the way to your heart.

Rampart Buffet (all ages)

(702) 507–5944. Daily except Thursday 11:00 A.M.–3:00 P.M., Thursday until 2:30 P.M.; reopens for dinner 4:00–9:30 P.M. $–$$.

This award-winning buffet offers nightly specials: Tuesday is T-bone steak, Thursday is seafood.

Spiedini Ristorante (all ages)

(702) 869–8500. Daily 5:00–10:00 P.M. $$–$$$.

Another spectacular entry by noted chef Gustav Mauler, this restaurant's delightfully modern decor is complemented by equally entertaining and wholesome soups, pastas, and spit-roasted meats.

Red Rock Canyon National Conservation Area

10 miles east of Las Vegas off Charleston Boulevard; (702) 363–1921; www.redrock canyon.blm.gov. Open from dawn until dusk year-round.

This place is so close to the Strip, one might almost trip over it, yet it seems as far away as a *Star Trek* voyage. Red Rock is one of the most beautiful desert landscapes in the Southwest. (We're not biased, of course.) The striking red Aztec sandstone combines with frosty gold limestone to create a multilayered rainbow of rock formations that range in color from pink to yellow to soft purple. Numerous springs and the protective shelter of the nearby Spring Mountains make this area surprisingly lush. Rock climbers, photographers, and even movie producers find this conservation area hard to resist. There is virtually something for everyone here. The Children's Discovery Trail features rock shelters, petroglyphs, and Native American roasting pits.

Stop by the visitor center to see the beautiful landscape photography that Red Rock has inspired, then pick up a map. Drive the one-way scenic loop, or take one of the numerous turnoffs

to stretch your legs and breathe the clean desert air. Native wildlife includes desert tortoises, wild horses, wild burros, coyotes, jackrabbits, roadrunners, hawks, and more. Those "ants" on the face of the cliffs are rock climbers. The cost is $5.00 per vehicle, $2.00 per bicycle, $20.00 yearly pass. $65 golden eagle pass or $10 over-62 golden age pass gets you into all national conservation areas, parks, and monuments.

Desert Tortoise Habitat (all ages)
Immediately behind the visitor center. Free.

Take a minute to look inside the 3-foot-high fence to spot a desert tortoise. Endangered through habitat destruction and the subsequent change in the desert environment caused by our increased population, these creatures take up to ten years to reach the size of a human hand. Before then, they are easy prey to those glossy black crows that circle above and appreciate our city dump sites as permanent feeding opportunities. At the far end of the habitat, the hatchlings are protected within a mesh cage from becoming crow dessert. Although the tortoises are hard to spot, patience is usually rewarded here. If you can't see anything, ask a ranger to help you out.

Adults' shells protect them from predators, but not from a four-wheel drive running over their bodies. When doing any four-wheeling, it is especially important to stay on the roads. Before you know it, the heavy tires of your vehicle may crush one of these shy creatures, which might otherwise have had eighty years more to live.

Adopt-a-Tortoise (all ages)
(702) 383–TORT. Free.

Tortoises make great pets for children because they are very easy to take care of and can be left for extended periods of time without danger. The Adopt-a-Tortoise program sends volunteers out to your house to tortoise-proof the property, answer questions, and help families get set up for their new pet. They are also available over the long haul, in case a question arises in five or ten years. Tortoises are fun to watch, hard to hurt, and require little care. They do, however, need a shady area and a way to get underground.

Spring Mountain Ranch State Park (all ages)
State Route 159 between Blue Diamond and Red Rock Canyon; (702) 875–4141. 8:00 A.M.–4:00 P.M.; house tours 10:00 A.M.–4:00 P.M. $ per car.

This 528-acre ranch was built along the old Spanish Trail and was one of the earliest settlements in the region. Once you've been there you'll see why it has since been owned by the rich and powerful. The dramatic red cliffs rise above a natural spring that feeds the grassy meadows. At one time it was owned by Vera Krupp, owner of the Krupp Diamond, which became world renowned when Richard Burton bought it for Elizabeth Taylor. Later the ranch was purchased by Howard Hughes, who used it as an executive retreat for visiting dignitaries and employees.

The ranch is open to the general public for picnicking. Entertainment, including Summer Outdoor Theater (702–594–PLAY), the Living History Program, and the Jazz Under the Stars Series (702–228–3780, www.mspjazz.com) are held throughout the summer.

Birding for All

Our family loves the places birds love, with running or standing water, lush vegetation, interesting scenery, or remote locations. There are birds literally everywhere, and birding has become an excuse to hike the backcountry, go to new territory, explore a hidden canyon, or rest in the shade as quietly as possible. Although birding may seem like a lone endeavor, in fact it can be quite social. Meet new friends, help save the environment, find out about exotic destinations, and bond with like-minded naturalists within these bird-watching clubs and organizations.

The Red Rock Audubon Society. P.O. Box 96691, Las Vegas, Nevada 89193; (702) 390–9890; www.audubon.org. Meetings are held the third Wednesday of each month from September through May at 7:30 P.M. at the Nevada Power Building, 6226 West Sahara, third floor, room 3. Park by the drive-up windows; obtain a guest badge at the information gate on the first floor.

The Las Vegas chapter of the National Audubon Society's mission is to "protect, restore, and improve the natural landscape, focusing on birds and other wildlife, and to educate the public about our unique Nevada environment." The society offers free field trips, hosts guest lecturers, and helps with annual bird counts. The social hour begins at 7:00 P.M.

Cornell Laboratory of Ornithology. 159 Sapsucker Woods Road, Ithaca, New York 14850-1999; (800) 843–2473 or (607) 254–2473; www.birds.cornell .edu. Your family can become citizen scientists under the direction of the Cornell Lab of Ornithology. Help with annual bird counts, build birdhouses to attract local and exotic birds, or visit the Nest Box Cam live video at www.birds.cornell.edu/birdhouse. Watch as birds nest and lay their eggs, hatchlings emerge, and hungry mouths are fed inside nest boxes across North America.

The site also offers a bird of the week, bird feeding tips, audio guides, slides, and sound recordings of birds and natural habitats. The sound of the week is fascinating; we could spend hours going through this site. What a hoot when the kids begin to recognize birds by their calls in our own natural habitats!

Birdsource. www.birdsource.org. A cooperative venture between Cornell and the Audubon Society, this is the site to choose when you are ready to take action. With various activities throughout the year, families can establish bird feeders, build a birdhouse, find out about local sightings, track bird migrations, and participate in the annual Great Backyard Bird Count. Go to the GBBC results and click on Nevada to find out which towns are participating and to see a list of birds seen here during the last bird count. Find out about our local birds, then see how your keen eyes can help monitor them.

Wild Birds Unlimited. www.wbu.com. This Web site's Junior Naturalist Program provides parents with the tools to make birding easy for younger watchers. It also provides equipment that may be hard to find including birdhouses, bird feeders, and other birding paraphernalia, as well as information and resources for certifying your yard as a Backyard Wildlife Habitat (www.nwf .org/habitats/index).

Nellis and Sunrise Mountain Area

Heading north on I–15, one quickly runs out of town. But take the time to vicariously enjoy the heart-thumping daring of the Las Vegas Motor Speedway or the Blue Thunderbirds when they are home, or quickly find yourself in a remote backcountry setting. Follow Lake Mead Boulevard/NV 147 east to the Rainbow Gardens Geological Preserve, a miniature version of the Grand Canyon, with stunning precipices and colorful rock caverns. (High-clearance vehicles are recommended.) Continue south along Lake Mead (NV 166/Northshore Road) to enjoy a scenic tour of the lake, then exit onto U.S. 93 within shouting distance of Hoover Dam (east) and Boulder City (west).

Planetarium (all ages)
Community College of Southern Nevada, 3200 East Cheyenne Avenue; (702) 651–4759 or 651–4505. Shows Friday at 6:30 and 7:30 P.M., Saturday at 3:30 and 7:30 P.M. (no late admissions). $.

Stargaze with the pros at these rotating shows and live presentations that start *on time!* When weather permits, the college telescopes are moved outside for real-life celestial viewing. Very small children might not be able to grasp the whole concept, but you'll be surprised how soon they catch on. If your child is afraid of the dark, you might wait until he or she gets a little older.

U.S. Air Force Thunderbirds Tour (all ages)
Nellis Air Force Base, Craig Road and Las Vegas Boulevard North; (702) 652–2754; www.nellis.af.mil. Tuesday and Thursday 2:00 P.M. Free. Reservations required.

Nellis Air Force Base is our local Top Gun training ground. Park along the freeway to watch planes land and take off or just fly overhead. For the **free** ninety-minute tour, which can get crowded, arrive a half hour early. After a ten-minute video, you'll tour a museum that

Summer **Desert** Safety

Summer desert travel comes with a string of cautions. With common sense, desert hiking can be very safe. Without it, you are courting disaster. Summer heat here can reach over 120 degrees Fahrenheit. Inside canyons, the temperature can exceed 140 degrees. Needless to say, even at temperatures that barely exceed 100 degrees, children can become dehydrated or overexerted. Watch for warning signs of heat exhaustion such as headaches, flushed skin, disorientation, or nausea.

Hiking

- Carry adequate drinking water, one gallon per person per day.

- Let someone know where you are going and when you plan to return. If something happens, someone will come looking for you and will know what area to look in.

- Wear hats to keep the sun off the top of your heads. If the temperature falls rapidly, the hats will help keep body temperatures regulated.

- Wear white or light colors. Black absorbs heat like crazy.

- Wear lightweight, loose clothing to protect your skin from the sun better than any sunscreen.

- If you have small children, ask which hikes are appropriate and how long an average person should take to get back to the trailhead. Plan on twice that time.

- Get small backpacks for all adventurers—as soon as they are out of the pack on your back. Fill accordingly and make sure each person carries water, a few snacks, and perhaps a miniature toy.

- If you can, freeze your bottle of water. It will melt throughout the day and keep the water refreshingly cold.

- Seasonal weather changes quickly. We've been sweating under the noonday sun to find ourselves freezing in a spring snowstorm by dusk. Be equipped for anything.

- And *drink* your water! It doesn't do you any good in the bottle.

Driving

- While driving, carry adequate drinking water, one gallon per person per day.

- Top off your gas tank. Services in the desert can be few and far between.

Even side trips off the main roads within the Mojave Desert may easily take you one to two hours from services.

- If you get into trouble, don't leave your car. Distances in the desert are deceptive. Waiting in (or in the shade under) a hot car might be uncomfortable, but you brought your water, right? Eventually someone will drive by. This is a desert, but it is not deserted.

- Heed air-conditioner turnoff warning signs. An overheated car is no picnic.

Now that you are prepared, have a great time and use common sense!

covers the Thunderbirds' history and collected memorabilia, and, safety permitting, the hangar. Between March and November the Thunderbirds are usually on the road.

From December through February you might be lucky enough to watch the Thunderbirds practicing their stuff. But even when they are on tour, this training facility is very active. To get a close-up glimpse of top-notch pilots flying F-15Cs, F-16s, F-15Es, A-10s, and HH-60 Pavehawk helicopters, a special **free** viewing area is open to the public. Pull off Las Vegas Boulevard North directly across from the Michael O'Callahan Federal Hospital to watch these pilots practice taking off, landing, and doing their precisely timed formations. Most of the activity takes place between sunrise and sunset, but there are occasional night flights.

Las Vegas Motor Speedway (all ages)

7000 Las Vegas Boulevard North; (702) 644–4444 or (800) 644–4444; www.lvms.com. Prices, times, and events vary.

What was a former dump was converted to a "diamond in the desert" and one of the top performance destinations in the country, at times holding 250,000 spectators. With twenty-two tracks and a dizzying array of races, including the prestigious NASCAR Nextel Cup, the NASCAR -sanctioned speedway has something for all race car enthusiasts. Fans can attend some of the top races in the country as well as weekly events that run the gamut of stock car spectator sports. Visitors cram the stadium for notable races like the NASCAR Busch Series, NASCAR Nextel West Series, and NASCAR Featherlite Southwest Series. Ticket prices for these events can exceed $100, but from March until November, weekly racing series are very pocketbook friendly, with tickets going for $10 or less. There is variety here as well, including everything from monster trucks and pulling competitions to motocross racing and freestyle. Kids love the World Mini event, the Air MX freestyle Motocross, the Penzoil World of Outlaws, National Hot Rod Association, and, of course, drag racing.

Las Vegas Motor Speedway Tour (all ages)

7000 Las Vegas Boulevard North; (702) 644–4444; www.lvms.com. Tours Monday through Saturday 9:00 A.M.–4:00 P.M., Sunday 11:00 A.M.–4:00 P.M. $, ages 3 and under free.

Tours start at the gift shop and move on to the fourth floor VIP suite for a sweeping view of the 1.5-mile speedway. Then visitors take a tram to the dirt track, drive strip, ⅜-mile Bullring, and the infield.

Carroll Shelby Factory and Museum Tour (all ages)

Shelby American World Headquarters, 6755 Speedway Boulevard; (702) 643–3000; www.shelbyamerican.com; www.carrollshelby.com. Weekdays 8:00 A.M.–4:00 P.M. Tours begin at 10:30 A.M. Free.

Carroll Shelby, race car driver and cool car designer, made his name in the '60s on the track and as a designer with the Ford Cobra and Shelby Mustang series cars. Called "the Farmer Boy" because of his trademark coveralls, his driving and his ability to design cars stirred race fans' imaginations and would-be drivers' souls. This museum features thirty-five years' worth of performance cars, including those that the factory is currently making in its 100,000-square-foot manufacturing facility. You'll also see some of the original designs, including Shelby Mustangs and Cobras.

Bandoleros (ages 9 and up)

600 Racing West; (702) 643–4386. Races are scheduled on the Bullring of the Las Vegas Motor Speedway. Spectator prices for the Bandoleros races are $.

Kids ages nine and up, with indulgent parents, can purchase and race Briggs and Stratton cars perfect for their small size, although adults can fit in them, and do. The private cars can go up to 55 mph and can be entered every other week in the Bullring races at the speedway. Kids go through a training program that qualifies them to race other kids in the same rookie program. After ten races, they can move up to the next level. Of course, we can all watch, which might be a more sound choice.

Dansey's Indoor Race Track (all ages)

741 North Nellis Boulevard; (702) 453–7223. Daily 10:00 A.M.–9:00 P.M. $ all day pass. Races for hobbyists of all ages are held at 7:00 P.M. Tuesday and Friday and 5:00 P.M. Sunday. $ per race.

This is the area's only indoor racetrack for radio-controlled cars. Watch the exciting races for free, but don't expect to stay uninvolved for long. Most people's fingers soon itch for their own radio controls. With 3,000 square feet of track, this can keep car enthusiasts busy for hours. Bring your own car or rent for $15.00 per hour, $8.00 per half hour.

Game Crazy (all ages)

5400 North Nellis Boulevard; (702) 437–9902. Monday through Saturday 10:00 A.M.–9:00 P.M., Sunday 11:00 A.M.–6:00 P.M.

Buy, sell, and trade games, collectibles, and cards at this second-hand gaming store.

The Sky's the Limit Guided Hikes and Rock Climbing (all ages)

(702) 363–4533 or (800) 733–7597. $$$–$$$$$ per person.

The Sky's the Limit provides customized soft-adventure hikes, including the Hike of the Day. Using professional guides trained in interpretive hikes, these off-the-beaten-trail adventures are educational and enjoyable. Discover Climbing is a half-day experiential-based climbing program that lets novices try their hand at climbing. Because these are customized tours, the programs can be adapted to your family's skill and age levels. For the more adventurous, or for a special family reunion bonding experience, the Sky Course lets groups of eight or more tackle more advanced climbing. This course includes zip lines, an aerial obstacle course, and more, with an emphasis on safety.

Owner Randal Grandstaff, who accompanied David Breshears to the top of Mt. Everest, designs all of the courses himself and just might be your personal guide. His company also conducts private guided programs for serious rock climbers. Adventurous families are more and more common, he says, and often book his company for a week at a crack, avoiding the city lights altogether.

Escape Mountain Bike Adventures (ages 10 and up)

8221 West Charleston Boulevard, Suite 101; (702) 596–2953; www.escapeadventures.com. $$$$ and up per person.

Escape Mountain Bike Adventures offers half-day and full-day hiking and mountain biking tours within the Red Rock Recreational area. Riders use 24-inch or larger mountain bikes. The cost includes transportation to and from the Strip, bicycle rental, safety gear, and a guide. Mountain bikers either cycle around the Red Rock Scenic Loop or tour Cottonwood Valley. Hikers can explore the White Rock/Willow Springs loop, Calico Hills, or the Icebox Canyon waterfalls. Tours can be geared for beginner or advanced trails or a combination of both.

Sagebrush Horse Ranch and Tours (ages 5 and up)

12000 West End Road; (702) 645–9422; www.sagebrush-ranch.com. $$–$$$ per person; horse camp $$$ per day, $$$$$ per week.

Head out to the "Ranch with all the Pretty Horses," nestled into the toes of the Spring Mountain Range, to experience children's horse camps, breakfast and sunset trail rides, and customized horseback tours into the Spring Mountains. The ranch, annexed to the Red Rock Canyon National Conservation Area, supports a herd of sixty-five horses, offering riders of all ages and abilities an appropriate mount. Parents can (and often do) sign up for camp along with their children to get a real taste of camp life. The camp trains kids in all aspects of horsemanship, including catching, grooming, saddling, and proper riding.

For More Information

Las Vegas Chamber of Commerce. 3720 Howard Hughes Parkway, Las Vegas, Nevada 89109-0320; (702) 735–1616. The chamber is accessible via e-mail at info@lvchamber.com or on the Web at www.lvchamber.com.

Las Vegas Convention and Visitors Bureau. 3150 Paradise Road, Las Vegas, Nevada 89109; (702) 892–7575 or (800) 332–5333.

Las Vegas Welcome Center. 3333 South Maryland Parkway, Suite 11, Las Vegas, Nevada 89109; (702) 451–7648 or (800) 821–6624.

A **Small** Gift

There's no place like home. No matter how wonderful a vacation is, there is nothing as magical as baking cookies with the kids. Find a great Las Vegas cookie cutter, then try my grandmother's famous sugar cookie recipe.

No-Stick Sugar Cookies

> 4 cups flour
> 2 cups sugar
> 1 cup butter
> 4 beaten eggs
> 1 tsp. baking soda mixed with 1 tbsp. hot coffee
> 2 tsp. vanilla

Mix flour, sugar, and butter to a piecrust consistency; make a well and add beaten eggs, baking soda, and vanilla. The dough can be rolled out on a floured surface as soon as you mix it. Roll dough about ¼-inch thick for chewy cookies, thinner for crispy. Flour the rolling pin to reduce sticking even more. Bake cookies at 375° F about ten minutes, or until golden. Sprinkle, paint, frost, or eat.

Tip: Instead of trying to transfer the cut cookies onto the sheet, roll and cut out the cookies on parchment paper, peel the excess from between the cookies, then transfer the whole sheet onto the baking tray. It's a lot less frustrating that way.

Appendix

Best Community Parks

Acacia Park. 50 Casa Del Fuego (Southwest of U.S. Highway 95 and Lake Mead Drive). This park hopes to promote desert-conscious landscaping and offers a water-play feature, a back-yard garden demonstration area, an edible garden, an allergy-free garden, an animal habitat garden, a wetlands demonstration area, and a Mojave Desert demonstration area as well as play areas and a dog park.

Alexander Villas Park. 3620 Lincoln Road. The park contains a baseball field, basketball court, fitness course, picnic area, playground, and walking course. The spray pool is arguably the best part, however, especially in the summer heat.

Angel Park. West Cliff and Durango Road. Kids will love jumping on the spray turtles located in the center of the park.

Buffalo Park. Buffalo Drive and Oakey Boulevard. Explore forty-five acres of sports amenities, five lighted football fields, picnic areas, walking paths, and a water play area.

Bunker Hill. Alexander Road and Tenaya Way. Great open space is studded with a skate park and bocce courts.

Centennial Hills Park. Elkhorn Road and Buffalo Drive. One of the city's newest and the largest park, the playground has equipment themed around bugs. With 120 acres to play with, the park will sport twelve new sand volleyball courts, soccer fields, state-of-the-art picnic pavilions, and walking trails. Over the next few years, other amenities will be phased in including natural trails, a recreation center, an amphitheater, a library, picnic shelters, and more playgrounds.

Cheyenne Sports Complex. 3500 East Cheyenne Avenue. The only track and field in the North Las Vegas area, this park also features a lighted baseball field and football field, as well as a lighted tennis court.

Doc Romeo Park. 7400 Peak Drive (behind the Rainbow Library); (702) 229–2296. Older kids can get extreme at this thirty-acre sports complex that features eight baseball/softball fields and a 40,000-square-foot skate bowl with toys, bends, and curves galore. Up your skills at the Leisure Services Extreme Sports Unit events and classes. The skate park was used as the host location for the First VegasX Skate Event and Concert.

Durango Hills Park. 3521 North Durango Drive; Gowan Road and Durango Road. Older kids will love this ten-acre park with its skate park, roller-hockey rink, and basketball courts. The multi-use paths include a special one for pet lovers. Two playground areas include a tot lot and a larger play area for kids twelve and up. Jump into the community center pool to cool off during summer months.The park is used for classes and events put on by Extreme Adventure Sports. Call (702) 229–2296 for upcoming events.

Ed Fountain Park. Vegas Drive and Decatur Boulevard. This twenty-two-acre park hosts five lighted soccer fields, two basketball courts, a rock climbing wall, a playground, restrooms, and picnic areas.

Firefighters Memorial Park. Redwood Street and Oakey Boulevard. This fifteen-acre park across from Bonanza High School is our local homage to the firefighters and others who died on September 11, and the southern Nevada firefighters who gave their lives in the line of duty. Local firefighter and artist John Banks designed the centerpiece, a magnificent 23-foot bronze-and-granite sculpture called the *Fallen Firefighter's Monument,* which rests at one of the park's corners.

Garehime Heights Park. Gilmore Avenue and Campbell Drive. Beginning skateboarders will appreciate a skate park designed for them. Tennis and basketball courts are also in this ten-acre park.

Hayley Hendricks Park. 811 Ithaca Avenue (next to Brown Jr. High School); (702) 565–4264. This spacious multi-use park offers Henderson's first skate park, a tot-lot playground, lighted horseshoe courts, an equestrian trail, lighted tennis courts, covered and trellised picnic areas, and a spray park. Open 9:00 A.M. to 8:00 P.M. during the summer.

Huntridge Circle Park. Maryland Parkway and Charleston Boulevard. One of the city's classic parks, the renovation has kept the verdant shade trees while adding a fence and rock climbing. The park may include art, a playground, a water feature, a gazebo, and a community garden.

Mission Hills Park. 551 East Mission Hills Drive. Enjoy the spray park between 9:00 A.M. and 8:00 P.M. during the summer as well as tube slides, fabulous concrete pathways to learn how to ride a bike or in-line skate, and acres of green grass.

Patriot Park. Next to Parson Elementary School, this park is designed for little ones. It has a shaded tot lot and playground equipment and a spray-fountain water feature as well as bocce and basketball courts, a skate park, and walking paths for older siblings.

Paul Meyer Park. 4525 New Forest Drive. The park's facilities cover baseball and softball fields, a picnic area, a playground, tennis courts, and a walking course. The spray pool is perfect for cooling off after playing in the sun.

Pavilion Center Pool. 101 North Pavilion Center Drive. Open May through September. This state-of-the-art Olympic-size pool is used for swim meets and boasts some of the best summer pool parties in the valley.

Pioneer Park. Pioneer Way and Braswell Drive. This lush seventeen-acre park designed by the community features playgrounds, picnic areas, a jogging track, basketball and horseshoe courts, bocce ball, and plenty of open space.

Sunny Springs Park. Elk Horn and Buffalo Drive. They packed this nine-acre park with four basketball courts, two tennis courts, a water-play feature, a beginners' skate park, an area to play horseshoes, and a large playground as well as a picnic area.

W. Wayne Bunker Family Park. Alexander Road and Tenaya Way. A skate park, horseshoe pits, a jogging track, and barbecue grills make this a local favorite.

Winchester Park. 3130 South McLeod. This park has things to do for kids of all ages. The spray pool is there for the little ones and there is a skate park for the older kids. There is also a community center, fitness course, picnic area, playground, tennis court, and walking course.

Community Centers

The city and the county have come a long way toward providing the kind of community centers that link families and provide kids with a safe place to hang out. The larger centers offer a wide range of low-cost classes in the arts and athletics and build community spirit by presenting special events that draw local families for special days of fun.

Community centers usually have **free** or low-cost open play areas, including basketball courts, tennis courts, swimming pools, and racquetball courts. What an easygoing way to spend some quality time with the family, hitting a few balls with your elementary school child while your toddler plays on the nearby climbing structure or works on a new piece of art.

Over time, you will find that your time at a community center will also expand your circle of friends and acquaintances as you and the kids meet easy playmates and new neighbors. Out-of-town visitors can meet the real people who are making Nevada home. Not all community centers offer the same equipment. The list below shows what amenities are available at some of the local facilities. Relax and enjoy!

Cambridge Community Center. 3827 South Maryland Parkway (at Flamingo Road); (702) 455–7169. Monday through Friday 8:00 A.M.–6:00 P.M., Saturday 8:00 A.M.–4:00 P.M. **Free.** This facility includes a game room, arts and crafts area, gymnasium, video games, kitchen, table games, and more. Special programs have included **free** open recreational activities for children ages six and up, or younger if accompanied by an adult; multicultural workshops; the aquatic facility; field trips; youth leadership training; **free** hip-hop and Mexican Folklore dance classes; and Peace Week.

Charleston Heights Arts Center. 800 South Brush Street (1 block west of Decatur off Charleston); (702) 229–6383. This facility contains a 375-seat theater with a fully equipped 30'x35' proscenium stage, a 60'x150' ballroom, a conference room and a 20'x30' art gallery with an 11-foot ceiling and wood floor.

Chester A. Stupak Center. 300 West Boston Avenue; (702) 229–2488; www.ci.las-vegas.nv.us/stupak_community_center.htm. Monday through Friday 7:30 A.M.–8:30 P.M., Saturday 9:00 A.M.–4:00 P.M. **Free.** Here you'll find a weight room, a library, a computer lab, a preschool room, and a family resource room.

Chuck Minker Sports Complex. 275 North Mojave Road; (702) 229–6563; www.ci.las-vegas.nv. us/chuck_minker_sports_complex.htm. Monday through Friday 7:00 A.M.–9:30 P.M., Saturday 9:00 A.M.–5:00 P.M., Sunday 10:00 A.M.–4:00 P.M. **Free.** A gymnasium, eight racquetball courts, cardiovascular equipment, a sauna and Jacuzzi, two weight rooms, a multipurpose room, and a video games area are included in this center. Special programs include kickboxing aerobics.

Desert Breeze Community Center. 8275 Spring Mountain Road; (702) 455–8334. Monday through Friday 8:00 A.M.–9:00 P.M., Saturday 9:00 A.M.–5:00 P.M. **Free.** This facility has a play pool and gymnasium.

Doolittle Community Center. 1950 North J Street; (702) 229–6374; www.ci.las-vegas.nv.us/doolittle_community_center.htm. Monday through Saturday 9:00 A.M.–4:00 P.M. **Free.** The Doolittle Center has a fitness room, a full basketball court, a game room, a gymnasium, and kitchen facilities. Special programs include a youth basketball camp during summer break and a yearly community block party.

Gibson Community Center. 3900 West Washington Avenue; (702) 229–5096; www.ci.las-vegas.nv.us/gibson_leisure_service_center.htm. Monday through Friday 2:15–9:00 P.M., Saturday 9:00 A.M.–4:00 P.M. **Free.** Facilities include a gymnasium and activities room.

Mirabelli Community Center. 6200 Elton Avenue; (702) 229–6359; www.ci.las-vegas.nv.us/mirabelli_community_center.htm. Monday through Friday 9:00 A.M.–7:00 P.M., Saturday 11:00 A.M.–3:00 P.M. **Free.** Situated near a park, this facility includes a kitchen, Talented Tykes room, a game room, a weight room, and a half gym.

Northwest Community Center. 6841 West Lone Mountain Road; (702) 229–4794; www.ci.las-vegas.nv.us/northwest_track_break_center.htm. Monday through Friday 7:00 A.M.–6:00 P.M. **Free.** A multipurpose room, a kitchen, playground equipment, and computers are available here. Past special events include **free** social/games nights and a Mother's Day pancake breakfast for $2.00 per person.

Orr Community Center. 1520 East Katie Avenue; (702) 455–7196. Monday through Friday 10:00 A.M.–7:00 P.M.; Saturday 8:30 A.M.–5:30 P.M. **Free.** The Orr Community Center has a soccer field, arts and crafts area, pool table, Foosball, video games, and a basketball court appropriate for ages four and up.

Paradise Community Center. 4770 South Harrison Drive; (702) 455–7513. Monday through Thursday 7:00 A.M.–8:00 P.M., Friday until 6:30 P.M., Saturday 9:00 A.M.–4:00 P.M. **Free.** Nestled in a park, you'll find a gymnasium, tennis courts, a craft area, and a large play pool with lap lanes.

Parkdale Community Center. 3200 Ferndale Street; (702) 455–7515. Monday through Friday 8:00 A.M.–5:00 P.M. **Free.** Facilities include a game room, arts and crafts area, dance floor, play pool, and computer lab. The center offers a **free** open recreation program for school-aged children 3:00–6:00 P.M. weekdays.

Rafael Rivera Community Center. 2900 East Stewart Avenue; (702) 229–4600; www.ci.las-vegas.nv.us/rafael_rivera_community_center.htm. Monday through Friday 9:00 A.M.–8:00 P.M., Saturday 9:00 A.M.–5:00 P.M. **Free.** This center has a game room, a multipurpose room, a kitchen, a soccer field, a baseball field, tennis courts, a children's playground, and a picnic area.

Reed Whipple Cultural Center. 821 Las Vegas Boulevard North; (702) 229–6211. Times and prices vary with performances. This facility contains a 300-seat multipurpose theater with state-of-the-art lighting and sound and a 45'x24' proscenium stage; an intimate eighty-seat studio theater; a 40'x60' dance studio with a specially designed resilient floor of particular benefit to dancers; meeting rooms, conference rooms, arts and crafts room, pottery studio, and a 35'x37' art gallery with a 9-foot ceiling and carpeted floor. It is the headquarters for the Rainbow Company, the Las Vegas Civic Ballet, the Las Vegas Civic Symphony, the Las Vegas Youth Orchestras, and the Las Vegas Symphonic Band. This facility offers **free** admission to all gallery exhibits.

West Las Vegas Arts Center. 947 West Lake Mead Boulevard; (702) 229–4800. Monday and Thursday 1:00–9:00 P.M., Tuesday and Wednesday 10:00 A.M.–9:00 P.M., Friday 10:00 A.M.–6:00 P.M., Saturday 9:00 A.M.–5:00 P.M.

Whitney Community Center. 5700 Missouri Avenue; (702) 455–7576. Monday through Friday 8:30 A.M.–9:00 P.M., Saturday 9:00 A.M.–3:00 P.M. **Free.** This facility offers table tennis, basketball courts, a kitchen, a music center, and an arts and crafts area. Special programs include a children's community garden and a drama program.

Winchester Community Center. 3130 South McLeod Drive; (702) 455–7340. This facility offers an outdoor basketball court, a theater and art gallery, walking trails, picnic areas, and classes.

Community Pools

What better place to hang out during the summer than a great community pool where the cost is low, the excitement high, and the chance to meet a friend nearly 100 percent? Exciting community pools have followed the commercial pools' lead, adding slides, sprays, beach entries, and other cool water features. Grab a pick-a-nick basket, some sunscreen, and a favorite book for a lazy day of watery relaxation at the best community pools in the Valley.

The pools are scattered throughout the Valley. The county has a special promotional swim punch card; once you have swum at all of the county pools, you win a **free** all-day swim pass.

Baker Swimming Pool. 1100 East St. Louis Avenue; (702) 229–6395. June through August, Monday through Friday 1:00–4:45 P.M. This pool has a diving board, playground water structure, a slide, and a shaded deck area. The adjacent park has a picnic area with barbecue facilities.

Black Mountain Aquatic Complex. 599 Greenway Road (Greenway and Horizon); (702) 565–2880. Summer only Monday through Saturday 11:00 A.M.–6:00 P.M., Friday until 8:00 P.M., Sunday noon–5:00 P.M. $, under 3 **free.** When this aquatic complex opened, it was the talk of the town. The beach-entry pool was perfect for families with toddlers to teens. A three-loop slide, play structures, water jets, a swing, a raindrop waterfall, and plenty of surrounding park greenery meant that moms would pack a cooler and have the day's agenda planned. Call a few friends and you have a summer party without the hosting hassle and with plenty of fun for everyone. The adjacent recreation center gives kids an alternative to spending the whole day in the water. Lap lanes, showers, and a concession stand complete the complex.

BMI Outdoor Swimming Pool. 107 West Basic Road; (702) 565–2168. Summer only; hours vary. $, under 3 **free.** This community pool doesn't have all of the fancy-dancy play equipment, but many of the newer pools also don't include diving boards, which my kids love.

Cambridge Community Pool. 3827 South Maryland Parkway (Maryland and Flamingo); (702) 455–7169. Open May through September, 11:00 A.M.–7:00 P.M. daily during peak summer season. $. Enjoy this beach-entry pool with a 40-foot water slide and interactive play equipment, including water fountains, squirt guns, and a mushroom spray for little ones. There are also a concession stand and picnic tables, shaded umbrella tables, a large deck, and, hopefully, deck chairs. The cost is 50 cents for those who don't meet the height requirement for the slide.

Desert Breeze Community Pool. 8275 Spring Mountain Road (Spring Mountain and Durango); (702) 455–8334. $, under 3 **free.** Desert Breeze has one of the larger pool complexes in the city. The outdoor pool has one enclosed slide and one open-top slide for kids 48 inches and taller. The smaller play center includes water fountains, and water wheels that let kids turn flumes on and off. A concession stand offers prepackaged foods, picnic tables, and a surrounding park.

The indoor competitive pool is 50 meters by 25 yards. Designed like Olympic competition pools, it's geared toward attracting national level competition. Special programs at the pool include the Itty Bitty Water Ballet, dive-in movies, family night, open swim on weekends, and birthday swim parties.

Lorin L. Williams Municipal Indoor Swimming Pool. 500 North Palo Verde Drive; (702) 565–2123. Daily in summer 11:00 A.M.–5:00 P.M. $, under 3 **free.** The indoor pool is open year-round for swimming or diving. The outdoor aquatic complex opens in the summer.

Municipal Pool. 431 East Bonanza Road. Monday through Friday 8:00 A.M.–9:00 P.M., Saturday 9:00 A.M.–6:00 P.M., Sunday 11:00 A.M.–5:00 P.M. $, 3 and under **free.** A feast of programs throughout the year includes synchronized swimming, diving classes, learn-to-swim classes for all ages, preschool swimming, and lifeguard training. One of the few year-round pools, during the summer the roof opens for a sky view. Outside is a picnic and special events area.

Parkdale and Paradise Community Pools. Parkdale: 3200 Ferndale Street; (702) 455–7515. Paradise: 4770 South Harrison Drive; (702) 455–7513. $. Each of these pools features a 40-foot slide, a children's play area, and lap lanes, all in a park setting. The cost is 50 cents for those who don't meet the height requirement for the slide.

Trails Park Pool Summerlin. 1921 Spring Gate Lane; (702) 229–4629. June through August, Monday through Friday 1:00–5:00 P.M., Saturday noon–5:00 P.M. $, under 3 **free.** This L-shaped pool has cool decking, a shaded area and a grass area, one diving board, and play activities.

Whitney Ranch Aquatic Complex. 1575 Galleria Drive; (702) 450–8813. Monday through Saturday 11:00 A.M.–6:00 P.M., Friday until 8:00 P.M., Sunday noon–5:00 P.M. $, under 3 **free.** The indoor pool is open year-round for swimming or diving. The outdoor aquatic complex opens in the summer and is similar to the Black Mountain facility.

Golf Courses

Golfing is becoming one of the more popular family sports, perhaps because of the leisurely pace and quiet surroundings that allow conversation and camaraderie to flow. Of course, the example of Tiger Woods and his dad doesn't hurt either. Las Vegas has some of the best golfing in the country, with prices to match. This list offers places that cater to beginners with modest budgets.

Callaway Golf Center. Las Vegas Boulevard at Sunset Road; (702) 896–4100. Daily 7:00 A.M.–9:00 P.M., Tuesday until 7:00 P.M. Juniors and adults $ (residents), $$ (nonresidents).

Desert Rose Golf Course. 5843 Club House Drive; (702) 431–4653. Daily 7:00 A.M.–9:00 P.M., 6:30 A.M.–10:00 P.M. in summer. $ for juniors after 3:00 P.M., $$ for Clark County residents. Call for specials.

Eagle Crest Golf Club. 2203 Thomas Ryan Boulevard; (702) 240–1320. Daily 6:00 A.M.–6:00 P.M. Juniors $$, adults $$$.

Green Valley Golf Range. 1351 Warm Springs Road; (702) 434–4300. Open twenty-four hours, Sunday and Monday close at 10:00 P.M. $ per bucket.

Las Vegas Golf Center. 4813 Paradise Road; (702) 798–8700. Daily 8:00 A.M.–10:00 P.M. $ per bucket.

Las Vegas (Municipal) Golf Club. 4349 Vegas Drive; (702) 646–3003. Daily dawn to dark. Juniors $ and up, adults $$.

Los Prados Country Club. 5150 Los Prados Circle; (702) 645–5696. Daily 5:30 A.M.–11:30 P.M. Juniors $, nonmembers $$.

North Las Vegas Municipal Golf Course. 324 East Brooks Avenue; (702) 633–1833. Daily dawn to midnight; winter until 9:00 P.M. $ for juniors. North Las Vegas recently added a junior golf program. Good job.

Special
Events

Throughout the Year

Rainbow Company Theatre, 821 Las Vegas Boulevard North; (702) 229–6553.

"Theatre for the Young and Young at Heart" is the slogan for this delightful theater for everyone. Throughout the year, the company produces five plays that vary from whimsical fairy tales to heartbreaking, meaty stories that will make viewers think. One recent season, for instance, included a story about a Japanese girl experiencing the aftermath of the atomic bomb, a play about Nevada's history, and a charming October story about a boy who needed to know about shivers.

February

Annual Las Vegas Marathon and Half Marathon, www.lvmarathon.com.

We have to admit, most kids will prefer to run the marathon lounging in one of those cool, laid-back running carts. But if they want to stretch their legs, there's plenty of opportunity. The Clark County–sponsored run, the seventeenth oldest annual marathon in the world, goes from Jean, Nevada, to Sunset Park. Registration is required; cash prizes are awarded to the fleetest of foot.

Leisure Awareness Fair, Meadows Mall; (702) 229–6297.

Who knows what you will see at this festive fair? Performances and demonstrations abound that showcase activities and cultural events from around the city. Former fairs have included everything from belly dancers to senior tap dancers.

March

Annual St. Patrick's Day Parade and Festival, Sahara Hotel and Casino parking lot; (702) 743–3977.

Celebrate the luck of the Irish with the Sons of Erin at this annual parade and festival. The downtown parade runs along Fourth Street from Hoover to Ogden. Held from 10:00 A.M. to 7:00 P.M., the Irish Festival includes Irish music (ooh, we are in love), food, crafts, and a children's carnival for the "Little People."

Kite Carnival, location varies; (702) 229–6297.

Kids can make kites and experience kite decorating contests, stunt kite demonstrations and a rock climbing wall, among other activities.

Spring Plant Sale, The Sweet Tomato Test Garden, 5910 Sheila Avenue; (702) 658–7585.

Whose kids don't love to dig in the garden? This annual fund-raiser for garden clubs and other charities helps locals find plants that will actually survive here. Several garden clubs and other nonprofit organizations join forces to offer more than 18,000 plants including orchids, roses, tomatoes, herbs, and more. As you enjoy this cornucopia of plants and information, take time to chat with local master gardeners, garden club members, and other Las Vegas landscape experts. Then go home and let your kids dig in.

Jazz Fest, West Las Vegas Arts Center's Amphitheater, 947 West Lake Mead Boulevard; (702) 229–6383.

Introduce your kids to the sound of jazz at this **free** annual outdoor Jazz Fest. Bring your armchairs and your favorite picnic items, as well as hand toys for the littlest ones.

Focus on Youth Talent Showcase, Cambridge Community Center, 3930 Cambridge Street; (702) 455–7169.

The center celebrates the talents of local youth in an evening of music, dance, and other performing arts, plus a gallery of fine arts and writing. Call ahead of time to see how your family can participate, or just come and marvel at the area's talented youth.

Easter Egg Hunt, almost every city community center and community school.

This Easter egg hunt is for all children, from those crawling all the way up to and including teens. Little kids come to see the Easter bunny and find eggs, prizes, candy, and pennies; older kids attend a Thursday or Friday night BYOF (bring your own flashlight) hunt.

April

Annual City of Lights Jazz Festival, Hills Park Amphitheater; (702) 228–3780; www.mspjazz.com.

Bring your picnic basket, a bottle of wine for the grown-ups, and milk for the baby to mingle with fellow east-siders, gaze at the stars, and get mellow with some of the best local jazz musicians in the area.

Annual Search for Talent, Reed Whipple Cultural Center Main Theatre, 821 Las Vegas Boulevard North; (702) 229–6211. $ to attend show.

For more than twenty-two years, area kids have been strutting their stuff in this annual talent show. Auditions are usually held in March, with performances in April. The Primary Division is for ages 6 through 9; the Junior Division is for ages 10 through 14; and the Senior Division is for ages 15 through 18. All ages are invited to attend the performance, which includes anything from magic to music to mime.

UNLV Annual Plant Sale, 4505 South Maryland Parkway; (702) 895–3182.

Usually held the first Saturday in April. Dedicated gardeners of all ages line up outside the gates for the UNLV plant sale. Smart buyers bring their own wagons, but we have seen strollers full of plants, people pushing tree-laden wheelchairs, and more at this most antic-ipated of events. What makes this so special? Sellers scour nurseries and gardens throughout the Southwest to find unusual plants or to search out particular plants that aren't available locally. Expect to find desert plants and trees, unusual garden perennials, lots of flowering plants, succulents, and cacti. Come to browse, find unique and unusual varieties of more common plants, or ask the experts about your particular garden needs, but don't expect to go home empty-handed. Let the kids fall in love with something spec-tacular or discover a variety of grasses to bed in their own garden. Wandering experts ("We look for people with perplexed faces") include Cooperative Extension master garden-ers, instructors from horticulture programs around the Valley, representatives from grow-ers and nurseries, the director of the arboretum, and other gardening experts.

Clark County Children's Festival, Winchester Park; (702) 455–7340.

This award-winning festival combines art, culture, food, and more for an entertaining day of fun in the park. Past celebrations have included free performances, egg decorating, kiddie-carnival rides, arts and crafts, face painting, roving artists, storytelling, and special community performances.

Annual Invitational Native American Arts Festival, Clark County Museum, 1830 South Boulder Highway; (702) 455–7955; www.co.clark.nv.us.

During this three-day program, the arts, crafts, and culture of the Native American are celebrated with demonstrations, lectures and films, food, and a chance to purchase work from the outdoor Native American Arts and Crafts market.

Earthfest, Silver Bowl Sports Complex, 5800 East Russell Road; (702) 455–7503.

Celebrate Earth Day with millions of people around the world at the local **EcoJam.** Tradi-tionally celebrated on the weekends before and after April 22, on March 21 during the vernal equinox, or on World Environment Day (June 6), EcoJam combines the best of edu-cating people about and celebrating our local environment. Past EcoJams have included the dedication of areas such as the Clark Country Wetlands Park and Nature Preserve.

Las Vegas Senior Classic, TPC at Summerlin; (702) 242–3000.

As golfing kids learn who the masters are, this is the local tournament to watch—as the best of the best play to win here. Top golfers from the Senior PGA tour meet on one of the finest courses in the area, up close and personal. You may even be able to get a few autographs as well.

Tastes & Tunes: A Festival for Your Senses, Civic Center Drive in front of North Las Vegas City Hall at 2200 Civic Center Drive, North Las Vegas; (702) 633–1612. **Free.**

An all-day event that features live entertainment, food, arts and crafts, and a "Romp and Stomp" kids area often draws upward of 5,000 people. Food and games may be purchased separately. Two stages are kept busy with classic rock, blues, reggae, Latin, and swing bands. Local talent is also featured throughout the day.

May

Children's Pop Concert, Las Vegas Civic Symphony; (702) 229–6211.

Each year the symphony gives kids a special treat in a concert designed just for them. Music usually includes kids' favorites such as Disney music and excerpts from kid-friendly classics.

Lei Day in Las Vegas, Main Street Station parking lot; (702) 251–5793.

Celebrate the Hawaiian culture with arts, crafts, food, and entertainment for the whole family.

Spring Jamboree and Craft Fair, Bicentennial Park, Boulder City; (702) 293–2034.

Lots of crafty stuff for the garden or as accents for the home. We like the food booths and the whirligigs.

Boulder City Folk Festival, Bicentennial Park, Boulder City; (702) 293–6634.

Master storytellers prove that the language isn't dead at this festival that features folk music, ethnic food, and artist demonstrations. The highlight for our family is always the evening stories by guest speakers. One year we heard a parable about life as seen through the eyes of a parent of a T-ball player. Then we heard how to create a perfect, unforgettable childhood memory. Whimsical, yet laugh-out-loud funny, once a year the art of the story lights up the night.

Art Fest of Henderson, Water Street in front of City Hall; (888) ARTFEST; www.888artfest .com or www.cityofhenderson.com/parks.

This annual arts fair showcases more than 200 invited artists and crafters from around the region who display and sell their creations. Stroll through downtown Henderson to watch people, listen to music and street entertainment, enjoy the kids' area, or sample the variety of foods. In the past, guests who visited the Web site were entitled to a free T-shirt.

A Day for Children, Mirabella Community Center, 6200 Elton Avenue; (702) 229–6359.

This daylong event is the biggest kids' event of the year and includes entertainment, crafts booths, face painting, bake sales, and a variety of food. Some of the previous activities have included Bubblemania, with a variety of bubble wands available for play; a climbing wall; and Tots and Trikes Town, a cardboard city for little ones, complete with a barbershop and a cardboard candy shop.

National Tourism Week, various locations; (702) 641–5822 option #2.

This annual event put on by the Las Vegas Chamber of Commerce is designed as a fun way to recognize both sides of our leading industry: the tourists and the people who serve them. Previous years have seen key events like the designation of the Strip as a National Historical Landmark (with radio station giveaways and a parade of antique cars), and the recognition of the 500 millionth visitor arriving at McCarran Airport, coupled with a series of local events, parades, and festivities staged throughout the Vegas Valley.

Cinco De Mayo, Cambridge Community Center; (702) 455–7169 or 455–7004; and Lorenzi Park; (702) 789–8345.

Celebrate our neighbor to the south at this annual party that includes games, music, dancing, cultural foods, piñatas, entertainment, and fun activities for all ages.

Las Vegas Folklife and International Food Festival, Government Center Amphitheater; (702) 455–8200.

Cosponsored by the Las Vegas International Food Festival, the Las Vegas/Clark County Library District, and the City of Las Vegas Parks and Leisure Services, this festival features music, dance, storytelling, ethnic food vendors, crafts demonstrations, and children's hands-on activities.

Whitney Spring eXtreme Thing, Whitney Community Center; (702) 455–7576.

Three categories of skateboarders and in-line skaters compete on a street course. Sign up early, as space is limited; there is a $6.00 entrance fee. Come watch kids in action amid music, food, and prizes for winning competitors.

Annual Arts and Crafts Fair, Lorenzi Park near the Senior Center; (702) 229–6601.

Live bluegrass music, refreshments, clowns, bake sales, games, and prizes for the kids; arts and crafts from the community.

May–June

National Historic Preservation Week, Desert Demonstration Gardens, 3701 West Alta Drive; (702) 822–8344.

This annual day of educational family fun invites city, county, environmental, archaeological, and Native American groups to explore our collective and distinct pasts.

Food & Folklife Festival, Clark County Government Center Amphitheater, 500 South Grand Central Parkway; (702) 455–8200 for times. $, under 13 **free.**

The name says it all. Celebrate our cultural diversity with food, fun, and dance.

Annual Unity Festival, Doolittle Community Center, Lake Mead Boulevard and J Street; (702) 229–1235. **Free.**

Join community members in the oldest program offered by the Las Vegas Department of Leisure Services. In an effort to bring the community together after the Rodney King riots in 1992, the festival attracts more than 3,000 people each year to the festivities, a pool party, entertainment, and food. Donate a bag of clothes for a free swim pass.

Las Vegas Chautauqua, Hills Park in Summerlin; (702) 895–1878.

Historical characters come alive during Chautauqua, when historians, actors, or just plain people obsessed with someone from the past re-create a favorite persona. Most Chau-tauquas have a theme, like World War II, American humorists, or flamboyant Western fig-ures. During the first half of the program, the historical figure recounts the highlights of his or her life. During the question-and-answer session, the audience gets to ask ques-tions, often trying to stump the expert. Enlightening, educational, and often very funny, it is one of our favorite family outings. Those with small children, however, will find that the lecture session is often over their heads, and older people appreciate relative silence in order to hear well. If you have brought a picnic basket and a few hand toys, you will prob-ably be fine. If your child starts crying, though, take him or her out for a brief break. Older children may just find themselves wanting to re-create a character of their own.

Summer

Neighborhood Family Film Festival, West Las Vegas Arts Center Amphitheatre, 947 West Lake Mead Boulevard; (702) 229–4800.

Join other families on Friday at 8:00 P.M. at the Arts Center's outdoor theater to enjoy recently released animated films.

July

Fourth of July Extravaganza Concert, Hills Park, Summerlin; (702) 229–6297.

Put on by the City of Las Vegas. Performance by the Las Vegas Philharmonic, this annual fireworks show draws families from throughout the Valley.

Children's Summer Concert Series, Charleston Heights Cultural Center, 821 Las Vegas Boulevard North (Wednesday); (702) 229–6297. Reed Whipple Cultural Center (Friday); (702) 229–6211.

The Summer Concert Series provides an opportunity for children to experience a variety of performing arts programs, from music and theater to fantasy and dance. Previous years included giant puppets performing to Mozart's music, a jazzy musical adaptation of

The Owl and the Pussycat, excerpts from a ballet version of *Beauty and the Beast,* and a hilarious Animal Band. Wednesday performances are at 2:00 P.M.; Friday shows are at 2:00 and 7:00 P.M. Admission is $3.00.

Fourth of July Damboree, Bicentennial Park, Boulder City; (702) 293–2034; www.bouldercitychamber.com.

A parade, food, festivities, and games throughout town; the Cub Scouts usually sell water balloons.

August

Street Party, Arizona Street, Boulder City; (702) 293–2034.

Boulder City attracts an artsy sort, including many musicians. The street party lets families listen to a variety of live bands while eating from a choice of food booths. Sometimes people even dance in the streets.

September

Terry Fox Fun Run and Walk, The Four Seasons, 3960 Las Vegas Boulevard South; (702) 632–5000.

This annual charity event raises money for cancer research and awareness in honor of Terry Fox, a young Canadian who ran across Canada despite losing his leg to cancer when he was eighteen years old. Sadly, after 143 days and 3,339 miles, the disease prevailed and he was forced to quit. In a tribute to his courage and bravery, each year, the fifty Four Seasons hotels worldwide host a run to continue his spirited commitment to cancer research.

The Las Vegas Four Seasons's annual fund-raiser is a weekend of fun and fulfilling activities topped by a run/walk in Summerlin. Past festivities have included a lavish dinner prepared by signature chefs from Four Seasons and Mandalay Bay restaurants, a silent auction featuring exotic trips to Four Seasons properties around the world, and special concerts at the Events Center. The 5K run/walk is very family friendly, letting parents show children a good time while instilling values. To encourage people of all ages and fitness levels to attend, the Four Seasons caters a breakfast buffet at which awards and prizes are presented. Massage therapists are on hand for complimentary minimassages to ease muscles strained from unexpected or overinspired use.

Boulder City Chautauqua, Bicentennial Park, Boulder City; (702) 293–2034; www.bouldercitychamber.com.

Gather under the big white tent to hear reenactments of historical figures' life stories, usually told with wit and humor. Past figures have included Mark Twain, P. T. Barnum, Calamity Jane, and James Thurber. Young Chautauquans perform on Saturday mornings with a series of children's activities that relate to the evening's main events. A nearby playground lets little ones relax within eyeball distance.

Rattlin' Rails Handcar Races, off Yucca Street, Boulder City; (702) 293–2034.

Handcar teams compete against male and female teams from across the country and Canada. Boulder City boasts one of the best teams around. Exciting, different, and slightly educational, this low-key, high-energy sport is getting more attention lately, as are other historical competitions.

Pacific Island Festival, location varies; (702) 229–6297.

Enjoy music, crafts, and performing arts from a variety of Pacific Island cultures.

Autumn

Desert Treasures, Clark County Museum, 1830 South Boulder Highway; (702) 455–7955; www.co.clark.nv.us.

This annual gem and mineral show features vendors from all different aspects of rocks and minerals, with speakers and museum exhibits that tie in with the theme. Previous years have featured "Minerals Go to War" posters with accompanying information on minerals used in defense, and a glass-themed event at which minerals used in making glass and the resulting glassware were exhibited.

October

Art in the Park, Bicentennial Park, Boulder City; (702) 293–2034; www.boulder citychamber.com.

Art in the Park, a fund-raiser for the Boulder City Hospital, is the largest art show in Nevada. It attracts tens of thousands of patrons annually, who all seem to walk away with something new and wonderful for their homes. This is a juried show with invited artists and craftspeople from throughout the country. A great place to pick up early holiday presents for the person who has it all, you can find everything from fine art prints to whimsical nuts-and-bolts sculptures. One year a young artist had exquisite dried leaves and flowers arrangements inside sleek frames. Garden sculptures, handcrafted wooden kitchen items, doll clothes and furniture, candlesticks, abstract sculptures, drawings, glass, paintings, lithographs, ceramics, pottery, and more are available each year.

Silver State Market Place (all ages), Sam Boyd Stadium parking lot, 4505 South Maryland Parkway; (702) 895–3900. Saturday and Sunday, October 19 through May, except during football games.

Vendors sell unique collectibles and merchandise to thousands of locals who enjoy this lively outdoor market.

Creature Feature, Summerlin Veteran's Memorial Leisure Services Center.

Enjoy "trunk or treating" as staff members decorate the backs of cars so children can trick-or-treat. There is also free entertainment, food booths, and a haunted house.

Las Vegas Basque Festival, Lorenzi Park; (702) 256–6219 or 361–6458.

The Lagun Onak Las Vegas Basque Club sponsors this yearly Basque bash, beginning with a colorful Roman Catholic mass with music. After mass, traditional Basque dancers perform on stage followed by weight lifting using a 700-pound steel ball. Basque food complements the celebration, with dishes such as lamb, salad, seafood paella, chorizo, and pork loin sandwiches with sweet roasted bell peppers.

Interested families with a Basque heritage can join the club for regular picnics, *mus* (a game of cards played with a forty-card deck) tournaments, and the opportunity to send their children to the annual summer music camp. At the camp, kids between the ages of ten and eighteen study Basque culture and history as they learn traditional activities, including handball, Basque songs and dances, *txistu* (a flutelike instrument), and the tambourine.

Invensys Classic at Las Vegas (formerly Wendy's Classic), TPC Summerlin, additional courses to be announced; (702) 242–3000; www.lasvegas.com/lvevents.

Top PGA golfers compete in Las Vegas for one of the largest purses on the circuit. The Invensys Classic is one of the few tournaments on tour with five rounds of golf action.

Scrappin' Safari 4 Scrapbook Convention, 231 Denver Way, Henderson; (702) 565–4863 or (702) 585–2587. $.

This annual scrapbook convention is a hands-on experience as well as a chance to check out the latest products, classes, and vendors.

Tomb of Darkness, 2828 Highland Drive; (702) 735–2257; www.tombofdarkness.com.

One of the area's innovative haunted houses, this tomb features the usual scary creatures, but also live radio broadcasts and guest appearances from some of the top stars in horror.

PBR Bud Light Cup World Championships, Thomas and Mack Center; (719) 471–3008; www.lasvegas.com/lvevents.

The top forty-five professional bull riders compete in Las Vegas for a $1 million purse. The competition includes four performances scheduled over three days.

November

Wendy's Three-Tour Challenge, Reflection Bay Golf Club; (702) 565–7400; www.lasvegas.com/lvevents.

Teams from the PGA, Senior PGA, and LPGA tours compete against each other in this made-for-television event.

December

National Finals Rodeo (NFR), Thomas and Mack Center; (702) 260–8605; www.lasvegas.com/lvevents.

Each year the whole city swarms with cowboy hats and boots when this World Series of rodeos returns to Las Vegas. Ten days of the world's best nonstop rodeo action features the top fifteen rodeo athletes, who compete in bull riding, saddle bronc riding, calf roping, steer wrestling, bareback riding, team roping, and barrel racing for more than $4.5 million in prize money and the coveted World Champion title.

National Finals Rodeo Cowboy Christmas Gift Show, Las Vegas Convention Center; (702) 260–8605; www.lasvegas.com/lvevents.

The tickets regularly sell out for the NFR as soon as they are offered. The best chance of getting in is through the ticket booth exchange at the Cowboy Christmas Gift Show. Season ticket holders who are not able to attend an event can turn in tickets for resale. Expect to stand in line.

The Cowboy Christmas Gift Show is the only official gift venue for the National Finals Rodeo. The show has everything your little cowboy needs for Christmas.

Las Vegas International Antiques Fair, Caesars Pavilion; (866) 225–1812 or (702) 796–3133; www.1812andco.com. $.

Leading dealers and galleries feature furniture, decorative arts, painting, prints, jewelry, sculpture, and other ancient through early-twentieth-century art.

Old-Fashioned Christmas, Clark County Museum, 1830 South Boulder Highway; (702) 455–7955; www.co.clark.nv.us. $.

We miss the holiday events that the museum used to include during the Christmas season, but it has kept up the tradition of adorning its historic homes with holiday decorations appropriate to the times. Take a breather and imagine a period when Christmas was less about getting and spending and more about homegrown cheer.

Christmas Parade and Santa's Party, Bicentennial Park and Old Town Boulder City; (702) 293–2034; www.bouldercitychamber.com.

Boulder City loves its parades. The annual Christmas parade features local groups, state and local politicians, floats, and handfuls of candy tossed to the crowd. Afterward, Santa listens to children's holiday wishes at the Bicentennial Park gazebo.

Holiday Village, The Four Seasons, 3960 Las Vegas Boulevard South; (702) 632–5000.

Each holiday season pastry chef Jean Luc Daul creates twenty gingerbread real estate "properties" and a working 7-foot carousel as a Terry Fox Foundation fund-raiser. Individuals or companies can purchase a "lot" in the village; their names are showcased beside their "properties." Although my family builds a gingerbread house each year, it is mostly just an excuse to layer on as much candy as possible. These houses show true artistry at work and are bewitching enough to lure your own Hansel and Gretel to take a nibble. Properties sell for $250 to $750 each; carousel, $2,500 (mechanism not included).

Elegant Santa, Excalibur, 3850 Las Vegas Boulevard South; (702) 597–7777.

Each year during the holiday season, the theme becomes one of medieval Christmas. This Santa is dressed like those wonderful European St. Nicks that you may sport on your fireplace mantel. Many families come in their best Christmas attire to get their pictures taken with this elegant Yuletide man, who is really our favorite Santa to tell secrets to.

AAUW Christmas Home Tour, (702) 293–2034; www.bouldercitychamber.com.

This annual American Association of University Women's event raises scholarship funds each year for a Boulder City girl entering college and a Boulder City woman returning to college. The tour is normally one of the first Saturdays in December, with tickets sold during November. Great if you or your kids love decorations—most of these homes are decorated to the hilt. This is a "look but don't touch" experience for grown-ups and kids alike.

General Index

R

Race for Atlantis, Forum Shops, 42
Rainbow Company, 76
Rampart Buffet, J. W. Marriott Las Vegas
    Resort, 146
recreation centers, Henderson, 113
Rebel Adventure Tours, 36
Red Rock Canyon National Conservation
    Area, 146–49
Red Rooster Antique Mall, 95
Re Society Gallery and Atelier, Paris
    Las Vegas, 30–31
Reynolds' Dolls Gifts & Collectibles,
    Boulder City, 127
Rio, The, 81, 83–87
Rita Rudner, New York–New York, 18
River Mountain Loop Trail,
    Boulder City, 127
Rock Tour, Hard Rock Hotel
    & Casino, 92
roller coasters, 57, 67
Ron Lee's World of Clowns, 109
Ronn Lucas, Rio, 86
Royal White Tigers Habitat, Mirage, 49
RV parks, 98

S

Sagebrush Horse Ranch and Tours, 153
Sahara, The, 58–59
Scandia Family Center, 96
Second City, The, Flamingo Las Vegas, 44
Secret Garden of Siegfried and Roy and
    the Dolphin Habitat, 48
Senator Howard Cannon Aviation
    Museum, 94
Shark Reef at Mandalay Bay, 6
Showcase Mall, The, 26–29
Sirens of TI, 50
Six Company Visitors Bureau, Boulder
    City, 127
skate parks, 141
Skateboard Park, Boulder City, 125
skating, ice, 138

Sky's the Limit Climbing Center,
    Henderson, 108
Sky's the Limit Guided Hikes and Rock
    Climbing, The, 153
Southern Nevada Paddling Club, Boulder
    City, 126
Southern Nevada Zoological-Botanical
    Park, 77
Spiedini Ristorante, J. W. Marriott Las
    Vegas Resort, 146
Speed—The Ride, Sahara, 59
sporting clubs and games, 77–79
sports parks, North Las Vegas, 137
spray parks, 132
Spring Mountain Ranch State Park, 147
Stars of the Strip, 69
Star Trek: The Experience, Las Vegas
    Hilton, 93
St. Jude's Chapel of the Holy Family,
    Boulder City, 127
St. Jude's Ranch for Children, Boulder
    City, 127
Stratosphere, The, 65–67
Summerlin, 140–45
Summer Pool Parties, Las Vegas
    Hilton, 93
Sundance Helicopters, 36
Sunset Park, 74

T

table tennis tournaments, 113
Talking Heads, Forum Shops, 41
taxis, 90
TI, The, 50–51
Time Traveler: The Ride, Venetian, 53
Tony 'n' Tina's Wedding, Rio, 86
Tournament of Kings, Excalibur, 14
Tower, Stratosphere, 65
trolley rides, 65
Tropical Aquarium, 6
Tropicana, 15–17
Tropicana Bird Show, 16

Activities Index

About the Author

Lynn Goya is a freelance writer based in Las Vegas and has been published in *Nevada Magazine, Family Life Magazine,* and *Las Vegas Life.* She is the author of *Ghost Towns, Legends and Levis* (2004) as well as an Emmy-nominated writer for the PBS series, *Outdoor Nevada.* A produced playwright, radio commentator, and national print journalist, she covers Las Vegas, travel, entertainment, art, business, and residential and commercial construction. She also teaches writing and politics at the Art Institute of Las Vegas. "I find people fascinating," she says, "who people are and how they live. Everyone has an amazing story to tell if you just listen."